# A VERY DOUBLE LIFE

## THE PRIVATE WORLD
## OF MACKENZIE KING

# A VERY DOUBLE LIFE

## THE PRIVATE WORLD OF MACKENZIE KING

## C. P. Stacey

cop. a

Macmillan of Canada
Toronto

ISBN 0-7705-1390-5

Printed in Canada for
The Macmillan Company of Canada
70 Bond Street, Toronto M5B 1X3

... those who knew him best will be the first to admit that in some respects his character was baffling.

VIOLET MARKHAM

There is no doubt I lead a very double life.

MACKENZIE KING'S DIARY
*13 February 1898*

# CONTENTS

*List of Illustrations*

(Between pages 96 and 97)

# THE MACKENZIE KING DIARIES

William Lyon Mackenzie King, who was Prime Minister of Canada longer than anyone else has ever been, was an inhabitant of two worlds.

One was the very practical world of politics and public affairs. In this world he worked for forty years, operating with remarkable and increasing sureness of touch and no little ruthlessness, a political leader whose efficiency was unparalleled in Canadian and perhaps in modern history. The other was his private world, a world populated by his family (and his dogs), his innumerable women friends, and in his later years the spirits of the dear and the great departed. He contrived with striking success to keep this emotional and frequently irrational private life separate from his rational public world, and in his lifetime very little knowledge of it reached his countrymen, who would certainly have been greatly interested.

After his death in 1950, however, it became evident that a means existed of illuminating the hitherto dark side of King's life. This was the remarkable diary which he kept from 1893, when he was an undergraduate at the University of Toronto, until three days before he died. This diary is even more extraordinary as a document than King's career is as an episode of politics. It is the most important single political document in twentieth-century Canadian history. It is also a social and a personal record of absorbing interest, chronicling in great detail, and with sometimes shattering frankness, the personal experience of one human being—and a very eminent one—from adolescence to the grave, and from the last decade of Queen Victoria's reign to the Korean War.

In the beginning, and for many years, King kept the record in his small, difficult handwriting in bound "daily diaries". Later, notably during the Second World War, he dictated it, sometimes at very great length. Although he must be regarded on balance, in terms of persistence at least — for his style is anything but distinguished — as one of the champion diarists of all time, he was still not entirely immune to the tendency to neglect that besets lesser ones. There were long periods when he made no entries. This was particularly true during the time that he was out of politics following the Liberal defeat in the election of 1911. In the year 1913 he wrote in the diary on only two days. But this neglect was exceptional. For years together he scarcely missed a day. In his last months, though he was no longer equal to keeping the diary in longhand as he had done for a time after his retirement from public life, he regularly dictated a page a day.

What drove King on to this long-continued effort? He told himself in the beginning that it was a means of self-improvement. On the flyleaf of the first diary, in 1893, the pompous eighteen-year-old wrote, "The chief object of my keeping this diary is that [I] may be ashamed to let even one day have nothing worthy of its showing; and it is hoped that through its pages the reader may be able to trace how the author has sought to *improve his time*." He went on to say that he also looked forward to "himself and friends" finding pleasure in the record "in future days". (At this moment, obviously, it did not occur to him that one day he would leave orders to destroy the diary.) On New Year's Day 1902, following the death of his friend Bert Harper, he returned to the diary after an interval, writing, "I am taking up this diary again as a means of keeping me true to my true purpose. It has kept me in the path from drifting more than I otherwise might have, it has helped to clear me in my thought and convictions, and it has been a real companion and friend. . . ." It was medicine for his chronic insecurity. One may ask why he made such a conscientious record of the sins which he so regretted, and must assume that he found in it some psychological relief; it was a form of confession. (The British politician who wrote that King "gave one the feeling that he was an entirely sexless creature" was far from being alone in his view; but it is clear that his impression was inaccurate.) Finally, it is apparent that the diary often served a mere business purpose, as a record of events for later reference. Witness, for example, the case of the Chanak Affair of 1922. The diary had lapsed for over a month and a half; but with the onset of the crisis on 16 September King at once returned to keeping it in detail, beginning with the words, "I was about to go into the temple of Peace at Sharon, when the Toronto Star reporter, about 2.45 handed me a despatch to the effect that Britain had invited Canada to participate in an attack against the Turks, & in the maintenance of the Dardanelles. . . ."

The history of the diary since Mackenzie King's death demands notice. His declared intention to leave instructions that it was to be destroyed caused consternation and brought protests from his friends, one of those who protested being John D. Rockefeller, Jr. In the end he relented to a limited extent, and the will he signed on 28 February 1950 directed his four literary executors "to destroy all of my diaries except those parts which I have indicated are and shall be available for publication and use". Perhaps fortunately, before his death he marked *no* parts of the diaries for preservation. It may seem difficult to believe that he really intended that the diaries should be burned—after all, he had spent a good proportion of his life writing them; but it must be remembered that he undoubtedly hoped that he would live to write, or to supervise the writing of, his memoirs, which would be based on the diaries and, supposedly, would incorporate much of the substance of them. However, no serious progress had been made with the memoirs before his final, fatal, illness.

The literary executors were thus faced with a singularly difficult problem. They were instructed to co-operate in the "preparation" of King's memoirs — to which it is clear he attached great importance—but also to destroy the diaries which were the essential foundation of the memoirs. On the basis of conversations that some of them—particularly Dr. W. Kaye Lamb, then Dominion Archivist — had had with King before his death, concerning the sort of passages he might mark for retention, they took legal advice. The lawyers told them they were not required to destroy any part of the diaries. Accordingly, no part of them was destroyed, and they were made available to King's authorized biographers, and later to some other people. Beginning in 1960, large portions of the diary for the years 1939–48 were published by Mr. J. W. Pickersgill (one of the literary executors), assisted by Mr. D. F. Forster, under the title *The Mackenzie King Record*. In general, however, the facts of King's private life are omitted from these volumes.

More recently, in the light of the passage of time and of the fact that most of the persons who figure significantly in the diaries are now dead, the literary executors have gone further. Some years since, the diaries (deposited with the rest of the King Papers in the Public Archives of Canada in Ottawa) were opened to students generally through the year 1931 (and the whole text for 1893–1931 has now been published in microfiche form by the University of Toronto Press). Still more recently, the decision has been taken to apply to the diaries the "thirty-year rule" which now governs access to government records, and at the moment of writing, accordingly, the Mackenzie King diaries are open to all and sundry through the year 1944.

The literary executors have been criticized for not destroying the diaries. Here, surely, is a question of "mixed ethics". The most poignant comment on the problem which I have seen is that of King's dear friend Mrs. Godfroy Patteson, who wrote in 1951 to Violet Markham (another dear friend) concerning her disagreement on the matter with one of the literary executors: "Mr. McGregor & I have not been at one over the diaries. Rex made me promise to see that Mr. McG. burned them without reading—and while I saw the need perhaps of reading them, the dying request was very sacred to me—and that I think is what I have suffered most [sic]. I have no knowledge of their contents—but I have wished that his wishes could be carried out."

These views are entitled to deep respect, but to the present writer it seems nevertheless that the literary executors acted rightly. The destruction of the diaries would have been a disaster for Canadian history, and this, I think, applies as much, or nearly as much, to the personal as to the political material. In any case, everyone who has examined the diaries, so far as I know, agrees that it would be an impossible task to separate the public from the private portions. King himself tried for a time in 1934 to keep separate records of what may be called his temporal and his spiritual experiences; but after a few months he gave up the attempt. The alternatives for the literary executors were to destroy everything, or to preserve everything. To any historian who has looked into the diaries, destruction seems utterly unthinkable. The executors have acted, I think, in a commendable spirit of responsibility, preserving the diaries but awaiting the passage of a long period of time before opening them generally to researchers. Mackenzie King has now been dead for a quarter of a century, and the sometimes curious facts recorded in his diaries are a part of history.

To King's official biographers, and particularly to the first of them, Robert MacGregor Dawson, whose volume covering the years 1874–1923 was published (posthumously) in 1958, the account of King's private life set down in the diaries presented problems. Writing within a very few years of King's death, and while many of his close associates were still living, Dawson could not possibly help being inhibited. Mrs. Patteson, for instance, who should have figured in the latter part of his volume, outlived the biographer, dying on 23 April 1960 at the age of ninety. The reader of the diaries soon realizes why Dawson subtitled the book *A Political Biography.* It is a valuable book. But it is not really practicable to tell the story of one half of a person's life and leave out the other half. The man inevitably affected the politician. The present little book is in a sense a supplement to Dawson. Mr. H. Blair Neatby, the author of the second volume of the authorized biography, published in 1963 and dealing with the years 1924–32, had in some respects an easier task. Writing about a mature man, he did not have to deal with the sowing of King's wild oats (which Dawson simply left out). Many actors in the story had passed on, and in general the lapse of time facilitated frankness. Mr. Neatby's volume is much better balanced than Dawson's, though, not surprisingly, the private world still gets slight attention by comparison with the political one. Mr. Neatby has another volume on the way, to which we shall all look forward.

My own acquaintance with Mackenzie King was slight, consisting of guiding him, to the best of my ability, over the Normandy and Dieppe battlefields in 1946, and, later, of speaking to him once or twice on the telephone about the project of his memoirs. This book is a by-product of two others. In the later stages of writing an official account of Canadian military policy in the Second World War, I was kindly given access to the King diaries by the literary executors, and it was thus that I became acquainted with these fascinating documents. Subsequently, while writing a book on Canadian external policies, I delved into the earlier diaries in the hope of finding something about King's views on these matters during his first days as party leader. I found a little on external policy, and a great deal on King's relations with women. I was drawn, as they say, to read on.

This volume is far from being the last word on its subject. When I read a paper on King to the Canadian Historical Association in 1974, I described it as an interim report. The present book is somewhat more complete, but it is still an interim report. I have read very widely in the King diaries, but have not read the whole enormous corpus of them. Some private correspondence and other documents in the King Papers are still closed, including some of the detailed records of King's spiritualistic activities. I am sure that various investigators — not only historians, but political scientists, psychologists, psychical researchers, and others — will find in the Papers material to occupy them for generations to come. Perhaps this book will do something to help them on their way.

I have told the story very largely in King's own words. He wrote quickly and carelessly, and even when he dictated he frequently did not bother to correct the typescript afterwards. I have interfered with his text as little as possible, but I have tried to make things easier for the reader by some adjustments of punctuation — usually involving merely adding commas, which King had a tendency to dispense with. I have not felt it necessary to indicate where this has been done.

I have to thank many friends for their help: members of the staff of the Public Archives of Canada, other people interested in King, who have called various points to my attention, and still others who have answered my questions: Peter Robertson, Carman Carroll, Jean Dryden, Frances Mallory, Harcourt Brown, Douglas LePan, Graeme Patterson, Richard Alway, Robert Bothwell, Ramsay Cook, Norman Hillmer, Brian Henley, Valerie Proctor, and, most particularly, Barbara Wilson. I am grateful to Diane Mew for very perceptive editorial assistance, and to Audrey Douglas for typing the manuscript.

C.P.S.

Massey College in the University of Toronto
November 1975

# INTRODUCTION
# THE MASTER POLITICIAN

The main facts of Mackenzie King's political life are moderately well known; but it is worth while to set them down here by way of background for the story of his private life, with which this book is chiefly concerned.

William Lyon Mackenzie King was born in Berlin, Ontario, on 17 December 1874. (Many of the city's people were of German origin; after bitter controversy it was to change its name to Kitchener in 1916.) His mother was Isabel Grace Mackenzie, thirteenth and last child of William Lyon Mackenzie (1795–1861), Scottish immigrant, radical newspaperman, first mayor of Toronto on its incorporation in 1834, and leader of the abortive Upper Canadian rebellion of 1837. As King many times recalled, she was born "in exile", in New York City, where Mackenzie was a refugee after the failure of his mismanaged *coup*. King's father, John King, Q.C., was an admirable but ineffective person, an unsuccessful lawyer with scholarly and literary ambitions. John's background was quite different from his wife's; his father, another John King, was a bombardier in the Royal Artillery. Thus Mackenzie King from the beginning had the best of both worlds. As the grandson of the "Little Rebel", his liberal and radical credentials were beyond criticism. On the other hand, on occasions when he wished to present himself as a pillar of the established order, he could recall Bombardier King, who had helped defend Canada against the filibustering attacks which his other grandfather had fomented.

Mackenzie King did well at the Berlin High School, and in 1891 he went on to University College at the University of Toronto. His father was a graduate of the University and a member of its Senate. The new freshman apparently made some ill-advised reference to this latter distinction, which produced a rude comment in the student paper, *The Varsity*, concerning the son of "Senator Rex" of Berlin. Claiming that he had been misrepresented, King brought the affair before a meeting of his class, which, he assured his parents, accepted his version and cheered him to the echo.[1] The permanent result of the incident was the nickname "Rex", by which those who knew him best called King until the end of his life.

King took his Toronto B.A. in the spring of 1895. For a time he worked as a newspaper reporter, combining this with spare-time study of law; and in June 1896 the University of Toronto conferred on him the LL.B. (which must have been a fairly cheap degree). He acquired a third Toronto degree in 1897, receiving an M.A. for a thesis on the International Typographical Union. By that time, however, King's Toronto period had ended.

In the autumn of 1896 King became a graduate student at the University of Chicago. Like many young idealists of that age, he had fallen under the spell of the University Settlement idea — the idea of university men helping slum-dwellers by living and working among them. King admired Jane Addams, and for a time he lived in her celebrated Chicago settlement, Hull House. But Chicago did not give him what he wanted—though it is clear that he was not sure at this stage just what that was. He would have liked to return to Toronto, but the University of Toronto refused him a graduate fellowship—a slight he did not forget.

In 1897 he moved on to Harvard. Here he found his academic ideal, and Harvard was good to him. He took a Harvard M.A. in

1898 — four university degrees in four years! — and in September 1899, financed by a Harvard travelling fellowship, he set off for Europe. London, Berlin, Paris, Rome—and in the Italian capital he received a cable that changed the course of his life. In 1897 he had written for a Toronto newspaper an article, based on first-hand investigation, on the evils of sweated labour. With his father's help he made what he had discovered known to a member of the Dominion Cabinet, William Mulock, the Postmaster General, who was a family friend. Mulock commissioned him to make an official investigation, and he submitted his report in January 1898. It was well received and even produced some government action. And when, in the summer of 1900, Sir Wilfrid Laurier's ministry set up for the first time a rudimentary Department of Labour, Mulock became its Minister, combining these duties with those of the Post Office. It was he who sent the cable to King. It offered him the editorship of a new publication to be called the *Labour Gazette*. After long and painful thought King accepted. On 24 July 1900 he arrived in Ottawa to take up his new duties. He was twenty-five. Ottawa was to be his home and the scene of his labours for the rest of his life.[2]

King did not remain merely an editor. Very shortly he was appointed in addition Deputy Minister of the new department; "probably the youngest Deputy Minister ever appointed in Canada", he later recorded happily.[3] He had always been poor; now he suddenly found himself comparatively affluent, and enjoying a position of official importance and social prestige. But he still had doubts as to whether this was really where he wanted to be. And ambition still pricked him on. His new post, enviable as it was, was only a way station. On 11 August 1900 he had reflected in his diary on the events of the past year: "I have seen more & had more of success than I could have imagined it possible to have . . . it reads like a fairy tale—yet it is true—& I am not satisfied." His own determination, energy, and ability, combined with good connections carefully exploited, had done much for him at a very early age. They would do a great deal more.

An incident of 1902 is worth noting. King had not been given initially the full statutory salary of a deputy minister ($3,200). Now Mulock put this in his estimates for the coming year. The Minister of Finance, W. S. Fielding, sent for King and told him there was some feeling in the Cabinet, first, that there would be criticism if the Labour Department were given full departmental status, and secondly, that King was very junior in the service and the government had done well by him already. Faced with comments like these from a senior Cabinet minister, most civil servants would have caved in and accepted the situation. Not so King. His firm rejoinder was that if the government felt that it could not give him the salary of a deputy minister, as provided by law, he would resign and "return to academic work". He threw in a reference to "my love for Canada inspired by grandfather's life & work". It was the Cabinet that caved in; King got his $3,200.[4] It was becoming apparent that there was a vein of iron in this pudgy young man.

Mackenzie King was a senior civil servant for eight years. During this time his activities as a conciliator in industrial disputes across the country made him something of a national figure. "We call him the Peace Maker," said Lord Grey, the Governor General, in 1905.[5] This was the laudatory term commonly applied in those days to the reigning sovereign, King Edward VII.

Grey also said in 1905 that King was a future Prime Minister of Canada. The young man's ambition was, in fact, already fixed upon that office; he had confided this to his mother as early as 1901.[6] Earlier aspirations—to be a minister of the gospel, to be a professor of political science or economics, to be president of the University of Toronto—had faded now, and politics more and more monopolized his imagination. Beginning late in 1905, he profited by his growing friendship with Sir Wilfrid Laurier, pressing the Prime Minister to help him find a seat in the House of Commons and to make the Department of Labour an independent department with King as its Minister. Laurier put up with a great deal from King at this time without turning against him; and after a long campaign King got what he wanted. In the general election of 26 October 1908 King was elected for his old home riding of North Waterloo. Almost immediately the Department of Labour received its independent status, and on 2 June 1909 Mackenzie King became a Privy Councillor and took his seat in the Cabinet as Minister of Labour.[7]

The government King joined was a very old one. Laurier had been Prime Minister since 1896 and had won four successive general elections. Now two external questions arose to bedevil Canadian politics: the question of naval defence (a by-product of the growing tension with Germany), and a project of tariff reciprocity with the United States. In the election of 1911 these combined to ruin Laurier and the Liberal party. Mackenzie King himself was defeated in North Waterloo. After only a little more than two years in the Cabinet he found himself no longer a Minister and no longer a Member of Parliament.

The next period was one of "casual employment". King was clearly anxious to get back into active politics, but no immediate opportunity presented itself. Then, in June 1914, the Rockefeller Foundation invited him to become head of its new Department of Industrial Relations, at an annual salary of $12,000, to carry on a program of research in this field. After his usual doubts and hesitations, King accepted, specifying that he would remain a Canadian citizen and be free to take part in Canadian politics. This new work brought him into association with John D. Rockefeller, Jr., and the two men remained close friends for the rest of their lives. In practice, King's first task in his new appointment was to restore peace to strike-torn Rockefeller mining properties in Colorado, which he did with conspicuous success.[8]

King's ill-wishers, who were legion, were to make much of his "desertion" of Canada at the moment when the First World War was breaking out. In fact, it is rather absurd to suggest that he ought to have gone into the army. He was in his fortieth year in 1914, and had had no military experience. It is, perhaps, a little strange that he apparently never thought of abandoning his Rockefeller project in favour of some kind of war work in Canada. But he had no difficulty in arguing later that keeping American mines and factories working smoothly—which was his chief wartime activity—was an important contribution to Allied victory. Ottawa was always his official domicile and base of operations. Nor did he lose touch with politics. In 1917 the Liberal party was disrupted by the conscription issue. The Conservative Prime Minister, Sir Robert Borden, formed a Union government, which a number of English-speaking conscriptionist Liberals joined; but conscription was anathema to French Canada, and Sir Wilfrid Laurier refused to have any part in the coalition. The Khaki Election of December 1917 was a Liberal disaster, except in French-speaking Quebec, where the Laurier Liberals took 62 of the 65 seats. Mackenzie King stood by Sir Wilfrid and ran in North York, a constituency associated with his political grandfather. He was defeated; but the defeat had in it the seeds of future victories.

At the end of the war King had to make a choice. His remarkable reputation in the United States is reflected in the fact that not only did he have the opportunity of staying with the Rockefeller Foundation, with an annual income of $30,000 or more, but he was also offered the post of Director of the Carnegie Corporation, with similar remuneration. But it was back to Canada and to politics that King's eyes mainly turned. It cannot be doubted that there lay the career he most craved—provided he could be assured of the probability of achieving his ambition of filling the highest office. It was evident that Sir Wilfrid Laurier would not be leader of the Liberal party much longer.

On 17 February 1919 he died. King clearly intended to be his successor if he could; and he thought he had important advantages in the contest for the leadership. During his first weeks in Ottawa, back in 1900, he had encountered the then Deputy Minister of Militia, and described him as "a Frenchman, slow and indifferent". "It seems a great shame," he went on, "that so much French should be perpetuated around here." He knew more about the facts of life and politics now. When he heard that Laurier was dead he wrote, "Quebec dominates the House of Commons, the Liberals of Quebec will never take as a leader any man who 'betrayed' Sir Wilfrid at the last election. . . . "[9] It turned out that he was right. In the convention that chose the leader, King's most formidable rival was old Mr. Fielding, whom he had bearded in 1902; but Fielding had been a conscriptionist, and Quebec would not have him. It was in the main, it seems; Quebec votes that elected King leader of the Liberal party on the third ballot (7 August 1919).[10] A couple of months later he was back in the House of Commons and on his way to the summit.

Borden's government was crumbling. In 1920 the wartime prime minister, broken in health, was succeeded by Arthur Meighen. As the drafter of the conscription law, Meighen had no hope of allaying the hostility of Quebec; as an outspoken defender of protection, he had equally little hope of overcoming the growing alienation of the western farmer, who was convinced that he was being exploited for the benefit of the eastern industrial community. In the campaign preceding the general election of 6 December 1921, King, while duly abusing the government, said little about issues; he let the situation work for him. These tactics succeeded admirably. Quebec this time gave every one of its 65 seats to the Liberals, who also took every seat in Nova Scotia and Prince Edward Island. The Progressives (the farmers' parties) swept the prairies and got many seats in Ontario. The Conservatives were ruined. King, with 117 supporters, had by far the largest group in the House of Commons but was just short of an absolute majority. On 29 December 1921 he took office as Prime Minister of Canada.[11]

King's policies during his first administration were characteristically cautious. He sought to complete the reunion of the Liberal party and to absorb the Progressives, or, failing that, to undermine them. Supported by the country's postwar isolationist mood, he reversed the Borden–Meighen imperial policy, founded on the concept of a single foreign policy arrived at by consultation between the Commonwealth countries, substituting the idea of a separate Canadian policy, with conference with Britain when circumstances might require. In the Chanak Affair of 1922, when the British government made a sudden and very ill-advised request for an offer of troops to support its forces confronting the Turks on the shore of the Dardanelles, King's reply was that Canadian public opinion would require the authority of Parliament — which was not in session — before a contingent could be sent. At his first Imperial Conference in London the following year, the Canadian prime minister, at the cost of making himself still more unpopular with the British government, successfully opposed the idea of a uniform Commonwealth foreign policy, and may indeed be said to have killed it.[12] It is obvious that King was following a line particularly acceptable to French Canadians, but many other Canadians also found it agreeable. Still others, of course, hated it.

These important questions of external policy were little discussed in the general election campaign of 1925. Indeed, no important issue emerged; and the result was very unsatisfactory to Mackenzie King. This time it was the Conservatives who got the largest group — 116 seats against the Liberals' 99. The Progressives, though much reduced in number, held the balance of power. King himself lost his North York seat and had to find another in Prince Albert, Saskatchewan. The Governor General, Lord Byng, thought King should resign his office and let Meighen form a government; but King, urged by his colleagues, decided to cling to power and to meet Parliament. Progressive support enabled the government to survive for the moment; but early in 1926 it was shaken by revelations of corruption in the Customs Department. In June, King, faced with the likelihood that the House of Commons would pass what amounted to a vote of censure on the government, asked Byng to dissolve Parliament. The Governor General, "right for the wrong reasons"[13]— he would have been on sounder ground if he had based his action on the attempt to escape censure rather than on his belief that Meighen's strength in Parliament entitled him to a chance to form a government — declined. King resigned; Meighen accepted office, and was promptly defeated by Progressive votes; and Byng then granted Meighen the dissolution that he had refused to King. The most curious aspect of the whole affair was the autonomist King's urging Byng to seek the advice of the Secretary of State for the Dominions in London. The Governor General refused to do so; he acted in fact the part of a Canadian constitutional monarch.

The country was now plunged into an election campaign which King fought on the "constitutional issue"; in effect he attacked Byng through Meighen. It is doubtful whether many voters fully understood the question; no doubt a considerable number resented what was vaguely considered an English appointee's interference in Canadian politics. Other questions, including economic ones, were doubtless important; there was a large return of western voters to the Liberal fold. If the constitutional issue was nothing else, it was an excellent red herring to divert attention from the customs scandal. At any rate, King won a great success, taking 128 seats and enjoying for the first time an absolute majority. (Quebec was faithful as always: 60 seats.)[14] After the 1926 election, moreover, King was master of his party as never before. He was credited with having turned impending defeat into resounding victory. He was now Canadian Liberalism's indispensable man.

In the autumn of 1926 King took a prominent, if hardly leading, part in the Imperial Conference that re-defined the British Commonwealth and prepared the way for the Statute of Westminster (1931) which established the Dominions' constitutional equality with the United Kingdom. Three years of peace and prosperity followed. But prosperity collapsed in 1929 and was succeeded by world depression. One of the first victims was Mackenzie King's government, which went down to defeat at the hands of the Conservatives, now led by R. B. Bennett, in a general election in July 1930. Liberal legend, of which King's political infallibility was an important part, later asserted that, foreseeing what was coming, he lost the election on purpose, to leave the Tories holding the very damp baby of the depression. This is not true (and, indeed, no one who, like the present writer, saw King performing on the Opposition front bench after that election, could have believed it; he was too obviously a bitter and disappointed man). He spent five years in the political wilderness. The early part of this period was made still more unpleasant for him by another scandal, involving revelations of large contributions to Liberal party funds by a beneficiary of actions of King's government, the Beauharnois Power Corporation. But in the end the depression, which had defeated King, defeated Bennett too. The election of October 1935 brought King the largest majority he had yet had, and he became Prime Minister for the third time.[15]

As the country began to pull out of the slump, the war clouds thickened over Europe and Asia. Canadians remembered the blood-bath of 1914–18; Canadian politicians remembered what conscription had done to national and party unity. The instinctive reaction was to go for peace and isolation at almost any price. This was reflected in the utterances of Conservatives and Liberals alike in the 1935 campaign, conducted under the shadow of Italy's war of aggression against Ethiopia. King, back in power, took refuge in a policy of postponing decisions. There would be "no commitments", to Britain or anybody else, in advance of an actual crisis; and when and if the guns opened fire, "Parliament would decide." Within himself, it seems clear, King never had the slightest doubt that if Britain became engaged in another great war, Canada would have to go to her aid. At the Imperial Conference of 1923, speaking of American influence on Canada, he had said, "If a great and clear call of duty comes, Canada will respond, whether or no the United States responds, as she did in 1914, but it is a most important consideration against intervention in lesser issues."[16] In other words, we do not intend to get involved in Chanaks; but a great crisis, with the existence of Britain and the Empire at stake, would be a different matter.

In the meantime, any policy that offered a hope of staving off war would have King's support. Neville Chamberlain, and his plan of appeasing Adolf Hitler, had a strong appeal for him. He had spent much of his life opposing any idea of a common Empire foreign policy; but he made an exception of appeasement.[17] He supported it strongly and publicly. When he had an interview with Hitler in 1937, he simple-mindedly accepted the dictator's protestations of his love for peace, writing, "He impressed me as a man of deep sincerity and a genuine patriot." But he also told Hitler something that he had not yet told the Canadian people: "I thought it was only right to say that if the time ever came when any part of the Empire felt that the freedom which we all enjoyed was being impaired through any act of aggression on the part of a foreign country, it would be seen that all would join together to protect the freedom which we were determined should not be imperilled."[18] It was a typically Kingly mist of words, but there was a hard fact concealed in it. Whether Hitler understood, or was much impressed, is not recorded.

By the spring of 1939 it was pretty evident that war was coming. King and the Liberals still held Quebec. The Conservatives, under a new leader, R. J. Manion, wanted Quebec. Manion, hearing that King was about to make a commitment against conscription, sought to anticipate him. If war came, he declared, Canada should fight beside Britain but should conscript nobody for overseas service.[19] Three days later King made a similar declaration against overseas conscription. Political expediency had produced a formula that would facilitate unity in case of war. Six months later war came. King and his colleagues, still clinging to the "no commitments" and "Parliament will decide" principle, summoned Parliament. Nobody had much doubt now what it would decide, and, one week after Britain's declaration, Canada declared war on Germany. There had been very few dissenting voices. For years Canadians had worried neurotically over what would happen in such a crisis. Could the country go to war without coming apart? It had done that now; and many people who had never been fond of him were inclined, however reluctantly, to give much of the credit to Mackenzie King.

The greater Allies had no desire to share the direction of the war with Canada or any other secondary power. King, no war-lord, made little complaint about this. He kept his eyes fixed primarily upon the domestic scene, intent upon maintaining the country's precarious unity and his own and his party's power. In the beginning he opted for a decidedly "moderate" war effort. During those first months he was challenged from both flanks: first by the provincial government of Quebec under Maurice Duplessis, which assailed the threat the federal government's war measures represented to provincial autonomy, and then by the Premier of Ontario, Mitchell Hepburn, who attacked its war effort as inadequate. King's Cabinet colleagues from Quebec took the field against Duplessis and persuaded the people of the province to replace his Union Nationale ministry with a Liberal one. The Ontario threat King met by dissolving Parliament. In the ensuing election (March 1940) he got the largest majority any Canadian government had ever had. It is evident that, in the circumstances of the time (the "phony war"), the people at large were quite happy with King's war policy. By a combination of luck and good judgement he had obtained, before the beginning of serious fighting in western Europe, a mandate that would last him until the end of the German war.[20]

When the phony war ended and Dunkirk shook the western world, Canada's "moderate" war effort ended too. The dollar was pushed out of the driver's seat, the armed forces were enlarged, and the industrial effort was expanded. In only one respect did limited liability survive. Conscription was invoked for home defence, but the government stood by its pledge against sending conscripts overseas. The election had removed Manion from the stage, and some—but not all—Conservatives were inclined to talk conscription. The chief of these was Meighen, who now returned briefly as party leader. He ran on a conscriptionist platform in a by-election in a Toronto riding and suffered a disastrous defeat. English-speaking Canadians were not yet ready to support compulsion. But, as the struggle went on, feeling began to change, and conscriptionist sentiment manifested itself inside King's Cabinet, notably in the Minister of National Defence, Colonel J. L. Ralston, a legendary battalion commander of the "old war". That French Canada had not altered its view of conscription had been made clear when a plebiscite on releasing the government from its pledge drew an affirmative vote in every province *except* Quebec.

The crisis came after the Normandy D-Day, 6 June 1944. For the first time the whole of the overseas army was in action; a shortage of infantry reinforcements developed; and the mood of English Canada was changing. Ralston recommended sending the trained home-defence conscripts overseas, and indicated that he would have to resign if the recommendation was refused. King declined to yield, but begged him to stay. Then, on 1 November, though Ralston was still prepared to seek a compromise, King suddenly dismissed him from the Cabinet, replacing him with General A. G. L. McNaughton, formerly commander of the First Canadian Army overseas. McNaughton failed to prevail upon any considerable proportion of the conscripts (the "zombies") to volunteer for overseas service. The conscriptionists in the Cabinet were now responding to the mood of their constituents, and by 22 November it was clear to King that his government was about to be disrupted by resignations. He now abruptly abandoned the position he had defended so long, and agreed to send 16,000 conscripts overseas. The government was saved, and for the rest of the war King ruled virtually unchallenged.[21]

The war made King a junior associate of Winston Churchill and Franklin D. Roosevelt. He had always disliked and distrusted Churchill — the man of Chanak — but from 1940 Churchill commanded unlimited admiration in Canada as elsewhere, and King trimmed his sails accordingly. He had established a friendly relationship with President Roosevelt before the war, and this contributed to producing in August 1940 the Ogdensburg Agreement, which brought Canada and the United States together in what amounted to a defensive alliance — an arrangement almost universally applauded in the circumstances of that summer. Next year King obtained Roosevelt's consent to what has come to be called the Hyde Park Declaration, which opened the way for considerable sales of Canadian-manufactured equipment to the United States and solved Canada's American exchange problem for the rest of the war. But however he might delight in his friendship with the President, as time passed he began to doubt whether the Americans' intentions towards Canada were entirely honourable. Several times in his last years he recorded in the diary his apprehensions of absorption by the overpowering neighbour.[22]

June 1945 witnessed King's last general election. The Germans had just surrendered. The fighting men had always disliked King intensely, and there was perhaps a certain poetic justice in the fact that he lost his own seat in Prince Albert by the service vote, and had to seek another constituency. Yet the servicemen generally gave a plurality of their votes to his party, and, though his parliamentary majority was reduced, it still existed—125 seats out of 245. It was a notable fact that Quebec still stood by him, giving him 53 seats. French Canada had not liked his capitulation to the conscriptionists, but clearly he was regarded as a lesser evil than the Conservatives. The socialists— the Co-operative Commonwealth Federation — had seemed to pose a serious threat, but King stole their thunder by a politic social measure, the introduction of family allowances, popularly called the "baby bonus". This was quite in accord with King's image of himself as the friend of the poor; it was also in accord with the economic advice of the National War Labour Board and the Department of Finance.[23]

Weakening health now forced King to think of retirement. In the summer of 1948 he completed twenty-one years as Prime Minister. In April he had passed the record supposedly set by Sir Robert Walpole and had held office longer than any other first minister in Commonwealth history; this gave him much simple pleasure. In August a Liberal convention elected Louis S. St. Laurent to succeed him as party leader. One of King's last official duties was going to London to attend the Commonwealth Prime Ministers' Conference in October 1948; but a strained heart kept him from the meetings. Returning to Canada, he resigned as Prime Minister on 15 November. He died at his much-loved Kingsmere estate near Ottawa on 22 July 1950.[24]

Such was the distinguished public career of Mackenzie King. It remains to try to tell the story of his other world.

## PART I

# THE BOY AND THE GIRLS

The King family was not large by Victorian standards. There were two sons and two daughters. The eldest child, Isabel (Bella or Bell), was born in 1873; Willie (also called Billy), we have seen, came the next year; Janet (Jennie) was born in 1876; and Dougall Macdougall (Max or Mac), the baby of the family, arrived in 1878. There is no doubt that the six Kings, parents and children, constituted an unusually close and affectionate family group.

When young Willie went off to University College, Toronto, in 1891, the family were still living in Berlin. In Toronto Willie lived in lodgings for the first two years of his course. But in 1893 John King was offered a part-time lectureship in Osgoode Hall Law School, and the Kings moved to Toronto. They occupied a moderately impressive semi-detached house, which still stands, at 147 Beverley Street, in what was then a superior district. The house was rented, for John King's name does not appear in the City Registry Office records. Willie now moved in with the family, and 147 Beverley became the base for his varied operations for the next three years. The Kings, always short of cash but always respected, soon acquired a place in Toronto society. Devout Presbyterians, they became members of St. Andrew's Church on King Street, and Willie formally joined that congregation "by certificate" on 27 October 1893. John King, almost inevitably, became an Elder of St. Andrew's. There was apparently a much earlier family connection with the church. The tablet which Willie (then Prime Minister) and Jennie put up in it in memory of their parents during the St. Andrew's centennial year records that William Lyon Mackenzie was "one of those members of the Legislative Assembly of Upper Canada and citizens of York who founded the Congregation in March, 1830".

It was at 147 Beverley Street that Mackenzie King, aged eighteen and about to begin his third year at University College, launched the project of keeping a diary.

# THE BLUSHING YOUNG LADIES

The diary began rather tentatively. Nobody would have thought that it was going to continue for fifty-seven years.

On 6 September 1893 Willie bought himself the first of many "daily diaries". That evening he wrote in it:

> After having been told by many that I could never keep a diary, I decided to make, at least, an attempt.... I purchased today Andrews' "Institutes of Economics" ($2.00) and a small copy of Mrs. Browning's poems to give to a young lady friend Miss Mab. Moss who leaves for England on Monday next. I spent this evening at her mother's home.
> ... After giving Miss Mab the little remembrance she said blushingly "It was very kind of you to remember me."

It need occasion no surprise that Miss Moss was a member of one of the best families of Toronto (her father, Charles Moss, Q.C., later became Sir Charles and Chief Justice of Ontario). She was not to play any great part in King's life. Her trip to England would seem to have had permanent consequences; for two years later Mary Ada Beatrice Moss married "Samuel Squire Sprigge, M.B., B.S. Cantab., eldest son of the late Squire Sprigge, of Watton, Norfolk".[1] But she occupies a unique position as the first girl in King's diary.

She was the first of very, very many. People did not think of the bachelor Prime Minister of later years as in any sense a ladies' man, but this was one of the many matters in which people were wrong about him. Miss Moss is a symbolic figure. She is the leader of an endless procession of females who glide through King's life as reflected in the diary. Some, like her, make only a brief appearance, accompanied by appreciative comment; others become permanent parts of the scene. Collectively, they are the subject matter of a tremendous proportion of the diary. Only one of those up-to-date historians who have called the computer to their aid could do full justice to this theme; for Mackenzie King's lady friends were as the sands of the sea for multitude.

Relatively few of them, in his student days, were found among his fellow undergraduates. Women students were still very much a minority at the University of Toronto. King seems to have had nothing against them — we find him for instance paying rather marked attention to a Miss F. L. Sheridan, a freshman of 1893, but he seems to have met her at a private dance, not at a university affair.[2] To a large extent he found his female friends among the "society" families of Toronto, and particularly the families connected with the law; this was doubt-less a result of his father's professional connections. A close parallel with the Moss friendship was that with the Falcon-bridges. Like Charles Moss, William Glenholme Falconbridge became a Knight and a Chief Justice; and incidentally they married sisters, daughters of Robert Baldwin Sullivan, another judge. (Charles Moss's elder brother Thomas was also a Chief Justice, and he also married a Sullivan daughter. Such people might seem strange associates for a grandson of William Lyon Mackenzie; but the members of this particular Family Compact were Liberals, so it was unquestionably all right.) Jack Falcon-bridge was a close friend of King's, and so were his numerous sisters. They, too, were travellers. On 14 December 1893 most of the family were off to France, and King went to the station "and said good-bye to Mr. and Mrs. Falconbridge and kissed Madeline, Evelyn, Emily, Adele & Amy (baby) good-bye. . . . They are all dear girls. . . ."[3]

King's physical energy was colossal. It found outlets, as the diary shows, in all sorts of sports: cricket, rugby football, running, skating, and others. He seems to have been not more than moderately good at these pursuits, but he was very persistent. At the same time he lived a very active social life and was extremely fond of dancing. He went to Lelia Lash's coming-out party, and listed his partners for seventeen dances; "I enjoyed my dances with Miss Street perhaps best of all" (he danced with her three times).[4] She was presumably a daughter of Judge W. P. R. Street —another legal family. At the college *conversazione*, "I had some very pleasant dances. . . . Miss Mackenzie & Miss Kerr were two splendid dancers."[5] The catalogue of girls' names goes on, repetitive but with constant additions. "Tonight Bella & I went to a small dance at Mulock's, had a lovely time. Took an exceedingly great liking to Miss Edith Jones, a girl with great depth of nature and character. We had a delightful talk together."[6] Miss Robertson; Miss Worthy; Miss Marwood; Edith and Flo Macdonald ("They are lovely");[7] Miss Dowd; Miss McQueston; Miss White; the Miss Lamports; and so many more — one wonders who they all were, and what became of them.

In the summer of 1895—a B.A. now, aged twenty and finding it necessary "to shave every second day to look respectable"[8] — King spent a holiday on an island in Muskoka, apparently as the guest of friends named Douglas. Another guest was Kitty Riordan, who was there with her mother and her brothers, one of whom seems to have been a college friend of King's. The Riordans were a papermaking family. Kitty was seventeen and attractive; and in the course of a few days, King recorded, he found himself "falling insensibly in love" with her. She, for her part, must have been attracted by the young man; at any rate, she apparently made no complaint when he sought to entertain her, day after day, by reading aloud long, long passages of Gibbon's *Decline and Fall of the Roman Empire*. In the end, King decided, perhaps unnecessarily, that he must take strong measures to extricate himself. "I knew it was not right for me to allow myself to become thus enraptured with this girl of 17, and felt that she could not but resent it. I . . . resolved to free myself by telling her all. . . ." He took her paddling one evening and "told her that I could not help becoming fascinated, but also said that I was desirous only that this should result in a life's friendship, and nothing more." Then he went back and set it all down in his diary: "as I have never experienced anything of the kind before I make a clean breast of it in these pages." According to King, his manifesto brought relief "to us both".[9] Three days later, however, he wrote that Kitty had been "very unpleasant all day". That, however, did not prevent him from continuing to read Gibbon to her on the days that followed.[10]

One important group of King's girls we have not yet mentioned. He was obsessed with nurses and hospitals. This was doubtless related to the religious obsession which the diary also makes evident. Nurses were dedicated to service—the service of humanity, and, according to King's ideas, the service of God. "Nurse Cooper" is a prominent figure in the diary from the beginning. (No doubt she had a Christian name, but it never appears in the diary.) She was on the staff of Toronto's Riverdale Hospital, in the city's east end, and King often undertook the long walk from Beverley Street or the University to see her. In Christmas Week of 1893 he recorded "a long and beautiful talk" with her: "I hope I may be of great help to her in her work for the Saviour." They frequently exchanged letters.[11] And at the end of 1893, in the first of those solemn, ceremonial, year-end summings-up that became a feature of the diary, special benison was reserved for her: "My last prayer was for all the family, that I might be a better man and that God would bless and help my friend Miss Cooper."[12]

However, Miss Cooper was not alone, or not for long. In March 1894 King's brother Max fell ill and nurses had to be brought into the family house. King was soon friendly with them, especially with one girl named Scott: "I had a lovely little talk with Nurse Scott in the kitchen." The friendship with Miss Scott flourished for some time.[13] We also find King corresponding with one "Nurse Rogers"; and then there was "Nurse Harding" of Grace Hospital, who wrote to King while he was in Muskoka in 1895, telling him she was ill and asking him to call and see her.[14] He retained this compelling interest in nurses for many years. Long afterwards, in 1916, he was in hospital in Baltimore for a minor operation. He described how, coming out of the anaesthetic, he "spoke to the nurse Miss Stairs": "I remember thinking she was a noble woman, a sweet woman & a good woman, and I told her so and that God would give her happiness, and enable her to have a life of useful service."[15] Miss Stairs must have been mildly surprised, but no doubt she reflected that people say strange things when coming out of the ether.

From his early days as a student at Toronto, Mackenzie King had been conducting religious services at the Children's Hospital on Sundays for groups of little girls. The diary constantly refers to the pleasure these occasions brought him.[16] In the spring of 1895 they came temporarily to an end. On 24 March something evidently happened which King does not explain. After his service he visited the hospital a second time, "went back for nurse but could not see her as she was very fatigued." On the following Sunday he found he could not take a service, "as they were fixing up things". Nor could he the next Sunday or the next; and when he visited the hospital's summer location on Toronto Island one Sunday in July he "could not get in . . . on account of some reason". One can only speculate as to what had happened. Was there some suspicion of King's motives or behaviour? Or had someone complained that he had no formal qualification to hold religious services? At any rate, the ban did not last. In October he was again recording "lovely mornings" with his brood of little girls.[17]

The tendencies and susceptibilities that appeared in Mackenzie King as a student stayed with him all his life. To state it in the most obvious and simple terms, this lifelong bachelor was enormously attracted by women. He greatly enjoyed the society of women, particularly of women who were handsome, vital, and intelligent. (If they were also wealthy and important, it was all to the good.) In his mature years the procession of interesting females continues to march across the pages of his diary as it did in the days of Mab Moss and Kitty Riordan.

We have been talking so far of King's association with what were called, in the language of the nineties, "respectable" women; those whom he would have thought of as belonging to "his own class". But by the time the young man had his brief passage with Kitty — having "never experienced anything of the kind before"—he had had much more intimate relations with girls on a lower level of society.

# STROLLS IN THE SUB-WORLD

The census of 1891, the year Mackenzie King came to Toronto as a student, gave the city 181,000 people. It liked to think of itself as a moral place, and presumably it was no worse than most North American cities of its size in those days. But one C. S. Clark published in 1898 a little book entitled *Of Toronto the Good* which contained considerable evidence that it was no better than it should have been.[1] Below the prosperity and the respectability, he revealed—not surprisingly to a modern eye—a sub-world of poverty and vice. In particular he went into details about the prevalence of what people called then "the social evil": prostitution. He gives an impression of the young men of Toronto's "better classes"—the future legislators, judges, and leaders of the professions—regularly trooping off to visit houses of ill-fame.

Clark doubtless exaggerated somewhat, but Mackenzie King's diary gives him a good deal of support. Precisely when the boy from Berlin first began to explore the seamy side of life in the city one cannot say, but the process was under way when he started the diary in 1893. On the second day he kept it, he made an entry in terms that were to be repeated a good many times: "Tonight was practically wasted, a little seen of the wickedness of the world." A month later there is a similar record that says a little more: "The night was worse than wasted. Went out about 8

P.M. and returned at 11.30. All the intervening time worse than wasted. Saw a little of the dark side of the world which results in my making a firm resolution which with God's help I will keep." "Worse than wasted": the reader should note the phrase, for it will recur. What the resolution was King does not say, but it would seem that he didn't keep it. About a fortnight later comes another entry: "I committed a sin today which reminded me of my weakness & so aroused me that I went over and had a long talk with Murray tonight. We had a short prayer which I hope will be answered. I must live a christian life." "Murray" was presumably J. L. Murray, one of King's classmates.[2]

To repeat all young King's reports of his sins would be to harrow or, more likely perhaps, to bore the reader; but we must give a couple more quotations from the early months of 1894. One night he records that his friend Charlie Cross, whom he usually studied with, went to a hockey match and left him alone. He found it difficult to concentrate on his notes of Professor George M. Wrong's history lectures:

> It was very hard for me to stay in. I felt I must go out & stroll round. Alas I have much to conquer as yet. Oh I wish I could overcome sin in some of its more terrible forms. Tonight has proven to me that I am very weak but I will pray to be made stronger. I wrote a little letter to Nurse Cooper & one to Nurse Rogers.

The following day he writes, "I cried after coming home tonight. I feel very sorry for something I did last night. What sort of man am I to become? is the question that is bothering me at present." On an evening about two months later, he says again that he "felt very much unsettled and could not read", so he "went out and strolled around for a while. I am ashamed to record all. I felt very sorry on coming home."[3]

The precise nature of his sins he does not tell us. But it can hardly be doubted that these "strolls" were visits to prostitutes—

the pattern of his life during the next few years strongly suggests this — or that he had learned how to find the prostitutes from fellow students who knew the way.

In the very midst of these experiences, in February 1894, something new appears. The nineteen-year-old amateur libertine launches a one-boy program to *rehabilitate* prostitutes. (Did he know that that other Liberal, William Ewart Gladstone, had been engaged in the same pursuit, to the scandal of his friends, for most of his life? To King it would have been an inspiring example; but there seems to be no evidence that he had heard of it.) King's first subject was a member of a poverty-stricken family he already knew. We shall call her Millie Gordon, though that was not her name; names mean little in this context. She had had a small sister who had been a member of King's little congregation at the Children's Hospital and who had died at the beginning of the year. Calling to see Millie on 6 February at a respectable house where she had been staying, King found that "she was not there but in a house on King St.". He followed her there and begged her "to stop her wicked life and turn to Christ". On the 8th he found she was still there. "We had a long and beautiful talk together":

> There was a young fellow there, a perfect scoundrel, I believe, who has wished to marry her, but she refused him and decided to come with me to Mrs.-----'s. . . . Miss Gordon and I left together. At Mrs.-----'s we had a long talk & a quiet talk together, a little hymn and a little prayer. . . .

Two days later King presented Millie with a 50-cent Bible, and wrote happily in his record, "This has been a poor week for college work but a blessed week for the cause of Christ.[4]

His rejoicing was premature, for Millie proved to be a backslider. A few days later she went back "to her place on King St.". King however did not give up easily. "I went down after her and after playing Detective for a while I found she was in the room but she got out a back way before I could find her. I went down again however & got her, she came back with me." Again they had a long talk; she "seemed more conscious of her sin than ever before" and "cried bitterly". "I was dreading this all along," the young man wrote. "I pray God that it will never happen again." Nevertheless, it did. Next week King heard that Millie had "gone back to her old life". At this point he seems to have given up the case for the moment. But we continue to hear of Millie getting into trouble and King attempting to help her.[5]

Later in the year another campaign began. It started dubiously with a post-theatre pick-up:

> I had dinner at residence with Dunc* then we went to the theatre. . . . We went out with 2 girls who live on King St. and down to their rooms, we were here till nearly 2 A.M. I got pretty well the history of the girls' lives. When we left we had some steak at a restaurant. I stayed all night with Dunc at the residence. We both felt rather badly.

The reader can interpret that for himself. But it is pretty clear that the affair didn't begin as an exercise in rehabilitation, and King's turning it into an exercise in sociological research somehow doesn't improve the taste. The best defence is to recall once more that we are dealing with a nineteen-year-old. At any rate, three days later he took another friend down to King Street to see the two girls. (This was the finale of what this remarkably energetic youth called "a red letter day"; during it he had taken a leading part in a Convocation riot at the Massey Music Hall, in the course of which, he says, "I had a fight with [James] Brebner the Registrar on the steps of the building, threw him down three times.") This time his object in visiting the girls was clearly to

---

*Two Duncans figure in the diary at this point. One, N.M., is probably Norman Duncan who became a novelist of some note; the other is David. Neither seems to be found in the University of Toronto *Class and Prize Lists* of King's time. Presumably neither ever passed an examination. It cannot be said with certainty which is referred to here.

reform them. The friend departed, but King remained to try to argue the girls out of their way of life. "I tried to point out the love of the Saviour to them, I must have spoken for nearly 4 hours."[6]

For the next few weeks, King's dominant interest — for he adjusted his little difficulty with the University authorities over his fight with the Registrar with remarkable ease*— was rescuing the two girls. One of them he prevailed upon to go into "the Haven", which was evidently a home for "fallen women"; a third girl from the same King Street house he found a place for in Grace Hospital; Millie reappeared and also went into the Haven. (King was "much impressed at hearing the girls at the Haven singing 'Rescue the Perishing' "; he wrote a verse from the hymn in the front of his diary for 1895.) But, sad to record, all or most of the girls slid back into the life of sin almost immediately.[7]

The private program of reforming prostitutes seems to have lapsed early in 1895 and never revived. University politics, involving a famous student "strike" in which King played a somewhat ambiguous part, claimed most of his attention for a time. But he continued to feel moved to devote himself to the service of the poor and wretched. Going to see the Gordons and other poor families in June 1894, he had used the phrase, "went over

*The only possible reference to any kind of penalty or amends is King's note on 7 October that he called at Brebner's house and "to some extent explained matters and apologized". Can young King have been a privileged character? The same Family Compact of King family friends that we have seen in the judiciary was represented in the University Senate (by Charles Moss and Glenholme Falconbridge); King's own father also sat there, and William Mulock, another family friend, was Vice-Chancellor. On the other hand, generations of students were well acquainted with "Jimmy" Brebner's ungovernable temper; and his colleagues may well have felt that he, and not King, was to blame. At any rate, King asserts that on 16 October he saw the President of the University and "had a laugh about Brebner's affair"! The "fight" is reported by the *Toronto Daily Mail* of 6 October, which says that it "appeared like an unwarranted assault upon the Registrar of the University"; no student is mentioned by name. The incident is not in Dawson's biography of King.

to my own little 'mission field' ". That summer he discovered the
writings of the first Arnold Toynbee (1852–83), the English
pioneer of social service, and was entranced; he had found, he
thought, "a model for my future work in life". Some weeks later,
in the midst of his excitement about the girls on King Street, he
wrote, "I am going to devote my whole life to mission work."[8]
Such were the urges that drove him on to Chicago and Hull
House in 1896.

Unfortunately, and inevitably, those other urges that drove
him on to sin, and the habits he had acquired in Toronto the
Good, continued to plague him. At times the diary becomes a
record of a struggle against temptation, with the young man
usually winning. But not always. Witness the sad entry of 19
November 1896 in Chicago:

> ... got into another trap, cost me $1—wasted time till 5
> came home on elevated.... I now feel terribly sorry &
> disgusted at my action.... I fought hard against temptation
> & this has broken my Chicago Record. I cannot bear to think
> of it.—Why am I so weak? Why cannot I keep where I strive
> so hard to be? — I will try harder the next time.

Not long afterwards he writes, "There has been a fierce war of
flesh & spirit all day. When shall I subdue the evil in me?"[9] The
episode of 19 November seems to have given him a bad fright.
Back in Chicago from a trip home to Toronto for the Christmas
holidays, he immediately "went to see a doctor, being haunted
with this dread hanging about me ... he examined me & said
there was absolutely nothing the matter with me that all my fears
were groundless."[10] The dread was pretty obviously that of what
our grandparents called (behind their hands) private disease.

The sociological researcher and the joyless voluptuary continued to co-exist in King. In April 1897 we find him, with a
companion named Symons, visiting "saloons and dives" in
Chicago. He writes, "We must have looked at or met over 500

prostitutes, mostly young girls & on the whole not very degraded in appearance. . . . I have never seen so much of the social evil. Came thro' untouched." But he was not untouched very long. Two nights afterwards he recorded that he intended going to St. Luke's Hospital, but did not get there "until nearly nine". "Meanwhile I spent $1.25 after being in the company of one I met" — an interesting turn of phrase.[11]

St. Luke's Hospital introduces us to a new phase of Mackenzie King's life. On 8 March 1897 he developed symptoms of typhoid fever and was admitted to St. Luke's. He remained there until the 27th, but was not so ill that he could not derive enjoyment from the situation. The hospital was just full of delightful nurses. On 9 March King recorded, "This morning Miss Rohrer and Miss Grossert came for day duty. They are both lovely, it would be hard indeed to express the unbounded admiration which one has for these nurses. I have seen here what is noblest and best in woman."

Another nurse, perhaps not from St. Luke's, appears in the diary at this period. We may call her Miss Hall. King was sure she was in love with him: "She showed it in her face. I told her that I did not know what life or love meant." Nevertheless, the foolish youngster, though he does not seem to have been serious about her, later exercised his romantic and literary talents in a letter to her that he was sufficiently pleased with to copy into his diary: "I will never forget our little romance. It was the one bit of true poetry which I carried away with me from the great commercial city. . . . But where is the face that will efface from my mind & heart, my Evangeline, My Marguerite, My Joan D'Arc? With these I have you, and if all are very dear to me I hope you will not mind." The girl to whom this extraordinary effusion was addressed wrote him months later from New York: "She still seems put out at my 'rejection' of her," he writes. "I am sorry my words were so wrongly construed."[12]

After he left the hospital, King is found taking more than one

of the nurses to the theatre.[13] Clearly, however, it was Miss
Grossert who had smitten him. He writes, "I love her, she is such
a beautiful christian character." The next day, she is "constantly
in my mind. . . . I cannot but love her deeply." Then a little later,
"I cannot help almost loving the nobility of character I find in
her."[14] (Take note of the word "almost".) Miss Grossert was to be
enormously important in King's existence during the next year
or so.

We have already seen that his hospital experiences did not end
his gallivanting in Chicago. In Toronto next summer he speaks
of nocturnal wanderings and temptations ("How the chains of
Hell pull on a man when he is tired!"), but his resistance seems to
have been successful.[15] Then, in September 1897, he goes to
Harvard, and immediately begins to make expeditions into the
sub-world of Cambridge and Boston. On his first evening in
Cambridge, "anxious to talk with some one, lonely a little &
restless", he goes for a "stroll" (that word again) and meets a
young girl. "We walked about a while together. Had I read my
diary before going out I wd. not have gone so far — returned
about 10. Went to bed tired & sorry at the mistake I had made."[16]
A few weeks later he gives us a picture of himself wandering "like
a lost child at the biddings of passion". "I got home by Heavenly
protect'n without having fallen, but O God what a struggle,
looked at sad picture of mother & resolved to start again." But at
the end of October there is a very explicit account of a defeat:

> Went to see factory inspector Mrs. Ames after wh. I wan-
> dered about streets of Boston. Oh fool that I am who will
> deliver me,—went completely to the devil with my passions,
> wasted money & came home sad. God only knows why I am
> so weak, He knows I fight hard.[17]

# MATHILDE GROSSERT

At the beginning of 1898 Mackenzie King, Harvard graduate student aged twenty-three, was in serious trouble. He was tormented by the sexual urges that drove him to associate with prostitutes, and by the religious beliefs that told him that associating with prostitutes was sin. In many ways this was to be the worst year of King's life. He himself frequently said that he came to the brink of insanity; and those who read his diary will be inclined to agree.

The young man's sad state is reflected in his record of his journey back from Toronto to Boston after the Christmas holidays. He missed a connection in Buffalo and had to wait until two in the morning for another train. Meanwhile, he says, he "went to a hotel where I wrote for over four hours finishing my report on the sweating system. In this way I avoided all temptation & turned to good advantage a misfortune." Having caught his train, he found himself thinking — as he often did — about books he would like to write. He thought he might write "a revelation of things as they are" under the powerful title *In the Sight of Almighty God.* He was in an upper berth. In the morning he found that the berths were so ill constructed that he could "see the lady in the berth below making her toilet". He proceeds:

What man could have resisted the temptation to look? I

should have, and might have but did not. However, I fought hard against possible temptations last night and won completely. I am determined that this year shall not witness some of the stains of the old. This resolve I have made above every other, to aim ever at becoming purer in thought & word & act.

This passage really seems beyond comment. Perhaps the best course is simply to quote the sentences immediately following: "I had a splendid breakfast but it cost me $1. When I saw I was in the trap I ate all the cheese that I could."[1] This is one of the very few attempts at a joke that are found in the fifty-seven years of the King diaries.

The record of the fight against the temptations of the flesh goes on, accompanied by orgies of self-contempt. King writes in February, "There is no doubt I lead a very double life. I strive to do right and continually do wrong. Yet I do not do the right I do to make it a cloak for evil. The evil that I do is done unwillingly, it comes of the frailty of my nature, I am sorry for it. . . . I fear I am much like Peter, I deny my Lord when the maid smiles at me, but with God's help I will overcome even this temptation. . . . During the past week I have been on slippery ground, but I have been kept from falling. . . ."[2] It was in such circumstances that King turned to Miss Grossert, the Chicago nurse whose "beautiful christian character" he had so admired.

Mathilde Hedwig Grossert was a recent immigrant from Germany. King recorded long afterwards that she was a grand-niece of the poet Schiller.[3] She was clearly a well educated and intelligent woman, a superior person in the best sense. She was older than King; they were both much aware of this. King's diary can be interpreted as indicating that she was thirty-six in 1898.*

*On Victoria Day 1898 King attended a Canadian Club dinner at Harvard, came home and kissed a lock of Mathilde's "beautiful hair" thirty-six times. For a parallel, see the account of Mrs. King's seventy-fourth birthday party, below, page 151. Other information, however, is that she was born

After he left Chicago in June 1897, King corresponded with Miss Grossert, and at Christmas he records receiving "by letter a pair of little blue shoes 'An das Kind' from my good little nurse in Chicago".[4] Possibly this was a Christmas card. After his return to Cambridge the correspondence with Chicago warms up and becomes a peculiar long-range courtship, undertaken with many doubts on both sides. On 5 January (just after that curious journey back from Toronto) King writes, "I carried in my pocket a letter from Miss Grossert. . . . What a beautiful girl she is. I love her with all my heart, though perhaps I should not. . . . But am I right to fall deeper in love, is she not right in keeping me away. . . . She loves me but her love is of another kind. I am still the child." Perhaps this showed a certain perspicacity, but King soon forgot it, at least for the moment.

Towards the end of February Miss Grossert becomes an obsession with him. On the 24th he got a letter from her in reply to one of his; she admitted, he says, "that she knew I admired her". He went out and consulted his most eminent Harvard acquaintance, Professor Charles Eliot Norton, a very great man in the world of scholarship. Norton, taking, it would seem, a considerable chance on the basis of what must have been only the sketchiest knowledge of the facts, advised him "not to lose a jewel". Next day King spent "nearly two hours" concocting a letter to her. As with a good many other letters of the period, he was evidently proud of it, for he copies part of it into the diary: "I find in your thoughts & your words & actions a truer expression of those graces and virtues which constitute the ideal woman than I have found the world over, my own mother & sisters alone excepted." On the 26th we find him reading William Lyon Mackenzie's biography and connecting his Mackenzie heritage with Mathilde; with her by his side he could stand "against all the

---

in January 1873, and was thus only about two years older than King. Her middle name, moreover, is given as Pauline, not Hedwig as in the diary. Perhaps she changed it.

world", and Mackenzie's voice "shall be heard in Canada again".[5]

Mathilde was backward about encouraging the young man, and for some days he waited for a letter that did not come. It was apparently without receiving any word from her that he then proceeded to write another letter himself. His record of this is so curious that it had better be quoted at length:[6]

> "I love you with all my heart. I have spoken of friendship and admiration but I never felt words so hollow before. It is not friendship, it is love, deep deep love, deep and true. It is not admiration, it is love, true, true love and it is all love of *you*. You, Mathilde Hedwig Grossert, you I love and with all my heart." These were the words I wrote this morning in a letter to Miss Grossert. . . . Strange[ly] enough I wrote the letter while I was in a dull cold mood or rather feeling as one does who is more or less tired and who has little hope. Yet I expressed my thoughts as I believed them to be most true. I mailed the letter at two and it is now beyond my reach, for good or ill Miss Grossert knows my heart and I have taken a step which a year ago I would have believed impossible. Indeed I had decided never to think of marriage till I had a home provided and now I have practically proposed.

The combination of the passionate words of love and King's description of his own hesitation and uncertainty is bizarre: "a dull cold mood"; "my thoughts as I believed them to be"; the letter "is now beyond my reach". He was, in fact, being dishonest with Mathilde; the letter was one of the romantic exercises to which he seemed to have become addicted; and anybody reading the passage just quoted could not have expected the attachment to have any good or permanent consequences.

It did not. But the affair went on for six miserable months, painful and tortuous.

On 10 March King received Mathilde's reply to his declaration. He copied it into the diary: "My dear Mr. King — I have received your letter and although I have not even had time to read it all [one suspects that it was very long], I will let you know that I shall answer it. But have patience with me, I implore you— Mathilde Grossert." It is a strange fact that King immediately assumed that he had been refused. His comment in the diary was, "The issue is practically settled and for the present, at least, I am to give up all hopes of gaining Miss Grossert. . . . The letter promised will have the whole soul of a beautiful woman running thro' it, but there will be reasons why Miss Grossert cannot love me. Perhaps it is better that it is so for the present at least. . . . " One gets the impression that the young man is immensely relieved. Yet a few days later he has totally changed his mind, and believes that the letter still awaited will say that Mathilde loves him. On 18 March he spends the whole morning composing another long and elaborate love-letter, large parts of which he copies into his record. He says at one point, "I promise you only a true & loving heart, a sincere and lasting devotion, a never failing but an ever increasing love. If you believe in these & trust me you are perhaps better able to judge what an earnest endeavor, a boundless ambition & an untiring zeal may be able to accomplish." In some respects, at least, King was an accurate judge of his own qualities. The letter concluded:

> As I have looked thro' my window in writing the last line, I saw a small wee bird fly from the ground to a tree with a long straw in his little beak. He is thinking of someone he loves and longs to build a home where his chosen companion may be happy while she lives. Won't you let me too begin to gather up the straws for you are the one I love.[7]

On 25 March he received the first letter from Mathilde since the note that came on the 10th. She was still uncertain. Here is King's version: "Dear little soul, she says 'If I can get a clear thought out of the chaos of feeling & if you think it worth while to wait a little longer I shall write tomorrow or the following day.'

I wrote and told her I could wait for all time for her, and thus I closed 'Oh, Miss Grossert, you must & will be mine, no matter what the barriers. . . . God bless you ever, for you are the most beautiful flower in the Master's garden here below. I have asked Him for it and He will not refuse me this I know. Ever with love.' " On the 29th he writes again: he is desperately in love with her, why does she make him wait? "Believe me if I ever get you in these arms you will never break from them in this world or the next." He got as far as the letter-box, and decided not to send it: "There are references in it too earthly in their nature and the truest love is far above all of these." Instead he sent Mathilde a telegram begging her to "write something soon", and followed it up with another letter.[8]

The agitation in Mathilde's mind we can only imagine. Doubtless she found young King attractive — it seems evident that many women did. Doubtless, also, she thought long about the difference in their ages. Perhaps, as he had thought, she did have some mother-feeling for him. At any rate, his persistent bombardment, extending over a month, finally seems to have begun to overcome her doubts. On 30 March King received from her a letter which he does not directly quote but which was, he says, "full of the most passionate love".[9] However, she still did not give him a final answer.

King himself immediately began to have doubts again. It is at this point that one begins to wonder whether the young man's reason is tottering. On 31 March he has a bad cold and is feverish, writes a letter to Mathilde and does not send it, writes another and sends it, goes to dinner with friends and has "a most delightful time", and ends the day by writing this extraordinary passage in his diary:

> There is this very night the eternal fight within my breast.
> Sin and wrong would tear her from me. Thoughts come to
> me which are begotten of the devil and which would ask me
> if I have gained all. They say she has never written and that

my love grows cold. Base & foul thoughts begotten in hell itself. Too often have you tried to lure me from heaven itself, I will have none of you. You offer me ambition and the world. You tell me to gain it alone, — to hell again with you all. For in my best my purest moments I love this woman most. I have not prayed since a child to be guided in this matter right to be deceived now. God has heard my prayer and he gives to me the one who will keep me nearest to Him. . . . I have had a long wait, but faith is strong.

Thus the twenty-three-year-old. On 4 April he wrote asking Mathilde not to delay any longer. But he had already written his family in Toronto telling them of his love for her, and the result was to multiply his troubles.

A flood of letters from 147 Beverley Street now broke over King. First one from his mother, "to which father added a line". "It was to come home & talk over everything first and a warning against too hasty a step." Next day another letter from his mother made him "sick at heart". Basically, the family argument was selfish; if King did what he planned to do, then he would be unable to help the family at home in the way they were counting on. His mother wrote,

> I have built castles without number for you. Are all these dreams but to end in dreams? I am getting old now Willie and disappointment wearies and the heart grows sick. Sometimes when I hear you talk so much what you would do for those that suffer I think charity begins at home and as you do so shall it be done unto you. I am not grasping for myself but I do feel for your sisters and I know you who have such a big heart will not forsake me.

His father said, "I think your first duty is to those at home." His sister Jennie added her voice to the onslaught.[10]

King had refrained from telling the family that Mathilde was older than he was. If she was really a dozen years older, this was the strongest argument against the marriage that King was (sometimes) dreaming of. Even leaving King's state of mind aside, it seems rather unlikely that such a union could have been a success. There is no need to defend the Kings' attitude, for which there is little enough to be said. Nevertheless, it is arguable that, like Lord Byng on a later occasion, they were right for the wrong reasons.

Willie King was now utterly distracted. In the midst of these miseries he received on 7 April a telegram from Mathilde. It began, "My answer, yes", and went on to tell him to return unopened a letter she had sent that day. It is evident that poor Mathilde, too, had been having terrible mental struggles. Her consent only made King's problems worse. There is no need to inflict on the reader the full text of the lamentations he set down in the diary day after day at this period. The entry for the day he got Mathilde's telegram concluded, "I wrote to Mathilde tonight, I wrote home, I mailed the letters at midnight. What storm is this what sea. Oh God bring peace and understanding soon. Let thy purpose be revealed. Bless us all."[11]

King did what his family had asked: he went home to Toronto to discuss the affair with them. Only afterwards did he go to Chicago to see Mathilde. When they heard of this intention his mother and father must have felt that they had won. Here is his record of his talk with them on 17 April: "Father thinks it would be a terrible mistake for me to become engaged, that it would cramp me in every way, it wd. be unfair to the girl, etc., etc. I see the truth of much of this now but is it not too late. I cannot be dishonourable, I cannot now retract. . . . My prayer is that Miss Grossert may not love me or if she does that she may or we may be led to see whether or not it is well for us to become engaged. I promised that I would not become engaged but I would not promise not to love the girl or not to engage myself at a later time to her."

King's diary of his visit to Chicago is long, confused, and

excited. As before, expressions of confident love alternate with doubts. The course of events was this. King reached Chicago early on 19 April, but he did not see Mathilde that day, presumably because of her hospital commitments. He visited a friend of hers, Mrs. Billin, who had written him a letter trying to explain Mathilde's difficulties; and he spoke to Mathilde on the telephone. On the evening of the 20th he met her. The reader who has put up with his peculiarities this far is entitled to know what he wrote in the diary afterwards:

> Oh life it does not become changed in a day. I have had Mathilde in my arms I have kissed her lips. I have seen she loves me and I am still the same. Oh God, Oh God, Oh God, Where! where! where! What! oh what! oh what! Where is the love that was so beautiful and strong in me, what are these feelings of pain and anguish that now fill my breast. The little one rushed to my arms, she said nothing for many minutes, she only clung to me, she looked at me, she kissed me, she would not let me leave her. I could not speak. I did not have the thoughts I longed to have. Nor was I carried as I had hoped I might to other worlds. I was more of the earth earthy. Oh miserable man that I am, what sort of man am I. We talked together, we had dinner together. I felt more like crying than eating. We walked together to the Lake shore drive & stood on the bridge together.... She was not altogether happy, nor was I....I left her at midnight....

Apparently King was shocked by the discovery that he felt physically attracted to Mathilde. Apparently also he had not yet dared to tell her about his family's attitude. On 21 April he wrote, "I am going to see Mathilde tonight and tell her all. I cannot go away without doing this, I will probably break down but that alone will bring rest."

Later he recorded what happened. They took a cab and drove along Michigan Avenue. "We stopped near a light and I read her some back pages of my diary shewing my love for her. I then told her how the last few weeks had destroyed so much." He goes on,

> We each really wanted the same thing. We wanted to know that we loved each other but no engagement yet. We agreed to go back to where we were in our writing before words of love were spoken of and learn whether we were each in love or not. We are neither of us ready for an engagement yet, and both are too sensible to trifle in the matter. But tonight I love her more than ever, and I somehow feel that she will some day be my wife. I have kept faith with those at home, with Mathilde & myself & I am happy now.

Thus for the moment he convinced himself that a compromise had been reached that would be satisfactory to all parties. For the moment.[12]

On 23 April he was back in Cambridge, and already his views were changing. He had now decided that he hated Mrs. Billin, whom he had described on the 19th as "a woman of much character". He also decided, extraordinary to relate, that Mathilde had deceived him. "Her whole manner towards me was not that of a woman in love and the truth is, I have been deceived. I was worshipping an ideal but Miss Grossert was not the ideal. Still there is much in the girl that I very truly and greatly admire. If she had been in a home instead of an institut'n she would have been the most beautiful and loving of girls. Oh it is a mistake — this new woman, worldly freedom idea. I have been like Peter. I denied my lord for a girl's sake, but I will do better."[13] (King was repeating himself, as he tended to do.) For a moment his regard for the nursing profession seems to have faltered. Woman's place, he says in almost so many words, is the home. So much for Henrik Ibsen, Bernard Shaw, and the New Woman. A couple of weeks later he was moved to further reflections on the subject when he saw Ada Rehan in *The Taming of the*

*Shrew.* "The last few words of the Shrew* pleased me greatly," he wrote. A man, he proceeded, "should be looked up to by his wife & be strong in her eyes. 'New women' are a perversion."[14] Mackenzie King clearly had no sympathy with the contemporary phase of the women's liberation movement.

Within a few weeks, however, everything was starting over again with Mathilde. On 19 May the incredible young man is inditing to her another of his elaborate literary love-letters. "Not until the sun, or the light or the moon or the stars be darkened or the clouds return after the rain, or ever the silver cord be loosed or the golden bowl be broken or the pitcher be broken at the fountain, or the wheel broken at the cistern will I forget you. . . . I think of you all the time, and have kissed your photo every night for two weeks past before I turned out my gas. . . ." And Mathilde, not altogether surprisingly, responded. On 7 June Willie recorded a "beautiful letter" in which she told him "for the first time in English that she loves me" (a letter received on 15 April had said, "Ich liebe dich").

Unfortunately, things soon began to go wrong again. King's religiosity gets involved with his love in a most unpromising way. He answers Mathilde's declaration by saying (as he puts it in the diary), "The path of duty will open up, God has His work for us to do, it will be the struggle I have looked forward to from youth." This was doubtless a very excited letter, for King writes the next day in the diary, "I was doing last night just what brought me so much trouble before, writing, writing—wildly, in mad haste, not reflecting — also talking only of myself and my plans. Oh God make me humble, very humble, make me very

---

*It will be remembered that Katharina's last speech includes the lines
    I am ashamed that women are so simple
    To offer war where they should kneel for peace;
    Or seek for rule, supremacy, and sway,
    When they are bound to serve, love, and obey.

humble. . . . " A little later he writes, "Christ and Toynbee and this girl all come to me together. When I love the one I love the other, and to turn from the one is to turn from the other"—and so on. He again begins (at times) to be overwhelmed with doubt. He writes a long letter to Mathilde, decides not to send it, writes a short one instead. "How strange I am, I really do not know myself."[15]

This could not go on, and the late summer of 1898 brought the end of the affair. King was increasingly distracted. Should he tell his family he loved Mathilde (as he sometimes did)? Could he tell Mathilde he had grave doubts about their relationship (as he sometimes had)? How should he plan his summer arrangements? He thought he might first go to Muskoka for two weeks' holiday, then to Toronto for two weeks with his family, then to Chicago for two weeks to see Mathilde. This was not an arrangement likely to commend itself to Mathilde. What was worse, he declined an invitation, received through Mathilde, to stay with a sister of Mrs. Billin's where Mathilde was to spend her holiday; he thought it, he told the diary, "by far the best" to accept instead an invitation from his friend Professor William Hill. But after desperate soul-searching he decided to go to Chicago first. On 12 August he writes, "I determined to write Mathilde at once and let Muskoka go." He proceeded to telegraph her that he was coming next week; then, he says, "I went to my room & cried on my bed in anguish. If I could only bring her before me, but she has [been] getting further & further from me. . . . I played the piano & cried while playing, cried bitterly." On 13 August he wrote in the diary, "I have decided to write home & tell them of my going to Chicago but am not able yet. I wrote Mathilde first a long letter with explanations then a short one telling her that I love her. I do love her, I can see that when my thoughts are at their best & when I can bring her before me. . . ."[16]

Apparently King wrote Mathilde, in addition to telegraphing, on Friday, 12 August; and it was this letter that did the damage. We know nothing of its content, but from King's state of mind and his past performances (and its consequences) we may deduce that it was a very "wild" document. The U.S. mails were swift in those days. On Tuesday the 16th King "found two letters in the box from Mathilde":

> I opened the large one first, found it had been written in great haste & anger in lead pencil, the day after she had received my telegram and showing clearly that she had mistaken my intention in sending it. She seemed to think I was angry because she had not answered my letters & that I was coming at once while she was on duty. Her letter was *too* hasty. She had kept it till she rec'd my letter of Friday, & then wrote another no name at either end. "My worst fears are confirmed — neither your letter nor your actions are those of a sane man". This relieved my mind greatly. I see that it will be impossible for us to come to any understanding other than that we must at least be friends. . . .

To use the argot of a later age, Mathilde had had it. The reader is unlikely to be surprised.[17]

On 17 August the "relieved" young man reflected, "The advice from home was after all wise and judicious and I had done better to have sought it before I wrote." The same day he wrote a formal five-sentence note to "My dear Miss Grossert", remarking, "If you feel that you would care to talk with me I should like to come to Chicago to see you when you are free. . . . I sincerely trust that we are not to be less than friends." His reflections in the diary exhibit the usual confusion. "Sometimes I think she may have tried to entrap me, but this I do not believe she did, yet if she is older than I, much older, etc., she may have had design[s], still I cannot think this of her. . . . I am to blame, she is a woman & had reason to believe I loved her, tho' I never said the words to her. She has never heard them from my lips." This is a thoroughly deplorable quibble. King may never have "said the words" to Mathilde, but the reader knows what he wrote to her. A day later he writes, "I love her now as I did a year ago, but it is a love of a child for his nurse, not that of lover & lover. I always feel she is older than I am, she is more to me like a mother than a sweetheart. . . ."[18]

King would surely have been wiser to forget about the trip to Chicago. However, with or without Mathilde's consent (the diary lapses for a time after 21 August), he went, and it seems that what happened there was too painful to record. He set down that he left for Chicago on 23 August and reached Toronto on 3 September: "Was truly thankful." That is all. A month later he makes a passing reference to the events "in Chic.". "All this was a terrible business. . . . It has nearly destroyed my mind & life. I feel effects on both even yet." He is probably speaking of the affair generally, rather than specifically of what took place in Chicago. Looking into his diary he says, "I could hardly bear the sight of my doings since March. They were disgraceful. I was completely beside myself." As late as January 1899 he was sufficiently disturbed to be moved to consult a doctor "& find out if I have reason to worry & what I had better do to quiet my nerves". What seems to have been oppressing him now was not the fear of venereal disease ("strolling" appears to have been suspended during the business with Mathilde) but the possibility of mental breakdown. The doctor told him there was nothing wrong with him; all he needed was "more variety of entertainment, to see more people & to stop worrying" (the doctors' sovereign remedy for worry). He prescribed "some powders", presumably the 1898 equivalent of tranquillizers.[19]

It remains to note one rather remarkable feature of the episode. To every university teacher the student whose work is ruined by emotional problems is a familiar figure. There has rarely been a student with emotional problems worse than those that beset Willie King in 1898; but they did not ruin his work. Far from it. His marks when he received them were "5 A's and one B on a half course last term". He had already been awarded one of Harvard's best fellowships. He himself was rather astonished.[20] It is worth remembering, also, that during the early part of 1898 he completed the report on sweated labour which put his feet on the road to success in the Canadian public service. One is tempted to say that he had already learned to live his life on two levels, separating emotion and business, as he was to do with marked success through a long career.

Would Mackenzie King have married Mathilde Grossert if his family had not objected? The family's interference was important, but probably less important than Dawson thought. The reader is acquainted with King's constantly recurring doubts, which would have been very hard to overcome. The family's attitude reinforced the effect of these doubts. If the marriage had taken place, it would probably have been disastrous for both parties. King might never have become Prime Minister of Canada. Mathilde did herself and King a great kindness when she put an end to the affair.

Older than King as she was, Mathilde may perhaps have had for "das Kind" feelings that were those of a mother for a child rather than those of a girl for her lover. King, it will be remembered, said this at the beginning of the episode, and at the end of it said that his own feelings for her were those of a child for his nurse. We shall see that almost every woman for whom Mackenzie King conceived a long and deep affection in the course of his lifetime was older than himself. It may be that for him Mathilde was primarily a mother figure. Or was she sometimes one thing and sometimes another? A further point of interest is that there was what may be called an element of fantasy in the attachment. King had not seen Mathilde for some eight months when he began to shower her with love-letters. His mind had been at work on the beloved object.

One may speculate on the permanent influence of this crisis on Mackenzie King's life. Did it help to mature him emotionally? It would be hard to imagine a more emotionally immature young man than the author of his 1898 diary. One wonders whether the episode offers any clue to his lifelong bachelorhood, whether it did something to encourage that condition. One notes the contrast between King's readiness to go with the girls of the streets—his strong sexual urges can hardly be doubted—and his awkward and timid approach to a "respectable" woman. One recalls his apparent disquiet at discovering his "earthy" feelings for Mathilde. Perhaps this is more evidence that he was looking for a nurse or a mother rather than a lover or a wife? I am content to let the psychologists and psychiatrists resolve these riddles, if they can.

Although the "affair" with Mathilde ended abruptly in August 1898, that was not the finish of Mackenzie King's connection with her. It went on for fifty-two years longer.

At Christmas 1898 King sent Mathilde a present. His motives do not seem to have been the highest, for he wrote in his diary, "the next thing will be to get my letters back for of them all without exception almost I am well ashamed." In the following March he got a letter from her. She sent him a Bible which he says she asked him "to carry, & to read". Was there a barb in this? She said she thought of returning to Germany. King wrote a long reply; he told her "that I was sorry for all I had done amiss . . . and asked her to forgive me". He also says, "I asked her to burn all of my letters with two exceptions, and said I wd return hers when she desired."[21] (Here we have to blush for King; immediately after the fatal 16 August 1898 he had busied himself in copying Mathilde's letters.[22] So he was in a position to return them and still have them.)

This exchange seems to have had no immediate sequel; but in December 1900 King, now a Deputy Minister in Ottawa, met a former St. Luke's nurse who told him Mathilde was married and living in Maryland. Her husband, he was told, was a cousin of hers "who came out with her & his uncle some six years ago". His name, although King did not get it right at first, was George Edward Barchet. King was delighted. "I feel a newer, freer, happier, better man because of the news I heard tonight." Clearly his behaviour to Mathilde had left a burden of guilt-feelings weighing upon him. But it had not prevented him from getting on. He reflected, "As I look back over the past I can see where I was nearly mad. The wonder is I have weathered the storm so well."[23]

The girl from St. Luke's must have reported to Mathilde, for a few months later King heard from Mathilde's husband asking for her letters and for an address to which she might return King's. Mathilde's letters had been left in Boston; King recovered them, and there was a scene in Ottawa in which, once more, the Deputy Minister does not appear to good advantage:

> Tonight I read aloud to [H.A.] Harper parts of Miss G's letters, then did them up in a bundle to return to her. Burb[idge] came in about 10, at which time I destroyed in the fire on the hearth all of mine. As I look at them I see them to have been the most worthless sort of trash. I am glad they are in ashes.

Reading a lady's love-letters to his room-mate was surely one of King's more regrettable performances. But the passage suggests that King had learned something, even if it was not gentlemanly behaviour. Incidentally, although the "worthless trash" was reduced to ashes in King's fireplace, much of it is preserved for posterity in his diary. As for Mathilde's letters, King finally appears to have destroyed most of the copies he had made; only a couple of fragments remain among his papers.[24]

Here one might have expected the thing to end; but there was a very long epilogue. Time removed the bitterness, and it would seem that a certain affection lingered. King and Mathilde acquired the habit of exchanging Christmas greetings (he was an insatiable Christmas greeter). At least once, in 1916, when medical treatment took him to Baltimore, King visited the Barchets at their farm outside Annapolis. Mathilde gave him a "beautiful" table cover she had worked for him. King wrote, "I debated after I came away if it [were] wise to have gone. She has such deep feelings & the friendship of 20 years ago remains strong. It has been a truly noble friendship." In 1932 a disastrous fire destroyed the Barchets' home, Belfield Farm, St. Margarets. King sent them $250 as "a little help".[25] The occasional correspondence continued. Mathilde outlived King. He wrote her a letter as late as 3 March 1950, only four and a half months before his death. She died in 1960. Her son, Stephen G. Barchet, became a Rear Admiral in the United States Navy.

# MOTHER

In the light of the part King's mother played in the affair with Mathilde, this may be a good place to say something about her.

Though it would be foolish to build much in the way of an argument on this slight foundation, Mrs. King (and the rest of the family) are not very prominent in the earliest months of Willie's diary, in 1893–95. But in June 1895 he began reading Charles Lindsey's *Life and Times* of William Lyon Mackenzie, apparently for the first time. "I felt quite inspired and intensely interested, I imagined I could feel his blood coursing through my veins, especially in his references to the poor." A few days later, "I have become a greater admirer of his than ever, prouder of my own mother and the race from which I am sprung." And then again, an excited and almost incoherent passage:

> As I read of his many marvellous excapes [*sic*] from death the thought occured [*sic*] to me, why should this man escape the many many attempts made to end his life, suffer imprisonment, experience poverty in its worst form, be exiled from his native country [*sic*], that to him a young child should be born, the 13th & last of a large family, who should bare of son [*sic*] to inherit the name of his grandfather W. L. Mackenzie. Surely I have some great work to accomplish before 'I die'. . . .[1]

King's special regard for his mother, it seems to me, did not stem merely from the fact that she was his mother. She was also William Lyon Mackenzie's daughter, and this was very important. King was constantly and acutely conscious that he was his grandfather's political heir. The passage just quoted is only one of many* in the diary that make this clear. On 2 September 1901 he first told his mother that he hoped to be Prime Minister. She was returning from Ottawa to Toronto because of the death of a relative. He gushes about her face. "Had it been the face of a Luther, a Savonarola, Elisha, or other great prophet of God, it could not have been more beautiful. . . . I could see the strongest resemblance to grandfather, & thought of him as he must have toured this country in election & rebellion times. She [such?] a face was born to lead & guide men. Partly because of the association, partly to comfort mother, partly to express my own ambition & partly because my soul was large, my spirit strong & resolve great, I whispered to mother that I believed, that if opportunity came in the future I might become the Premier of this country." And it was not just heredity, it was literally a sacred mission, the result of "the ways of God". Mackenzie King was a man of destiny, appointed by Divine Providence to carry on his grandfather's work. No one who seeks to understand him should forget this.

Mrs. King's performance when her son was threatening to marry Mathilde Grossert gives us an impression of selfishness and possessiveness which is perhaps exaggerated. But she was a strong-minded little woman, the central personality of the King household.[2] And Dawson is I think right when he says that the Grossert episode brought "a new intensity" into King's relationship to his mother. It left King with guilt-feelings not only about Mathilde but also about the family and particularly his mother. Back in Cambridge after the final crisis, he writes, "I have suffered much pain today at my terrible selfishness while at

*See particularly below, pages 151-2.

home. Why was I not always with mother. I should have shown more love to her. If God spares her & me may he give me strength to prove my love. I must work now for all at home, keep them before me, deny self, work for my mother, father, sisters & brother *first*."[3] In London in 1899–1900 he had "no less than five" photographs of his mother displayed in his room. Increasingly he rhapsodizes about her in his diary. In the course of one such passage (September 1900) he writes, "She is, I think, the purest and sweetest soul that God ever made." (His biographer Dawson noted a little sourly in the margin, "First Real Rave about Ma".)[4]

For King her physical charms were as striking as her moral ones. In the same passage just quoted he writes, "in beauty she is wonderfully fair. Everyone looks with admiration on her." Photographs of her move him to write, "She has a finer face I think than that of any woman I have ever seen."[5] Readers of the diary become accustomed to King's accounts of public occasions at which his mother was the most beautiful woman present. She was a good-looking woman for her age, but surely scarcely as handsome as King thought. King's panegyrics tell us less about his mother than about himself. When he thinks of marriage, he thinks of a wife like his mother. Witness this remark (29 July 1899): "If I can only win such a wife as I have such a mother, how infinitely happy!" Another comment, early in 1901, probably tells us a good deal. It is his mother's birthday, 6 February, always a festival. King telegraphs her, and then writes in the diary, "I love her with all my heart and I would never feeling [feel?] a longing for the love of another if she were always with me, so pure so almost holy. . . ." But of course she was not always with him. Willie was now a civil servant in Ottawa, while his parents continued to live in Toronto. They came to visit him in the summers, and he often visited the family home in Toronto (the Kings moved to 22 Wellington Place about 1903, to 4 Grange Road in 1904, and finally to 236 Avenue Road in 1916;

King spent a week in Toronto supervising this last move).[6] But there are considerable periods in his early years in Ottawa when the family is seldom mentioned in the diary. An isolated reference to Mrs. King is this of 1904: "Wrote short letter to mother— dear little Mother. I am too neglectful of home, & its love."[7] There were, as we shall see, other interests in Ottawa.

# PART II
# THREE FRIENDS

As a young man Mackenzie King had a great many friends, male and female. It is sad to reflect that in later life, when he was a senior politician, he had a great many associates and acquaintances, but his real friends were comparatively few.

Most of King's private life during the half-century from his arrival in Ottawa in 1900 until his death can be described within the compass of three friendships: one with a young man, his college friend Bert Harper; two with mature married women, Marjorie Herridge and Joan Patteson. There were, of course, other friends, whom we must look at in their place. The short association with Harper really belongs to King's youth, when he was still living an active social life not unlike that of their university days. Harper was his closest friend at that time, but there were many others. The friendship with Mrs. Herridge overlaps that with Harper and continues as King's star rises until he becomes a Cabinet minister. The friendship with Mrs. Patteson virtually coincides with his career as Prime Minister.

It is important to note that all these three people, in their times, played essential parts in King's *daily life*. We have said that as Prime Minister he had few real friends. Even so, there were other people besides the Pattesons who deserved that term. But they lived in parts of Canada distant from Ottawa, in the United States, or in Britain, and he saw them rarely. In Ottawa, his home, there was in those days nobody like the Pattesons. They were the confidential partners of his private world, as Harper and Mrs. Herridge had been earlier. There seems no doubt that, at the centre, King was an insecure person. He felt the need of support, and he found it in constant close, private, quasi-domestic companionship with trusted friends. He got it from his family, and particularly from his mother while she was alive and with him; he sought to get it from her still by spiritualistic contact after she was dead; but he got it also from these three special friends.

He got it likewise, in later years, from his dogs. One is tempted to say that they were at least as important as any human friend. Anyone who reads King's account of the death of the first Pat (15 July 1941) — perhaps the most embarrassing passage in all the long years of the diary — realizes that he is confronting something more than an old gentleman's ordinary affection for a pet. And should one not list Kingsmere also among the solaces of his insecurity? In his first year in Ottawa he became devoted to this green forest tract in the lap of the Gatineau hills (it is "old Kingsmere" to him as early as August 1901), and as he gradually built up his modest estate there, the devotion grew. All the three special friends — and certainly the dogs — were specifically associated in his mind with Kingsmere. The place was his refuge and his pride. It seems to have become for him almost a personal presence — as it were that of some benevolent woodland goddess. In his last illness he refused to leave it, and at Kingsmere he died.

# BERT HARPER: "THE LOSS
WAS IRREPARABLE"

During the period of nearly two years between the end of the Mathilde Grossert affair and the beginning of King's work in Ottawa (September 1898 to July 1900) the young man went through a variety of experiences which no doubt did something to mature him—to make him a little less the silly youth who had lately behaved so absurdly, and a little more a man of the world.

For one thing, he took his First Drink. (It is curious that it came so long after the first woman.) The King household, one would gather, was strictly teetotal, as were many middle-class homes in Ontario, where, nevertheless, there was a great deal of hard drinking. Willie was definitely priggish about it, and about other things. In Cambridge early in 1899 he confides to his diary a description of a party with a group of "classical students" who told "filthy stories" and drank liquor. He writes, "How vice seems to creep into the lives of men! A drop of whiskey has never passed my lips & never will so long as I possess health & strength & a will of my own. I am glad I find no enjoyment in such gatherings." The first drink comes six months later in Toronto, but it is not whiskey. King is having dinner with two of his closest university friends, Professor and Mrs. William Clark. Says King, "I took a little claret at dinner, the first I have ever taken. I took it only because so often pressed by Mr. and Mrs. Clark, my reason against it being one of principle only, not fear."[1] One speculates that the Clarks were trying to ease their young friend out of a little of his priggery.

Many an Ontario youngster of that generation and the next, brought up to teetotalism, managed to overcome it. King overcame it, but very incompletely; its ghost haunted him all his life. He never became more than an abstemious drinker, but many references in the later diaries show that he worried enormously when he found himself moved even to small indulgences of this sort.[2] It is evident that an aura of sin continued to hang about the brown bottle.* His experiences with bibulous politicians — including ministers — did not make him more tolerant. When Chubby Power, the Air Minister, missed a Cabinet meeting on 23 May 1944, King wrote, "What a curse liquor is. The devil's principal agent, I believe."

Later in that summer of 1899 he first drank champagne. He was catapulted for a few weeks into the orbit of the American plutocracy when he went to Newport to tutor two young members of it, Bob and Peter Gerry. It was a genuine Arcadian adventure with the idle rich. King filled his diary with denunciations of their manners and customs, but it is pretty clear that he was enjoying himself. It is rather comical to find the penniless Canadian graduate student writing a letter of condolence to his new friend Reggie Vanderbilt on the death of his father. No other Canadian prime minister has ever had the connections with the world of American big business and big money that Mackenzie King had, and those weeks at Newport made their contribution. He never lost touch with the Gerrys, who for all their wealth were nice youngsters. He also met a Miss Julia Grant, a granddaughter of President Ulysses S. Grant, who was

---

* At a Government House party at Christmas of 1930, King records, "I took no wine or spirits of any kind, kept a glass of sherry in front of me, just to make clear to myself I could resist any temptation, refused a glass of champagne with His Ex. before coming away."

about to marry a Russian, Prince Cantacuzene, whom King thought "a poor affair". Miss Grant, on the other hand, he liked "very much": "she is pleasant & natural". She will appear again.[3]

Immediately after the Newport episode, King was off for Europe. Here a recurrence of "strolling" was to be expected. With his record, and London's reputation? The expected duly happened. On 13 October, "only the angels have kept me from falling, but they have". But the following evening, a dull lecture on the Transvaal (the South African War was just breaking out) drove him to take a walk: "Came back about midnight. — I have been wasting much valuable time, worse than wasting it." Familiar phrases! The cash account in the back of the diary records the sad little transaction of 14 October: "Wasted" — two shillings. In February 1900 he writes that the past two weeks "have been marked by no resolution or purpose, a drifting & wilful wrongdoing". "I must overcome again this selfish & sensual self, and free my soul from the peril in which I daily bring it."[4] The diary seems to contain no definite indication of "strolling" during his swing around the Continent, and there are no more "Wasted" entries in the cash account; but the news, received in Berlin, that his friend Bert Harper had lost both his parents produced another outburst of self-condemnation, including a word that King does not seem to have applied to himself before: "The truth is I am not the man I ought to be, I am the sort of man I most despise, a hypocrite, who plays fast & loose with life, & deals lightly with holy things."[5]

The strolling story may be carried somewhat further here. July of 1900 finds King in Ottawa. That prim little capital, a place of some 60,000 people, had its own sub-world. It was apparently not destined to see much of William Lyon Mackenzie King, but it saw something. King was now twenty-five, a relatively mature man, and (very suddenly) an important public official. For such a person, "strolling" seems scarcely conceivable. Yet the diary of 1901 chronicles one expedition below the surface, and the circumstances were curious. On 10 October 1901 the brilliant young Deputy Minister of Labour (a Presbyterian, but clearly no bigot) addressed an Epworth League convention at Bell Street Methodist Church. His subject was "the economic world of today" and the relation of the church thereto. He ended on an inspirational note: the church should make it its business to "inspire love in the hearts of men". It is evident that he quoted two of his favourite authors, Carlyle and Matthew Arnold (his discovery of Arnold we shall hear about in due course). The Reverend Salem Bland, seconding the vote of thanks, said "the apostle of Sweetness & Light wd. have rejoiced & Carlyle lost his pessimism had both been there". But the day ended sadly. The old phrases appear in the diary again:

> Tonight I wasted the time & worse than wasted it, being overtired & worn I should have gone to bed, a restless fit came on & I gave way to it by going out—Oh fool. When will I learn self control, the first element of greatness.[6]

Hypocrisy? The hostile critic could hardly find a better example than this respectable official encouraging lofty thoughts among his Methodist hearers, and then straightway going out onto the streets of Ottawa to look for a woman. To the people of 1901 it would have looked worse than it does in our permissive time. If it strains the reader's charity, he may perhaps reflect that it is a parable of miserable humanity: "I strive to do right and continually do wrong."

This is not the last time those telltale words "worse than wasted" appear in King's diary. We shall see them again, at a bitter moment in his life, in 1917 (below, pages 153-4). No doubt there were other journeys into the shadows, perhaps unrecorded (one remembers those long gaps in the record). Nevertheless, after this apparently isolated episode of 1901 the street-girls, who have been background figures in the diary since its beginning, no longer appear as they once did. Henceforth

King's dealings with women are more exclusively with the "respectable" members of the sex.

And if anyone should ask whether Mackenzie King ever had physical relations with a woman apart from those which he obviously had with the streetwalkers, the author of this truthful memoir can only reply that he, at least, does not know. There were some things that King did not put down in the diary.

On the day Mackenzie King arrived in Ottawa to become editor of the *Labour Gazette* (24 July 1900) he had lunch with his friend Bert, Henry Albert Harper, who was working in the city as correspondent for the Montreal *Herald*. From that time on they were close companions.

The diary for 1893–95 does not suggest that Harper was King's most intimate friend at the University of Toronto, where they were both in the class of 1895. References to Harper are not as numerous as those to some other students. But it is evident that by the end of their course they had established a special relationship. On his way back from his holiday in Muskoka in September 1895 King stayed with Bert for three days at the Harpers' family home in Barrie, Ontario. And in 1898, at Harvard, King records receiving a "splendid" twenty-page letter from Harper telling of newspaper articles on the "welfare of industrial classes" which he was going to publish. King's comment was, "We certainly have a true affection for each other, I will glory in all his successes."[7]

When King found himself in Ottawa saddled with the responsibility of creating a new government department out of nothing — for that was essentially the situation — it was natural enough that he should recruit Harper. He knew him, he was familiar with his abilities, and he knew that his views on social questions coincided with his own. By 19 October 1900 (the diary does not give a more precise date) Harper had severed his connection with the *Herald* and had become Associate Editor of the *Labour*

*Gazette*. He and King were already sharing living quarters; King proposed this three weeks after his arrival in Ottawa, and Harper evidently liked the idea. The two young men embarked on their partnership with sententious expressions of idealism. King wrote, "We can strive together after an earnest christian manhood seeking to inspire in each other what is most noble and to lop off the sins and shortcomings which so easily beset us. . . . I have one little doubt about a certain loss of privacy and a danger on my part of talking too much. . . ." (Had King thought that living with Harper would help him to curb his "strolling" propensities? It seems quite likely.) On 14-15 October they set themselves up at 202 Maria Street (now Laurier Avenue West), where they had found an establishment with separate bedrooms and a common sitting-room. In September 1901 they moved to 331 Somerset Street, where, King wrote, "I have the two large rooms and Harper the two small ones."[8]

Some present-day readers will nod wisely and say, "Homosexuality." They will, I think, be wrong. It was a consciously romantic and affectionate friendship, but the picture King's diary gives us is not of what C. S. Clark called "sinners of Oscar Wilde's type".[9] It was certainly not an exclusive relationship. Harper and King were very active in the young society of Ottawa. A third Toronto classmate of 1895, Henry A. Burbidge, was living in Ottawa, where his family had their home. "Burb" is very prominent in the diary, both in 1893–95 and the years beginning in 1900. Long afterwards he averred that he, King, and Harper were known as the Three Musketeers. "Until I went to Winnipeg in the winter of 1905 Mr. King was a constant visitor at our home."[10] In January of 1901 Burb told King that one of his sisters was being sent to Bishop Strachan's School in Toronto; and King then wrote, "I do not know why I should but I sort of feel that the family have decided on this because of my evident attentions to her. . . . She is, I think, the first girl, younger than myself to whom I have ever felt closely drawn." King foxed the family, up to a point; on his next trip to Toronto he got into Bishop Strachan's to see Beatrice Burbidge, on the basis of being convoyed by his father.[11] In March 1901 the Three Musketeers gave a sleighing party: "Four horses with plumes."[12] Such were the simple, strenuous amusements of Ottawa as the twentieth century dawned.

King was clearly as much a lady's man as ever, and he noted the same tendencies in Harper. He could recognize his own symptoms: "H. has gone out tonight. He has been restless all day. Hope he will keep up the fight for noble Christian manhood. I must do all I can to have it so for us both."[13] When Harper returned from his vacation in the summer of 1901 and described his experiences, King recorded, "I fear Bert has a weakness for the fair sex."[14] All this is not conclusive, but it is interesting. I feel sure that what King thought he was setting up at 202 Maria Street was not a male love-nest but a sort of family circle, a private world where he could find refuge and support. He had arrived in the new, strange society of the capital to undertake work of which he had no previous experience. At first glance he did not like Ottawa. "I find myself bearing up against a load in this place," he wrote on his first evening.[15] Bert was a providential gift from the familiar past, and King seized upon him.

The establishment at 202 Maria was not Wildean but Tennysonian. The two serious young men frequently read aloud together, and one of their favourite readings was *The Idylls of the King*. King writes on one occasion, "Tonight I felt like going to the theatre, but stayed in on Harper's suggestion, & read aloud 'Lancelot & Elaine'. He was greatly charmed with it. He then began reading Carlyle's 'Past & Present', a great book. . . ." The next day (Sunday) after breakfast King read aloud *The Holy Grail*, "a perfectly beautiful Idyll. . . . The whole is wonderfully beautiful."[16] They seem to have gone right through *Past and Present*, and they read other prose works.

The King-Harper partnership is pictured in the little memoir of his dead friend that Rex wrote later, and particularly, perhaps, in Bert's two final letters to Rex printed in that book.[17] The two young men emerge as utterly earnest, wholly humourless, and ineffably pompous. They had a strong sense of mission. Their object was to help the workingman to better himself. For "selfish employers", organized in such bodies as the Canadian Manufacturers' Association, which took a poor view of the Department of Labour and specifically of the Labour Gazette, they had no good word. Along these lines they worked happily together. When Rex was called to distant parts of the country on mediation tasks, Bert functioned as acting Deputy Minister, keeping his friend informed of developments in Ottawa. The last letter is signed "With best wishes and much love, Affectionately yours, Bert." (Would King have published this letter if the relationship had been anything but "innocent"?)

In his last will King stated that he made his first visit to Kingsmere on Thanksgiving Day of 1900. The little Kingsmere Lake lies among the hills on the Quebec side of the Ottawa, some eight miles as the crow flies from Parliament Hill. King recorded elsewhere that he and Harper cycled there together that day and ate their lunch on the summit of King Mountain, overlooking the land that King would one day own.[18] They spent much of the summer of 1901 at Kingsmere, living in a boarding-house run by a Mrs. McMinn and usually travelling by train from Ottawa to Chelsea when the day's work was over. King's mother was there for four weeks, and the Herridge family were also staying at Mrs. McMinn's.[19] Thus began the mystical association of Kingsmere with King's family and friends. But the association with Bert Harper was almost over.

On 6 December 1901, while Rex was returning from a mediation mission in British Columbia, Bert and other young people went skating on the ice of the Ottawa River near Kettle Island, just below the capital. In the gathering darkness a man and a girl skated into a patch of open water. The girl was Bessie Blair, a daughter of the Minister of Railways and Canals. The Bert Harper who looks out at us from his portrait, with the pince-nez and, if the whole truth be told, the rather bovine expression, has not the appearance of a hero. Later in the century, nevertheless, a great many young men more ordinary than Bert would discover that they were capable of heroism at the call of duty. On that winter night on the Ottawa duty called to Bert Harper. Knowing that it was almost certain death, he went into the black water to try to save the girl. He failed; both he and Miss Blair lost their lives.[20]

A telegram sent to Mackenzie King on the train bringing him back from the West did not reach him, and he first heard of the tragedy from the Toronto newspapers when he reached there on the 7th. He returned to Ottawa at once. Bert's friends "viewed the remains" (horrible phrase) at the Herridges' (St. Andrew's Manse, 293 Somerset Street) and Dr. Herridge conducted the funeral service there. Among the "floral tributes", we learn from the press, was a "pillow of roses with [the] word 'Bert' and three links, one broken, from W. L. Mackenzie King and H. A. Burbidge". The Musketeers had been disbanded.[21]

According to the Ottawa *Citizen*, King and Burbidge managed to attend both the further services at Barrie and Cookstown on 10 December, and a public meeting at the Ottawa City Hall the previous evening. That meeting decided to open a subscription list to pay for a monument in memory of Harper. The Hon. William Mulock, Harper's Minister, moved the resolution and headed the list with a donation of $100. Mackenzie King gave $50. The committee appointed to supervise the work was headed by the mayor and included King and Burbidge, as well as Mr. Justice Burbidge, Burb's father.[22]

There is no doubt that King was a moving spirit, if not *the* moving spirit, in the monument project. A month after Bert's death we find him talking to a Cabinet minister about it. The minister "thought the suggestion of the 'Sir Galahad' as a statue or relief a good one and was inclined to favour it."[23] The suggestion was undoubtedly King's; we remember the two friends reading that "wonderfully beautiful" idyll, *The Holy Grail*. And it was carried out; the little statue of Sir Galahad still stands on Wellington Street in front of the Parliament Buildings to prove it, with the quotation from *The Holy Grail* below it:

Galahad . . .
Cried, "If I lose myself, I save myself!"

The project moved slowly. The sculptor ultimately selected was Ernest Wise Keyser, a young American living in Paris. A real King touch: "Subsequent to the making of the award it was learned that he had been born on the same day of the same year on which Harper was born."[24] Early in November 1905 King had the satisfaction of seeing the statue unboxed in Ottawa, and reflected happily on the success of his "endeavours to secure the head of Metcalfe St. as a site".[25] On 18 November the Governor General, Lord Grey, unveiled the monument. The Deputy Minister of Labour presented it to the Prime Minister, Sir Wilfrid Laurier, and Sir Wilfrid accepted it on behalf of the government. "The regimental band of the Governor-General's Footguards [*sic*], which had volunteered its services, played 'The Maple Leaf' as the King's representative unveiled the monument; at the same moment the sun came out from behind a cloud."[26]

There is one other visible memorial to Bert Harper. In 1906 King published his memoir, *The Secret of Heroism*, dedicating it to his mother. King's biographer Dawson comments that the little book "displayed King's literary talent at its best".[27] This is probably true, though it is not saying a very great deal. But the book is an obviously sincere and sometimes a moving tribute to the dead friend. Its worst feature is the fact that in printing Bert's final letters King could not bring himself to omit passages praising William Lyon Mackenzie King.* Bert had once written in his diary, "Vanity is Rex's great weakness . . . and will I fear remain an alloy in his character to the close."[28] He obviously knew his man. But one thing we must give King credit for. In his account of the unveiling of the monument he leaves out his own speech, though he prints all the others. (The *Citizen* assures us that he spoke "with his usual fluency and eloquence".)

King's diary for 1901 is blank after 23 November, so we have no contemporary account from him of the shock of Harper's death and his own sense of loss. But he took the diary up again on New Year's Day 1902, and his first thought was of Bert: "He has gone quickly, the soul of the man that I loved as I have loved no other man, my father & brother alone excepted." He went on to observe that he himself was left because God had not yet had from him "the fulfilment of purpose for which I was created"—the task of bringing his fellow men "to realize the capacities of their natures".

King remembered Bert Harper. As late as 6 December 1944 he noted in the diary, "the anniversary of Harper's death 43 years ago". But a more striking passage occurs in 1909. On 6 December in that year King made his long-delayed maiden speech in the House of Commons. Of that evening he wrote:

> Before going to the House at 8 I put ten little white roses† on the base of the Harper Monument. It was beautiful to leave it [*sic*] there to look at when I came out. It was in thinking

*Notably: "My dear Rex, I assure you it is not the prejudice of a friendship, which makes me miss you more than I care to confess, that tells me that it is not the strong arm of a commission, nor yet the power of public opinion, that is your strongest weapon in this important crisis; but the commanding influence of a high-minded manhood moved by noble impulses, and unalloyed by selfish motive. Success must crown your efforts."

†Why ten? Why not eight, or perhaps a dozen? Remembering King's later concern with numbers, one feels sure there was a reason; but it is not evident.

before the debate that I was alone—no single soul to really share a discussion with, or to share a supreme hour of one's life with—that I was suddenly reminded it was the anniversary of Bert's death, and I knew that the loss was irreparable.

With those last words the diary forsakes its usual level of shabby and careless prose and rises, for an instant, to something higher.

# MARJORIE HERRIDGE: "HAPPINESS AND PAIN"

The Very Reverend Dr. William Thomas Herridge—he was to be Moderator of the Presbyterian Church in Canada in 1914—was English by birth, but a graduate of the University of Toronto. (He sat for a time on the University's Senate with John King.)[1] In 1883 he became minister of St. Andrew's, Ottawa, considered the wealthiest Presbyterian congregation in Canada; and he held that post until the connection was broken by tragic differences over the question of Church Union.* In 1885 he married Marjorie Duncan, the daughter of an eminent Scottish divine. They had two sons and two daughters. The elder son, William Duncan Herridge, born in 1886, was to have a distinguished record in the First World War and play an important part in public affairs in the 1930s. It is a point of interest that Marjorie Herridge was born in 1858.[2] She was thus some sixteen years older than Mackenzie King.

Piety and Presbyterian background made it natural for King to gravitate towards St. Andrew's. On 21 October 1900 he records, "We [that is, Harper and himself] went to Herridge's church"; and on 9 December, communion Sunday, he again notes that they went to St. Andrew's. It is quite likely that they

*Both St. Andrew's congregations of which King was a member, in Toronto and Ottawa, stood out against union with the Methodists and Congregationalists and remained Presbyterian. So did King.

had joined the church in the interim; there are gaps in the diary. The first indication of personal friendship with the Herridges comes in February 1901, when we find the two young men going to supper at the manse after church, and King expressing in his diary a low opinion of Dr. Herridge—"a man of ability but most conceited & vain, a teacher of Ethics not a preacher of religion".[3] March brings the sleighing party; Mrs. Herridge chaperoned it, and King says, "She was very full of life and kept those around her in good spirits." About a week later King and Burb go to church with Mrs. Herridge. Partly shocked, partly charmed, it seems, King records, "There was a strange Minister & when he prayed for the Minister's wife, she grabbed me by the knee & began to laugh. She was inclined to laugh too much, if opportunity given at all."[4] Here there is a parallel which psychologists and others will note: King's mother, another vivacious lady, is recorded as getting into trouble because of "her inability to behave with proper gravity" in church.[5]

By the summer of 1901, the friendship of King and Harper with the Herridges was well established. Though the diary does not say so, it was probably the Herridges who suggested that Rex and Bert should spend the summer at Mrs. McMinn's at Kingsmere, where, it is evident, the Herridges themselves stayed, though Dr. Herridge was visiting England and did not join the party until September. In the meantime King's mother was present and would seem to have got on very well with Mrs. Herridge. She returned home the same day that Dr. Herridge arrived.[6]

Saturday, 7 September 1901, is a day of some importance in King's life, for that evening Marjorie Herridge introduced him to the writings of Matthew Arnold.[7] As King came out from Ottawa, Dr. and Mrs. Herridge met him. The Doctor went on into town, presumably to perform his Sunday duties. King and Marjorie had supper together, and later began to read aloud some of Arnold's poems. Here is King's account:

My whole nature roused as I read them, & Mrs. H. and I gave her [our?] whole thought and mind to their beauty. We did not wish to leave them & read on till nearly half past one. The night was a revelation to me of a new soul, a supremely refined intellectual & spiritual beauty characterized its thought & expression. I became an admirer of Matthew Arnold's.

On Sunday night again they read Arnold "till nearly one or after". "I shall never forget these two nights," wrote King, "no not so long as I live. They have added too much to my life."[8]

That exalted week-end witnessed another turning-point: King took the first step towards acquiring land at Kingsmere. On Friday evening King and the Herridges had spent the evening talking of "securing houses out here". Mrs. Herridge pressed the Doctor to build one. "I drew a plan of the house," King recorded, "& we agreed — the entire night discussing it, framing dimensions etc. etc." This no doubt was the origin of the Herridge house, which at a day still far in the future would pass into King's hands and be named "Moorside". Now, on Sunday morning, King arranged to buy a "lot by the lake at $200" from one Allen, provided the seller would give him until next spring to pay, which he did. It was the beginning of one of the most important things in King's life.[9]

His devotion to Matthew Arnold was only less deep and lasting than his devotion to Kingsmere. He and Harper at once began reading Arnold together; by October they were into *Culture and Anarchy*.[10] Although the inspiration for the Harper memorial came from Tennyson, a quotation from Arnold's poem "Rugby Chapel" introduces *The Secret of Heroism*. References to Arnold occur in the diary for many years, often in connection with Mrs. Herridge.

Why did Arnold have such a strong appeal for King? No

doubt the fact that Arnold was introduced to him by a woman to whom he was clearly beginning to feel attracted had something to do with it. It is not surprising that a person accustomed to reading poetry aloud should fall in love with Arnold's often-melodious verse. His strong and varied prose style doubtless also impressed King. But it is hard to imagine King being attracted by Arnold's indictment of middle-class, puritan philistinism. From what we know of King's family they were very precise embodiments of that narrow tradition, of which, Arnold once observed, their friend Goldwin Smith had probably had abundant experience in "the long winter evenings of Toronto".[11] (Did King ever come across that passage?) But there is no evidence that Mackenzie King ever had doubts on any such score; he accepted Arnold as his literary hero without hesitation or qualification, and it is a fair assumption that he never thought of himself as a Philistine.

In the autumn of 1901 it became apparent that stuffy Ottawa was talking about Marjorie Herridge and the two young men. Rex and Bert took Alice Burbidge and her cousin to the theatre. On the way there Alice spoke to Bert, and on the way home to King, "about our going about with Mrs. Herridge". King remarked to his diary, "I thought it extremely impertinent. We have only been on one occasion anywhere with Mrs. Herridge where Alice B. or her friends cld. have seen us, & that was when we sat in Mrs. H.'s pew at church." He added, "The more impulsive in her goodness of heart, Mrs. H. has twice the head & heart of these other people & not their meanness."[12] It seems likely that the young ladies were in fact jealous of the older woman.

Two months later Bert was gone, and it can hardly be doubted that Rex, overwhelmed by his loss, turned naturally to Marjorie as a substitute friend. An entry in the diary at New Year's demonstrates rather curiously the extent to which he had now become virtually a member of the Herridge household:

> The New Year came in as Mrs. Herridge and I stood before
> an open grate* with bowed heads. Thoughts of all at home,
> of the new purposes of a New Year, of her beside me, of he
> [*sic* ] who is gone passed quickly by, each borne aloft on the
> wings of prayer and noble resolve. The children had re-
> turned from a party, and we kissed them anew, Gwennie
> was asleep, Dr. Herridge in bed beside two lighted candles, I
> kissed him & Miss Duncan and Willy later. Then Mrs. H. & I
> read a little from Emerson's Essay on Friendship by the
> fire's light, and at the half hour I came to my room, with her
> word for God's blessing as I went out into the new world of a
> new year.

Later that day King had New Year's dinner with the Herridges:
"Gordon played a while of [*sic*] the violin, the Dr. on the piano,
Gwennie with her arm around my neck, and Irene beside me sat
as we looked over some pictures together. Later in the evening
Mrs. Herridge read aloud most of the essay on 'Self Reliance'
(Emerson) which the Dr. finished, and at the close Dr. H. read
Browning's 'Abt Vogler' a magnificent poem revealing the har-
mony of music and verse, each as soul's embodiment of thought.
There is real strength in Emerson. . . ."[13]
   Unfortunately this rather idyllic picture began to alter almost
at once. We read of Dr. Herridge becoming ill with "melan-
cholia" and going away. After his return there is tension, and on
the night of 25 February an explosion. King escorts Mrs. Herridge back to the manse after midnight (she had been at his
rooms, where his mother was visiting him).

> When we came to the front door it was locked, Mrs. H. rang
> twice and then the Dr. came himself unlocked the door &

---

*The diary abounds in almost sacramental references to King's love of
"open" fires. One speculates that Miss Duncan, mentioned in this passage,
was Mrs. Herridge's sister.

stepped back. When I sd. good night to him, he did not reply, but in the most direct manner possible slammed the inside door shut on both of us. It was in so many words 'You may both go your way, I scorn you both'.

Next morning King had a long talk with Marjorie, in which each spoke "of things known to the other but unspoken before, Dr. Herridge's indifference to her, the want of any true love between them,—for years past, his going his way and she hers, his justifying her action by his friendship with other women, his leaving her alone for months each summer, & the rest." All this gave him, King records, "a tacit understanding that so long as honour could suffer no reproach there could be no objection to a closer friendship—where it was as ours has been, on intellectual and spiritual lines,—only of the purest & of the best—than might be enjoyed by others less fortunate in the purpose of their lives."

Later in the day King went to see Dr. Herridge. "He sd. that he had been annoyed with his wife, (I told him the fault was mine) he sd. the only reason was, what the neighbours might say. If there were but the three of us, I was welcome to go where & when & be where & when I liked with Mrs. H. but we had to consider the outside world, which I frankly admitted.... I stayed only a few minutes." That evening Mrs. Herridge went with King and his mother to the theatre, and after that there was a small supper party in King's rooms. "Mrs. H. stayed the night with Mother."[14]

A few days later Herridge came to see King and in effect apologized, saying he was glad that his wife and King had each other as friends. "He spoke only of the need of considering outside opinion. I spoke to him of my going so often to church with her. This he sd. he quite approved of. He did not think a word could be said against us. He then asked me if I wd. not come over and see Mrs. Herridge, that she was ill, & had been since Friday." King went, and Herridge took him up to her bedroom and "withdrew closing the door". Says King, "No man ever did an act more nobly or gracefully, and the man wd. be a dog who would profit by it, unfairly." After a talk she felt better and came downstairs. King wrote in his diary that night, "The truth is she loves me, and my problem is here. I am determined to do nothing that will cause any estrangement of feeling between her and the doctor."

King now had a revulsion of feeling in favour of the Doctor. That evening (it was Sunday) he walked to church with him, "taking his arm". Herridge preached "a grand sermon on Saul", and they went back to the manse for supper. Then, says King, "I told Mrs. Herridge she must do what she cld. for the Dr. to love him well. When she seemed to resent my being drawn closer to him, my soul rose against her. It will do this. When I think he is responsible for the lack of love, I sympathize, when I think she is the cause, or fosters it, it turns my heart against her. I fear she loves him little. I wd. to God she loved him more. Miss Duncan sd. she thought this was going to draw them closer together than they had been for some time. May it be so." Marjorie doubtless felt, as the modern reader is likely to feel, that her friend was a rather curious young man.[15]

We now come to the enigmatic summer of 1902. Enigmatic, because King's diary fails us. There are no entries between 11 July and 21 September. We know that in the early part of the summer, at least, King was paying for board and room at Kingsmere, presumably at Mrs. McMinn's. Undoubtedly Mrs. Herridge and her children were there, but it is not clear whether they, too, were at Mrs. McMinn's or whether their new cottage was ready; the latter seems rather unlikely. We know from King's cash account that in July he bought a silk hat for Dr. Herridge ($5.50).[16] We know from the press that Dr. Herridge went on one of his solitary holidays, this time to the Maritime Provinces.[17] And when King starts to keep the diary again, the first entry brings us up with a start. Apart from everything else, there is a new name for Mrs. Herridge:

After a lapse of several months I take up this little volume again. It is a return of self to conscience, the cry of a lonely soul seeking companionship in the expression of its own grief. The story of my life for the present is the story of its relation to the Child. Our summer has been lived together, lived to ourselves, and now the fall and winter has [*sic*] come and we are to live apart, and the duties of life rather than its pleasures are to receive their emphasis. What is to be the outcome of this love, the love which binds her to me and me to her, that is the problem now. She loves me more deeply than ever before if that is possible, and can do less well without me. I have reason to love her as I never had reason to before. I tremble at moments when I think of what our lives are to each other. The solution will not come in seeking to turn away, or in ceasing to be, it must be worked out in the full presence of each other by a fuller presence of God. I see no other path, either certain or right.... To do right, because it is right to do right. To follow Duty, and to listen more to conscience in discovering its dictates, to speak only truth, and never to act a lie....

King proceeds to record that he "went over to talk with the Child". "Her love," he says, "is such that she is unhappy one minute alone." The entry ends, "The Child looked beautiful today, so fair — oh Child!"[18]

What are we to make of this mass of words? An obvious interpretation is that during the summer Rex and Marjorie had become lovers—that their relationship was no longer merely "on intellectual and spiritual lines". Indeed, this seems not unlikely. However, dealing with the particular man and the particular period we are concerned with, it would perhaps be dangerous to jump to conclusions. King's late-Victorian romanticism and his capacity for fantasy must be allowed for. It is best to admit that we do not know how far things had gone. One curious fact in particular makes one wonder. Immediately after King wrote the passages just quoted, he left Ottawa to speak at a meeting in Hamilton, Ontario. A letter from the Child after his arrival there "made me happier, for I was lonely without her, and have missed her much." But the next day he met another married woman, Mrs. William Hendrie, Jr., "and was perfectly charmed with her". He arranged to see her again, and wrote in his diary, "She rouses the whole of my nature & makes me feel I could fight worlds."[19] Nor was this a mere passing fancy. Lily Hendrie, the lady who made him feel he could fight worlds, became a life-long friend.

One thing seems clear, if we are to believe the diary. Mackenzie King may have been in love with Marjorie Herridge, and probably was; but he was not so much in love with her as she was with him.

King continued to frequent the manse (one is tempted to say, a sort of cuckoo in the nest). We have a picture of the reception of another New Year, that of 1903:

> As the New Year came in Dr. Herridge Mrs. Herridge & I were sitting before the open grate fire or rather the Dr. & I were sitting, Mrs. H. was standing. He rose & kissed her then me, then I kissed her. We went together into the parlour & sang a few hymns then kissed the children—who were all asleep & talked till Miss Duncan came in from a midnight party at the Crannell's. I was invited but preferred to spend the last night of the old year with the "Child". We read thro' "the story of the Other Wise Man" by Van Dyke.

A fortnight or so later King gives a lecture on Social Settlements ("really an illustrated sermon," he says, "aimed at the indifferent well-to-do for their *own sakes*".) "The Child was very pleased & looked at me with her whole soul in her face & like a little child." The lecturer has "a bite of supper at the Herridges" before catching a train.[20] In April King leaves for a trip west on departmental business. "At 10 I went over to the manse and had a last hour's talk with the Child. It was hard to part for so long a time but she was brave, and we said 'Good-bye'."[21] During his absence they constantly exchanged notes and letters. On 6 May King writes in the diary, " ... two beautiful letters from the Child. It took me to a sort of Elysian field as I lay in bed reading the beautiful words & thoughts of this beautiful soul." (The Deputy Minister's vocabulary sometimes seems a trifle limited.) On 21 May the diary lapses, with King anxiously awaiting another letter.

Only on 5 October does King take up the diary again ("as a means to personal betterment"). And there has been a change. No longer is Marjorie called "the Child" (he practically never calls her Marjorie): "At 9 [p.m.] called on Mrs. Herridge & read her part of a sermon Mr. McCaughan sent me on 'Burden Bearing'. ... " One hopes she was edified. On the 6th he meets her walking with a woman friend. "We had a pleasant walk back to the city together, tho' she was somewhat depressed in spirits. ... " And on the 7th the young dog is up to his old tricks. At a dinner party he meets a Miss Catherine Keith from Kansas City. "After dinner I made for her, and we sang songs together at the piano, and then sat out on a window seat under a palm tree, where we talked all evening." On 10 October the diary lapses again, to be taken up only after the New Year.

The fact is that the passionate phase of the Herridge affair was over. What had happened between May and October we do not know. Perhaps more will be known when letters in the King Papers that are still under lock and key are opened.

This does not mean that the connection with the Herridge household was broken; far from it. King continued to flit in and out of the manse, continued to read constantly with Mrs. Herridge, and at intervals continued to write indictments of her husband. "The man is a cad and I can only class him as such. ... I feel so sorry, oh so sorry for Mrs. H. Her life with him can be only a continuous trial and pain."[22] This went on for years, with King, one feels, using Marjorie Herridge as a substitute mother and a source of the constant friendship and support which his nature needed. We get glimpses of the relationship between the two households at Kingsmere. By 1904 King had his own small cottage overlooking the lake, the Herridges had their larger house on the higher ground some distance back. Dr. Herridge had again gone off somewhere, and King was worrying about "the Child" (a name he rarely used now) and her children being alone at night: "She is an heroic woman to stay alone in that large solitary house, with two little children & neither servant nor even dog about." King seems to have spent several nights at the Herridge house as a result; at this point one feels pretty sure that everything was proper.[23]

Three years later King was hard at work preparing the way for his entry into politics. He clearly knew exactly what he wanted to do; but he consulted "Mrs. H.", getting her to come for a walk with him at Kingsmere. "She is a true friend to me," he wrote, "& is a woman who has great discernment in some things and none in others. She always helps me in my belief that self-reliance, being the master of one's own actions & life is the thing to be aimed at. She feels that public life with all its risks would be better for me than the civil service. She has often told me I should be my own master, & would only realize my best self when I was."[24]

At this time Marjorie had her grown-up son Bill living with her. A few days after this conversation Bill was struck down by illness. Mackenzie King—a good friend himself in an emergency like this — came tearing out from Ottawa with two doctors in "Mrs. Seybold's automobile", making it to Kingsmere in forty-five minutes. King writes, "I will never forget the sadness on Mrs. Herridge's face when she came down to my house about 6. I was getting ready to go up to see what the Dr. had said when I met her. She burst out crying & wept bitterly telling me that it was tuberculosis of the spine that Bill had, 'My beautiful, my strong Bill', she said. . . . I did all I could to comfort Mrs. H.

1. *Willie King was about fourteen when this photograph was taken showing him with his parents and his sister Isabel, whom the family called Bell or Bella.*

2. *Willie King (left) with his father and his brother Max in 1899, just before he left for his visit to Newport and his trip to Europe.*

3. *John King, Mackenzie King's father, rented the left half of this pair of semi-detached houses on Beverley Street, Toronto, for a decade from 1893. Mackenzie King lived here until he went to Chicago in 1896.*

**Q6349**

MONDAY 4.

WEDNESDAY 6.

**Q6350**

THURSDAY 7.

FRIDAY 8.

SATURDAY 9.

*Occasional Memoranda.*

4. *These first pages of King's diary mention, among other things, his present to Mab Moss, his seeing a little of "the wickedness of the world", and a family outing to Niagara. In later years King used diaries that gave him a full page for every day.*

5. Mab Moss gave Mackenzie King this photograph, dated 8 September 1893, when she was leaving for England, as mentioned on the first page of his diary.

6. Mathilde Grossert was the nurse in Chicago with whom King had a passionat love affair (mostly by correspondence) in 1898. They remained friends, and this is o of a group of photographs she sent him in 1916. There is no identifiable photograph her in 1898.

Lady Ruby Elliot (afterwards Countess of
mer) was a daughter of Lord Minto,
ernor General of Canada, 1898-1904.
ckenzie King convinced himself that he
in love with Lady Ruby, and she gave him
photograph; but the affair lapsed when the
tos left Canada.

8. Violet Markham, a wealthy and
high-minded Englishwoman, was a close
friend of Mackenzie King for forty-five years,
and in his younger days she gave him
financial assistance on several occasions.

*Mackenzie King met Lily Hendrie (right) at Hamilton in 1902, and ⸱nd her very attractive. They were friends until his death. This is one of a ⸱up of snapshots Mrs. Hendrie sent him showing what seems to be a garden ⸱ty, doubtless held for some good cause, during the First World War.*

*Mrs. Beatrix Henderson Robb, a New ⸱k divorcée, seems to have met Mackenzie ⸱ng in Europe in 1928. The next year he ⸱alled their "days in Geneva & Paris which ⸱e unique & happy". When visiting New ⸱k thereafter he never failed to see her.*

*11. Julia Grant, who became Princess Cantacuzene, was a granddaughter of President Ulysses S. Grant. King first met her at Newport in 1899, and in later life they were close friends.*

12. *Henry Albert Harper,*
*King's closest male friend*
*and his associate in the*
*Department of Labour, was*
*drowned in the Ottawa*
*River in 1901 while trying*
*to save the life of Bessie*
*Blair.*

13. *Mackenzie King in*
*Privy Councillor's*
*uniform, as Minister of*
*Labour in the Laurier*
*Cabinet. He wears the*
*C.M.G. awarded him in*
*1906.*

14. *The memorial to Bert Harper, erected largely through King's efforts, on Wellington Street, Ottawa. It still stands in front of the Parliament Buildings, though it has been moved a short distance. (The hydrant is no longer in evidence.)*

15. *King's friendship with Marjorie Herridge, the wife of the minister of St. Andrew's Presbyterian Church, Ottawa, was one of the most important associations of his life. By the time this picture was taken, in 1914, the friendship had cooled.*

16. *Joan Patteson at Kingsmere Lake. Mrs. Patteson, who, King said, "filled the place of his mother in his heart", was his devoted friend. She and her husband were his closest associates for thirty years.*

17. *Mrs. King frequently visited her son at his Kingsmere cottage. This picture, probably taken about 1914, suggests the roughness of Kingsmere in the early days. The sundial is mentioned in King's book* Industry and Humanity.

18. *The squire, the medium, and the lady — Mackenzie King, Mrs. Etta Wriedt, and Mrs. Patteson, at Kingsmere about 1934. The dogs are presumably Pat I and Derry. The picture reflects the improvements King had made to his estate.*

19. *The "Abbey Ruin" at Kingsmere: at the right is the bay window of the Parent house in Ottawa, which King thought was "like the Acropolis at Athens".*

20. *King at Laurier House surrounded by portraits of his mentors. Above him is Sir Wilfrid Laurier, at left Abraham Lincoln, and at right his grandfather, William Lyon Mackenzie. In the oval frame are portraits of the members of the Quebec Conference of 1864, the Fathers of Confederation.*

21. A page of one of King's memoranda of séances over the "little table". The date is 13 October 1935, the evening before the general election that returned King to power. King's father reports Sir Wilfrid Laurier's forecast of the result: "Sir Wilfrid says that you will win handsomely." His grandfather, William Lyon Mackenzie, says he loves to hear King say that this is Mackenzie's fight.

22. *The family shrine, Laurier House—King before the portrait of his mother painted by J. W. L. Forster in 1905. King often prayed here. He recorded that the book in his mother's portrait was Morley's* Life of Gladstone, *open at the chapter "Prime Minister". Above King's left hand are the books written by his father and his brother. Below the portrait is a model of the Iona Cross, the pattern for the family monument in Mount Pleasant Cemetery, Toronto.*

23. *"My grave plot is at her side at Mount Pleasant." King was buried beside his mother in Toronto, as arranged long before, under the Iona Cross, the family monument that he had erected. The monument to his brother Max, modelled on Pasteur's tomb, is hidden by the flowers at left. Prime Minister Louis St. Laurent, King's successor, stands beside the grave.*

tonight, but it was hard to know what to say. . . . " Next day King is busy "constructing a bed that would wheel about for Bill H. to lie on and doing what I could to cheer up him and his mother. . . . "[25] Happily, Bill recovered to play his own part in history. For some time, it seems, he regarded King almost as an elder brother, and it seems likely that King was responsible for his joining his own fraternity, Kappa Alpha, at the University of Toronto.[26] This pleasant relationship, unfortunately, was later to be disrupted by political differences.

While counting on Marjorie Herridge for companionship and advice, King in these years was having enjoyable relationships with other women, and in some cases at least considering matrimony. In 1904 he sees a good deal of "Mrs. Cheney, a very wealthy widow (reported to be a millionairess) who has come to Ottawa for the winter". He doubts severely "if her sympathies are with the mass of men in their struggle for a fuller life", but he keeps on seeing her all the same.[27] But his chief interest at this time was on a higher social level. He became devoted to Lady Ruby Elliot, the second daughter of Lord Minto, the Governor General. In January 1904 they have "a sweet talk on the stairs" at Government House, and she promises him a photograph (it is still extant; indeed, there are two). Almost immediately she leaves for Germany to study music, but King's mind continues to dwell upon her: "Such character, such strength, such beauty of soul. She is the only woman of younger years than myself that I have ever looked to as above & beyond me."[28] (Had he forgotten Beatrice Burbidge?)

The fact is that momentarily King convinced himself that he was in love with Lady Ruby. He had an ingenious argument to justify the attachment. He evidently believed, mistakenly, that Lady Minto's father was Lord Grey of the Reform Bill of 1832 (he was actually a younger brother): "We have traditions not unlike. Her mother's father got for the people in England their liberties in the 30's, my mother's father got for the people of

Canada theirs in the 30's here. Our sympathies are alike, only the barriers of custom & prejudice can keep us apart if her heart could care for me." Thus the King interpretation of history. But he was also looking into the future. "I felt...that if Lady Ruby ever wd. care for me & be mine, I could become the leader of the Reform Party in Canada & Prime Minister."[29] Of course, it all passed off. In November 1904 the Mintos finally left Canada. King asked Lady Ruby if he might write to her, "to which she replied, 'Now and then'. From that moment my feelings towards her seemed to undergo a change. . . ."[30] On the same day in August 1907 on which King writes Mrs. Cheney and a Mr. Scholfield congratulating them on their engagement, he hears of Lady Ruby's engagement to the son of Lord Hopetoun.[31] (In due course she became Countess of Cromer.) End of a chapter; but there are plenty of other chapters.

King was now thirty-two, and still a bachelor; and some of his official friends clearly felt that something should be done about it. In this year, 1907, Sir Wilfrid and Lady Laurier had a shot at matchmaking. On 27 August the Prime Minister abruptly asked his *protégé* (a term that could now fairly be applied to King), "Why don't you get married?" King says he replied "that I had set my mind on public life and had kept myself free from obligations which might make the course difficult for me". When he had established himself in public life he would be in a better position to "ask for the hand of a lady". Sir Wilfrid then argued that, on the contrary, "the right person would be a great help to you in public life", and proceeded to mention a young woman whom King had met at the Lauriers' a couple of days before. She was a widow, a daughter of the late Senator Fulford of Brockville, Ontario, a millionaire manufacturer of patent medicines. King went through the motions of accompanying her and Lady Laurier to the theatre, and it is clear that he saw nothing against her; but he was determined in such a matter to make his own decision. He wrote in the diary, "As to the choosing of a wife my heart alone must control that absolutely. I pray that God may guide me in the choice, and order all things to His own best end."[32]

Another friendship which lasted all King's life began in these years. In 1905 King met Violet Markham at Government House, where she was a guest of the Greys. Miss Markham was a wealthy and serious young Englishwoman who was visiting Canada largely to investigate social and industrial conditions. She tells us that she described King in her diary as "a most charming and able young man, full of the right ideals". King's own diary is silent at this point, but Violet says, "Subsequently I paid several visits to Mackenzie King's office and made some expeditions under his guidance—one to a pulp and match factory [undoubtedly the Eddy plant] and one to the government experimental farm. We spoke a common language about social and industrial questions and had the same enthusiasm for Settlement work. . . . We took almost identical views about Capital and Labour. . . . We were both young and enthusiastic, so friendship between us was natural."[33]

For forty-five years these two discussed their common interests and their problems, in letters and in many meetings. Their correspondence was, in Fred McGregor's words, "warmhearted and affectionate on both sides but without any trace of romantic attachment".[34] Miss Markham, whose conscience troubled her about the possession of wealth, decided that Mackenzie King was a suitable object on which to spend some of it. She helped with his election expenses, and after his defeat in 1911 she sent him £200 to give him the "sense of freedom" which she felt he needed at that moment. Almost immediately she made a further generous offer, in terms that made it difficult to refuse:[35]

> Now my dear friend into this crisis & into this breach, you must let me step. You are a poor man, a poverty most

honourable to yourself. I am a rich woman & because my wants are few, relatively a very rich woman. The whole problem of riches is a most difficult one to me. . . .

The simple fact is that I want to help you at this crisis, for Canada's sake as fully as your own. For the next three years I want you to take from me £300 a year so that your hands may be free & your independance assured through this time of crisis. There is nothing in such a gift which may not be offered by me & accepted by you in most perfect simplicity. . . . Any obligation to one of your fellow countrymen might tie your hands in some way. With me the word obligation could never arise — there is no obligation between us save that of a deep & enduring affection. So dear Rex for three years feel you are free to work & to *rest*, to lie fallow & study & read & think, without your life being obsessed by the harassing cares of daily bread.

King accepted, and surely no one need think the worse of him for doing it.

Rex and Violet kept each other informed about their family problems, and in 1914 we find King recording, "Violet Markham's help has made possible my brother [Max] & May [his wife] being together."[36] Max was a victim of tuberculosis, and had moved to Colorado in the hope of improvement. It is not surprising that Rex wrote of Violet a little later, "How wonderfully true and kind and generous she has been! She has a heart of gold, no purer heart or greater ever lodged in a woman's breast. Her help has meant much to me, and her presence is like that of an angel in all that surrounds."[37] In 1915 Miss Markham married Lt.-Col. James Carruthers, a professional soldier and an owner of racehorses. It seemed an ill-assorted match, but in fact they are said to have lived very happily until Colonel Carruthers died in 1936.[38] She had continued to use the name Markham in her active public life. One of King's interests she did not share: the spiritualism which so dominated his private life in later years. In the often perceptive memoir of him which she published after his death she wrote, "I listened to his views with interest if without conviction." She did not mention that she had shared in one of his little-table *séances* at her house in Kent in 1934.[39] In another matter she did not enjoy King's confidence (virtually no one did)—that of the extent of his fortune in those latter days. At the time of his retirement she explored the possibility of making a gift to add to the comfort of his final years, though certainly no such provision was necessary.[40]

Here it is suitable to bring to a close the story of King's friendship with Marjorie Herridge.

There was a gradual unhappy estrangement. We would know more about it if there were not so many long gaps in the diary (1913, notably, is almost a complete blank). It seems evident, however, that the ties slackened as a result of King's entering politics. The fact is—and King's whole career henceforth bears witness to this—that when he was in office the concerns of his private life were much less important than at other times. He was simply too busy to pay all the attention he would have paid in other circumstances to his women friends and—at a later stage — to the spirits. Politics and administration were his first priorities. We get an indication of this on 23 October 1911, a month after the disastrous electoral defeat that deprived King of his status as a Minister and his seat in Parliament. He records that he spent the evening reading aloud to Mrs. Herridge — reading his own book, *The Secret of Heroism*: "The first night's reading I have done for years. It recalled the happiest & best days of my years in Ottawa."

The Herridge children were now all grown up. The two girls "married money". King apparently could not refrain from making comments about Irene's marriage that her mother did not appreciate. There was a discussion on 19 November 1911 that made no difficulties, but early in 1912 there was trouble. King admits he made "a tactless remark, and hurt her, so that she was angered somewhat, and spoke hastily." It must have been a very unpleasant moment, for—a rare thing indeed—half a page has been cut out of the diary.[41] Presumably the record was so painful that King, at some later time, decided to suppress it. Here, it would seem, is the beginning of the end.

This episode is strange. Why should King apparently so resent Irene's marriage, and in particular her marriage to a wealthy young man, that it had a permanent ill-effect on his relations with the Herridges? From this time he repeatedly uses the words "selfish" and "selfishness" in connection with the Herridges, usually in a context related to these prosperous marriages. At the time of Marjorie's death he spoke of her having "perhaps injured my life a little thro' selfishness" (below, page 104). Can he possibly have played with the idea of Irene Herridge as a future wife for himself? The fact that in 1912, as we shall see, he was actively searching elsewhere for a wealthy woman to marry surely makes this rather improbable. But we are dealing, as we know, with a very peculiar personality. Perhaps the explanation was on that half-page that he cut out of the diary; in which case it is gone for ever.

In the spring of 1914 Mrs. King was making one of her visits to Ottawa, and King took her more than once to the Herridges' in the old way; but things were not as they had been. "It hurts me deeply to see the indifference of one and all after much that has been done," he wrote. "The more wealth, the more selfishness with most people." He seems to imply that the Herridges had forgotten all he had done for them. The reader may have his own ideas about this. King goes on to write, "There is no longer a welcome for me, because I have drawn away, & now I see it was selfishness that lay at the root of friendship, tho perhaps I am wrong in this. Lives change beyond our control at times."[42] As King himself might have said, How true. That the end had finally come was made clear on the mystical 17th of December:

"Mrs. Herridge has forgotten my birthday. How strange & sad! What changes the years bring." King was now forty; Marjorie was fifty-six.

All contact, of course, did not end. Mrs. Herridge busied herself with war work (she was later decorated by the King of the Belgians). We catch glimpses of King helping her, and admiring her performance.[43] When he was in Ottawa he still occasionally called on her as of old.[44] He prevailed upon her to come to his mother's seventy-fourth birthday party — an occasion we must deal with later—and writes, not very pleasantly, "I hope the visit may help to soften her heart, when she sees what Love and prayer can do—and filial devotion."[45] One would like to know what was said in the Herridge household when King became Prime Minister. When Marjorie's younger son, Gordon, was killed in a gun accident in 1922 it must have been a painful blow. It appears that her mind failed a year or so before her death.[46]

On 22 March 1924 the Prime Minister received word that "Mrs. Herridge Sr." had died that afternoon. This is what he wrote in his diary:

I thought of Matthew Arnold's lines as I drove home, "Strew on me roses roses & never a spray of yew."* I recall her reciting it years ago at [the] time Bessie Blair died, with a mystic sort of feeling that it applied to herself. Often very often since she has repeated the lines & often said there were many worse things than death, often too has she lately expressed the desire to die. Her life has been a great tragedy, the greatest I have known in a human life. The past ten years our friendship has meant little, my first ten years in Ottawa it was in some respects, apart from home ties &

*The quotation is not entirely accurate. "Strew on me" should be "Strew on her". The last word in the original may be either "yew" or "rue"; I have given King the benefit of the doubt. The two following lines, which King obviously had in mind, read,
  In quiet she reposes;
  Ah, would that I did too!

affiliations the most real expression of my life — full of happiness & pain. Selfishness marred it in the end, selfishness & self-indulgence. I could not have believed I could have felt so little the word of her death. Of course it is now a release a great release, but a sort of bitterness has since entered my nature, a feeling that she had perhaps injured my life a little thro' selfishness, *perhaps the greater injury was mine to her in ever having been such friends*. But it is over now. . . .

The italics are the present writer's. That evening King went to Bill's house and saw Marjorie in her coffin. At the funeral he saw her again, with a familiar expression on her face: "it was the earnest look I liked best of all." He still thought it necessary to say something unkind about her husband, but "Bill looked like a real son." A little later Bill sent King some mementoes of his mother, including (says the Prime Minister) "a little watch I gave her & which she carried always".[47]

Let us drop an old-fashioned tear for Marjorie Herridge. She was unlucky in her relations with the men in her life, always excepting, it would seem, her beautiful, strong Bill.

I said that Mackenzie King did not forget Bert Harper. Even though he "felt so little the word of her death", he did not forget Marjorie either. Ten years after she died, when Matthew Arnold was brought to his mind, the diary rose again above its usual commonplace level:[48]

> On reaching Laurier House, . . . I took from the little table in the hall a parcel which I opened and found to be the portrait of Matthew Arnold sent me by Eleanor Whitridge which M.A. had given to her mother, who was his daughter. I took it into the sunroom and hung it on the wall. . . . On the way, looking at it, . . . I repeated the lines*

*Again the quotation is not wholly accurate. "Falter" should read "shiver". The passage is from one of the seven poems making up "Switzerland",

In this fair stranger's eyes of gray
Thine eyes my love I see
I falter for the passing day
Had borne thee far from me   etc.

I thought of Marjory Herridge and the days of the reading of Matthew Arnold when Harper was still alive and at the time of his death and afterwards when "The Child" introduced me to "Sweetness and Light".

Through it all, sometimes in the background, sometimes in the foreground, was Mother. Four days after the election that made him a member of the House of Commons, Mackenzie King made to Sir Wilfrid Laurier a declaration such, surely, as few political leaders have listened to:[49]

I told him I was glad to be in prlmt. under his leadership and while my mother was spared to me. That my mother & he had been inspirations to me. I told him how mother had suffered poverty while a child because of her father's exile, and of inheriting through her a hatred of injustice and love for the poor, & a determination to vindicate the justice of the cause Grandfather contended for. Sir Wilfrid said he expected to [see] me go to the very front & rapidly. I told him he would find me faithful to him.

Mother, Grandfather, and Sir Wilfrid: these were, and would continue to be, his inspirations. Two of them were still with him when he spoke. When they died it would make surprisingly little difference.

Sir Wilfrid's private thoughts, unfortunately, are not on record.

---

which King and Marjorie read on the evening when she introduced him to Arnold (7 September 1901). The extraordinary thing is not that King should make errors, but that he should remember the poems, on the whole, so very accurately.

# SEARCHING FOR A WIFE

About the end of the year 1910, it would seem, Mackenzie King began to think seriously about marriage. If we are to accept the idea he had propounded to Laurier in 1907, that it was undesirable to think in such terms until he was established in political life, there was nothing to hold him back now. And in fact he now committed himself to the doctrine that a suitable marriage and a happy home were essential to success in politics. (He did not know that he would go down in history as the bachelor Prime Minister who was the most successful politician in Canadian annals.) This was not entirely new; had he not written in 1904 that if he could but win Lady Ruby Elliot he could become leader of the Reform Party and Prime Minister of Canada? He was now to record precisely the same opinion, in almost precisely the same words, about other ladies.

We speculated earlier as to whether King's various experiences had in any degree matured him emotionally. Early in 1911 he gave a performance which suggests that the process of maturity was far from complete. The thirty-six-year-old Cabinet minister acted, in fact, like an unusually callow adolescent.

In 1907 Sir Wilfrid Laurier had tried matchmaking and had failed. Now Lord Grey had a go. King was invited to "dine quietly" at Government House and introduced to "Miss Fowler of New York". Miss Fowler is one of the ladies in the diary who have no Christian names. I conjecture that she was a daughter of Thomas Powell Fowler, a railroad president, who died in 1915. King was instantly smitten. A major factor in his overthrow was the fact that the lady had been working as a volunteer with the famous medical missionary Dr. (later Sir) Wilfred Grenfell in Labrador. King had been corresponding with Grenfell and was one of his admirers.* Here undoubtedly we must remember the deep regard for nurses and their life of service that we have noted in King since the earliest days of the diary. He wrote of Miss Fowler, "She is interested in human life, in the saving of men, in the betterment of conditions for the poor." He pursued her while she was in Ottawa, and when she left he accompanied her on the train as far as Vankleek Hill. He left with her some of Dr. Grenfell's letters to himself and a copy of *The Secret of Heroism*, "which she told me yesterday Lord Grey had given her to read". When he got his first letter from her he wrote, "I love to think of that little one alone on the Labrador Coast."[1] Fantasy, fantasy.

Not only was King smitten, he told everybody who was any-body that he *was* smitten and intended to marry the girl. He told Sir Wilfrid Laurier, sweetening the pill by saying he "sometimes regretted" not having seen more of Sir Wilfrid's candidate in 1907. (Sir Wilfrid told him the Canadian girls would never forgive him if he married an American.) He told Lord Grey ("I think you have found for me the one I have been seeking for years.") He told Lady Tilley (the widow of one of Sir John Macdonald's finance ministers). Finally, he telephoned his mother. "I told her I had a great secret to tell her, that Earl Grey had been like a father to me. This seemed to cheer her a little. I am sorry to be away on her birthday."[2]

The reason he was away on her birthday was that he was

---

*Perhaps there is some connection here with King's contemporary at university, Norman Duncan (above, page 44n.), who had published *Dr. Luke of the Labrador* and *Dr. Grenfell's Parish* some years before.

following Miss Fowler to New York. There, alas, things began to go wrong. He had tea at the Fowlers'. His beloved, he says, has "a very beautiful disposition", but "it is hopeless for me to try to get to know her within four walls". "I must admit to experiencing a wounded feeling when I spoke of Harper's letters [undoubtedly, those splendid letters in *The Secret of Heroism* which speak so well of King], and she mentioned not having had time to read since her return. I think she had in mind the Toynbee book,* which has just come to hand. If she has not read the little memoir, it wd. be strange." Then there was some discussion about a mutual acquaintance, the Reverend Mr. Dickie of Berlin, Ontario. Just as King was about to remark that Dickie had baptized him, Miss Fowler observed that she had taken an "intense dislike" to the man. King admitted to himself that Dickie was a bad preacher, "but it was another knock in the interview. I really felt so ill at ease for a time that I hardly knew what to say." Mrs. Fowler invited him to supper for the following day. He wrote, "This looks favourable—but what chances are there. I want the girl to know me & I want to know her. That is the curse of this artificial life."[3] There the diary ends for the better part of three months, and when it resumes Miss Fowler has vanished from it. What happened at that supper party, and how this promising attachment came to an end, we shall probably never know. Can it be that the lady's apparent failure to read and admire *The Secret of Heroism* was intended as a signal that she was not anxious for things to proceed further? Was she really quite as serious-minded as King's fantasies had pictured her? Is it possible that she was finding this Canadian politician a bit of a bore? Is it possible that the charm that Violet Markham had felt when she met him in 1905 was beginning to weaken six years later?

One cannot help wondering what explanation King gave to Lord Grey, and Sir Wilfrid, and Lady Tilley, and, not least, to his mother.

*I am not sure what book this was.

This reverse must have discouraged King somewhat; but in the absence of help from the diary it is impossible to assess his state of mind. Except for one entry on 28 April the diary does not begin again until after the great Liberal defeat in the autumn. And at that point he is determined to seek a wife:[4]

> . . . I feel I should seek to become married. If I can only find the one that will be the helpmate needed thro life I will certainly marry. It is a mistake not to, and if my life is to be what I wish it to be I believe a home is all important. I cannot but believe that this good will come out of the present misfortune.

Reviewing his situation at the end of the year, he wrote, "I have a little leisure, opportunity to make with care & prudence the great step in life — the choosing of a wife — This I hope to do during the coming year. God grant I may, & may He guide me in the choice."[5] In effect, King now launched a campaign to find himself the helpmate he needed.*

Indeed, he had already fired the first gun on 18 December, when he wrote to Miss Frances Howard in Montreal. At the New Year of 1912 she was in Ottawa. King, with his usual penchant for making private matters public, talked to Laurier about her. Sir Wilfrid was enthusiastic, not least because she was a Canadian. She was a granddaughter of Lord Strathcona. Is it relevant that Strathcona, in addition to being a multi-millionaire, was a prime benefactor of the Grenfell Mission? But when King spent an evening with her in Montreal, things went wrong again: "Somehow I did not feel at ease. . . . It seemed to me it was the same with her, at any rate I came away feeling it was not wise to 'follow up' our friendship. There is something lacking. . . . I feel

*The campaign is described, rather respectfully, in F. A. McGregor, *The Fall & Rise of Mackenzie King*, Chapter 3. McGregor felt that in this book, published in 1962, he must suppress the ladies' names. At this date, and with the text of the diary universally available, there seems no point in following his example.

like despairing sometimes & wondering if I will ever see anyone I can truly & deeply love." But he intended to persist with the search. "I know that if I can find the right one to share my life with, & can be freed from dependence on others, I can be the Leader of the Liberal Party & ultimately Premier of Canada. . . . This year I must decide, either to leave politics altogether or be the framer of future policies, and that decision seems to me to depend on the woman I marry.—Marry I must if I can, it is the right life for a man. I have delayed it already too long."[6]

The Canadian contender having been scratched, King went on to New York. Here he confided in his old pupil, wealthy Bob Gerry, who was anxious to help in his quest and did in fact introduce him to various charming ladies. And he re-established contact on his own with another woman he had known before; he had written in Montreal, "My thoughts turn of late to Miss McCook, and have from the very start."[7] Miss McCook had the special recommendation of being interested in the Grenfell work in Labrador. All this activity had no practical result.*

It seems very likely that if the diary were more complete we would know the names of several more women whom King reconnoitred with the object of matrimony. The year 1913 is almost wholly blank. Then in May 1914 we find him undertaking a visit to Cleveland, Ohio, to meet a Miss Mather, whom he had been corresponding with for some time. She was probably a daughter of Samuel Mather, a coal and iron tycoon. She too apparently had Grenfell Mission connections. But, just before leaving, he got a letter from her telling him that she had become engaged to a Dr. Bishop. Wrote King, "It was a shock for a moment or two. I felt that I had allowed to pass one of the great

---

*Frances Margaret Palmer Howard married a British naval officer in 1913. Colonel J. J. McCook was a prominent New York lawyer with Republican political connections; he had been responsible for King's being invited to the White House in 1908 to discuss Japanese immigration with President Theodore Roosevelt. He died in 1911.[8]

opportunities of my life, but also that, perhaps, it was as well, as I had never been too sure that it was the path to happiness." When he had actually met the lady, his feeling remained the same: "a wistful sort of regretfulness, at a great opportunity missed . . . intermingles oddly enough with a feeling entirely the opposite, one of genuine relief at the thought of a complete freedom."[9]

On the day he got back to Ottawa from Cleveland, he launched another offensive. The lady this time was Miss Dorothy Stirling, the daughter of William R. Stirling, a wealthy Chicago lawyer, to whom he had had "a note of introduction for over two years". The note was from none other than Mrs. Grenfell. Mr. Stirling was not only a large contributor to the Grenfell Mission, but an adviser in its affairs. King wrote to Miss Stirling. If she would be at home, he would go to Chicago for a Harvard gathering in June. They duly met; and for some years after, apparently, King took Miss Stirling to dinner or the theatre on his fairly frequent visits to Chicago.[10] But, it is hardly necessary to add, he did not marry her.

Somewhat later came one of King's most truly extraordinary projects. On 9 March 1917, in New York, he went with Allan Baker, M.P., to call on Mr. and Mrs. Andrew Carnegie. During the call he had "only a few words with Miss Carnegie". Back in Ottawa, it is obvious that King's mind conceived the idea of marrying the multi-millionaire's only child. He consulted his mother. "I told her of my purpose to get to know that home, and avail myself of the chances to know the inner life and thought of Miss Carnegie. She told me to do so.—How wonderfully beautiful and as the very gift of God Himself it would be, if we should find in each other that which we have each sought in our heart of hearts." At the end of the month he is back in New York (without telling his business associate Rockefeller), with a view to penetrating "that home". The mission was a total failure. Whether the Carnegies suspected his purpose may be doubted, for he later had very friendly relations with them. But all he got from their private secretary was polite excuses; he went back to Ottawa without seeing any member of the family. On 4 April he wrote in the diary, "I was a little ashamed today that I had ever let my thoughts turn towards wealth in association with marriage. God knows it was not in terms of wealth that I considered the idea. It was the need of freedom & independence to do the big work of a nation as it can only be done with the necessary support."[11]

It may be well at this point to leap still further ahead in time and tell the story of what appears to be the one occasion—apart from the affair of Mathilde Grossert back in 1898 — when Mackenzie King did actually propose marriage to a woman.

In December 1917 King's mother died. Early in 1918, as soon as the first shock of his loss is over, King is found seriously paying court to a "noble and beautiful Christian woman"[12] in New York City.

The Christian credentials of Miss Jean Greer — her family seem to have called her Daisy—were indeed impeccable. She was a daughter of the Right Reverend David Hummell Greer, Protestant Episcopal Bishop of New York and a great figure in New York City.[13] When and how King met her I have not been able to discover; but the absence of references in the diary suggests that he had not known her long or well. The diary for February 1918 indicates that King had met her earlier and had given her a copy of *The Secret of Heroism* (he must have had a large supply of copies of that little book); but he had never heard from her about it, and (he now told Mrs. John D. Rockefeller, Jr.) "feared I had offended her by being precipitate". Mrs. Rockefeller, however, was able to tell him that the book had been received and that Miss Greer "had enjoyed the talk we had had together".[14] (That phrase suggests to me that they had met just once.) Thus encouraged, he telephoned Miss Greer and obtained permission to call on her. This he did on the evening of 21 February.

King was utterly overwhelmed. He wrote afterwards, "I see in her all that I most wish to find in a woman—more than I believed

I should ever find in anyone." Hundreds of words follow in praise of the virtues of Jean Greer. He arranged to meet her again at church the following Sunday, the 24th, in the front pew of the Cathedral of St. John the Divine.[15] Of this meeting he writes, "It made me very happy to be sitting at her side, though God knows I felt unworthy enough...." He goes on, "I reverence that girl with all my heart. If I can win her I will, I should like to give my life into her keeping for I know that there it would not only be safe but redeemed. She would make a true & perhaps a great man of me." That evening he "sent her a few flowers & a note" before catching the train for Ottawa.[16] What was in the note he does not say.

Unlike so many other cases, from Mathilde Grossert onwards, King expresses no doubts at all about Jean Greer. One reason, perhaps, is that he had convinced himself that she had been sent to him by his dead mother. He writes,[17]

> ... Who told Miss Greer to begin to talk to me of the contrast of the materialistic and the spiritual interpretations of life! Was it the answer to my mother's prayer? That is what I want to know! As she lay there through that long year of suffering was not the prayer of her heart that God would send her boy,—"my boy" as she called me,—a true woman to guard his life, and bring him to the altar of God unsullied and unstained from the hour he left the altar in the House of God on earth....

A replacement for his mother, in fact. Back in his apartment in the Roxborough on 25 February, King "Found 2 beautiful white flowers in bloom on little plant mother loved.—Spoke to them as to a voice from her—thought of Miss Greer [he never once uses her Christian name] as being sent by mother.... I anxiously await a letter from her."

It is a curious fact that King nowhere records that he actually proposed to Jean Greer. But he must have made his feelings quite clear — probably in that note he sent before leaving for home — for his life for weeks to come centres on the expected letter from New York. Day by day he watches for the postman: "Surely I shall hear from her tomorrow."[18] But the days became weeks, and—it appears—the letter never came. (There are some gaps in the diary, so it is difficult to be absolutely dogmatic.) What did happen was that John D. Rockefeller, Jr., came to Ottawa on a visit and talked to King about his problem. It is just possible that Jean had appealed to Rockefeller to straighten out his excited friend if he could. Rockefeller (who must have been greatly embarrassed) evidently tried to discourage the whole attachment. "He seemed to think she had no thoughts of marriage. He spoke of her as being his age,* & of the critical period of life it was for a woman & the greater wisdom of a marriage which would make possible the having children." Rockefeller seems also to have attempted to warn King against his disastrous tendency to fantasy: "He felt I was inclined to interpret her actions in accordance with my own feelings & wishes." His final word was, "He advised my going slowly,—treating her only as a friend & await[ing] developments."[20]

Beyond what King recorded Rockefeller as saying, there is no evidence of Jean Greer's feelings. It may seem strange that she never acknowledged his flowers or his letters (he seems to have sent at least one more letter from Ottawa when that sent in New York produced no rejoinder).[21] Undoubtedly she was greatly troubled, and not without reason. She had received an offer of marriage, or what amounted to an offer, from a man she hardly knew — a man whom, it would seem, she had met just three times. It is conceivable that Miss Greer felt that she was dealing with an individual who was the next thing to a madman.

After Rockefeller's visit the Greer episode was essentially over. King, however, was slow to abandon all hope. In his papers there is a note to him from Jean Greer, undated but probably of 1919,

*Rockefeller was born in the same year as King (1874).[19] Thus Miss Greer was approximately King's age (forty-three).

the following year. It is in reply to a letter with which he had forwarded some letters from Sir Wilfrid Laurier; presumably King had hoped to use these to impress her with the fact that he had a brilliant future before him. The tone of the note is friendly but distant; Miss Greer was clearly not interested. On 23 July 1919 she married Franklin Whitman Robinson, an instructor at the Institute of Musical Art in New York.[22]

Almost at the end of his life (13 March 1949) King wrote a postscript to the affair. Quite accidentally he looked at his diary for 1918 and read about Miss Greer. He wrote, "There is a case of a door closing, all to one's advantage. . . . Had I married her as I evidently had been prepared to do [!] I wd have become in all probability a citizen of the U.S. in association with large interests, not P.M. of Canada fulfilling my grandfather's life."

How did it come about that Mackenzie King, a man who so often got what he wanted, who set out with much apparent determination to find himself a wife, and who persisted in the project for a decade, ended up still a bachelor?

There is no simple answer, but we can suggest a few obvious points. First, King wanted too much; he had in mind a paragon, and paragons are hard to find. Secondly, he had extreme difficulty in making up his mind; those doubts that had assailed him as long ago as 1898, when he was worrying about Mathilde Grossert, assailed him still.

Dread in woman, doubt in man. . . .
So the Infinite runs away.

In these years the Infinite gradually ran away for Mackenzie King. Finally, in the one case in which he had no doubts at all he seems to have made a fool of himself and frightened the lady off. However, the case here may have been hopeless anyway; it is quite possible that Miss Greer was already interested in the man she married in the following year.

There is no evidence that King's mother offered any opposition (except in the very early Grossert case) to the idea of his marrying. We have seen her attitude in the Fowler and Carnegie affairs. In the summer of 1917 he writes, "I may be rewarded yet with her life for a long time with me and the desire of my heart realized for her to live till I am married & the leader of my party in Canada." A little earlier, when Max writes about the possibility of their mother coming to live with him, "she said no, she was going to stay with me. When I got married she would take a corner of the house."[23] By this time the old lady's health was so ruined that it was out of the question for her to live alone.

What did King want in a wife? He certainly valued physical beauty, as a thousand references in the diary show. He demanded high ideals, a social conscience, religious belief. (Did not at least four of his candidates have Grenfell Mission connections?) Clearly also he demanded wealth or position, or both. He would have angrily denied this, but his practice wholly nullifies his professions. The women he went after were too uniformly from the upper crust. King's theoretical love for "the poor" is amply documented; but he clearly had no intention of marrying one of them. His ideal, Jean Greer, had the stamp of religious orthodoxy upon her (after all, she was a bishop's daughter). At the time of her marriage it was reported of her that she had "given up much of her time to church and philanthropic work".[24] And she probably riveted his devotion when she made that reference to "the contrast of the materialistic and the spiritual interpretations of life". Position, of course, she had; and though Bishop Greer was no millionaire, he was not poor either (he left an estate of $188,000).[25]

King's remark about Miss Carnegie gives his attitude away. He was not interested (so he thought, or at least said) in wealth for its own sake; what he wanted was "the necessary support" to provide the "freedom and independence" required if one was to do "the big work of a nation". He still wanted wealth; and it is evident that he was very much aware of the possibility of acquiring it by marriage. It is extraordinary that he so fully accepted this idea for himself, when in connection with the Herridge girls it aroused his strong indignation. There is a whiff of hypocrisy here.

He wanted wealth; and where was the wealth pre-eminently to be found? In the United States. When King seriously decided to marry, he simply disregarded his range of female friends in Ottawa and Toronto, some of whom he had spoken of in the diary at earlier times as possible wives. The implied opinion is that none of these suited his purpose; he had to "find" a wife. His hunting-grounds were New York, Chicago, and Cleveland. It was rather strange procedure for a man with political ambitions in Canada, as indeed Sir Wilfrid Laurier twice hinted to him. It seems evident that the American plutocracy, which King had first encountered at Newport in the summer of 1899, had a powerful fascination for him.

# JOAN PATTESON: "SHE HAS FILLED THE PLACE OF MY MOTHER IN MY HEART"

Considering a return to politics at the beginning of 1919, King was still convinced that a politician should be married. He wrote in the diary, "To go into politics without marrying would be folly. I cannot live that cruel life without a home & someone to love & to be loved by. . . . Marry then I must. There are three noble women each of whom I think highly of above words." The three were Miss Greer (of whom at this time King still had hopes); Dorothy Stirling of Chicago; and a young woman who now appears for the first time, Aileen Larkin of Toronto. Miss Larkin was a daughter of Peter C. Larkin, a merchant prince (Salada Tea) and a sound Liberal who had already done much for King and was to be his greatest benefactor in the years ahead. King wrote, "I shall learn soon which one I love—if it is to be one of the three."[1] It will be noted that, of the three, only one was Canadian. King, of course, was to marry none of the three, and, for that matter, nobody else.* But by this time he had already met the lady who was to be, one may probably say, the second most important woman in his life.

*Mrs. Robinson, the former Miss Greer, died in 1945. Dorothy Stirling died unmarried in 1963. King was writing to her as late as 1949. Aileen Larkin, evidently a woman of strong religious feelings, corresponded with King occasionally to the end of his life. She turned Roman Catholic and in 1933

On 2 October 1918 King gave "a little dinner party at the Golf Club. . . as a sort of celebration". The reason for the celebration was the completion of the book *Industry and Humanity,* which he had been working on somewhat desultorily for years past. It was a study of the relations of labour and capital in industry, based upon King's wide experience. Full of his characteristic idealism and optimism, it exuded simple faith in the efficacy of "investigation" and "conciliation", principles that King believed would revolutionize international as well as industrial relations if mankind would pay proper attention to them. Unfortunately, most people then and since have found the book almost unreadable. King nevertheless was enormously proud of it, expected it to give him "a place perhaps in the world's thought",[3] and continued to refer to it, in Parliament and elsewhere, in season and out of season, for the rest of his life.

King had another reason for the dinner party. He wrote, "I wanted to have Mr. and Mrs. Pattison [*sic*] who are next door neighbours, & one or two friends. . . . Mr. and Mrs. Pattison came into my rooms after & spent an hour there. It was quite a happy evening."[4] Thus Godfroy and Joan Patteson make their appearance in the diary and in King's life. There were to be many more such happy evenings, for thirty years to come.

Godfroy Barkworth Patteson was manager of the Ottawa branch of Molson's Bank (which was later merged into the Bank of Montreal). He was the son of Thomas Charles Patteson, who had been for many years Postmaster of Toronto. His wife was born Mary Joan MacWhirter. She may have been a relative of the Scottish landscape painter John MacWhirter (1839–1911). In 1918 she was forty-nine years of age, five years older than King. The Pattesons had one son, John Coleridge Patteson, born in

---

entered a Catholic convent, where, however, she did not remain. She died in 1967.[2]

1896; a daughter, Rose A. Patteson, had died in infancy in 1906. Under the name Nancy she appears in *séances* in later years.[5]

The fact that they were neighbours in the Roxborough Apartments* made friendship natural and easy. As the months passed King began to spend more and more time in the Patteson apartment. In August 1919 he became leader of the Liberal party (without the advantage of marriage, which he had once seemed to consider essential to achieving that distinction). Later that month he is going out to a state dinner for the Prince of Wales: "Mrs. Patteson fixed my decoration for me, first time I wore it around my neck" (this was his C.M.G., awarded to him in 1906, which he later came to think was below him).[6] In October, King is elected to the House of Commons; he has dinner with the Pattesons, and Mrs. Patteson was, he notes, "the first lady to congratulate me". A fortnight later he records, "talked with Mrs. Godfrey [*sic*] Patteson & played gramophone. Had most happy evening. Tried to influence Mrs. Patteson to read more."[7] Once again, as at St. Andrew's Manse in the old days, King is moving in: a cuckoo in the nest.

By the spring of 1920 King is beginning to worry about the relationship. He writes, "spent the evening with Mrs. Patteson. Stayed and talked till after 1.30.—It is apparent to me that I am sitting up too late in these visits to the Pattesons. It is so delightful to have the time free & quiet, and I am very fond of Mrs. Patteson, but I realize it is not in the interest of my work, and perhaps it is better for each of us to see less of each other".[8] King talks again of marriage: "I have allowed myself to drift in a shameless fashion, . . . losing interest, ambition & power in poli-

---

*The *Ottawa City Directory* (the diary does not help) makes it evident that King stayed on at 331 Somerset Street, where he had lived with Bert Harper, until he moved to the Roxborough (a more "prestigious" address, as it would be called today) when that famous structure was opened some time in 1910–11. He stayed at the Roxborough until he moved to Laurier House on 11 January 1923. That was his last move in Ottawa.

tics. It all comes of living alone, not being married. Mrs. P. sees this plainly: never ceases to urge me to marry. If I could only find the one my nature seeks I wd. not lose an hour. Pray God in His Providence there may still be some one not too far away."[9] But things do not change. By the late summer the Pattesons have become "Godfroy & Joan Patteson" in the diary, and have begun to spend time at King's place at Kingsmere.[10]

It has been generally, and I am sure rightly, assumed that the relationship that developed between King and Joan Patteson was "purely platonic".[11] Nevertheless, there was clearly one moment in the early days when it threatened to become something different. At the end of August 1920 King is found going to the movies with Joan and Godfroy. Then, "This afternoon when [I was] talking with Joan, Godfroy phoned about going to a show tonight. It made me sick at heart to have her interested in these poor performances, when her life might count for so much." Now comes the Labour Day week-end, with the Pattesons staying with King at the Kingsmere cottage. Joan reads aloud Carlyle's "Essay on Mahomet". Writes King, "She has a nimble mind, a fine appreciation of literature, keen intelligence and wit, a most delightful intellectual companion, she could rise to the greatest heights, but in Godfrey she has not her equal intellectually. His tastes are on a different level. Her nature needs the spiritual, and that side is far from developed in him. . . . " We see a bright red danger-signal. The next day, back in Ottawa, King has an emotional conversation with Joan. "It seems so hard to overcome oneself, and this morning it was nearly desperation. . . . These storms of passion — for that is what they are, are madness and wrong. They 'rock the mind' and must cease. We both have strength enough to see that, and we will help each other to what is best for each, hard as the struggle may be — and it is hard in this lonely solitary life. . . . "[12]

Clearly, a crisis was impending, and it came on 9 September. What happened, however—whether it was triangular, involving

Godfroy, or was merely emotional passages between King and Joan—we shall never know. For a second time a knife is used on the diary, presumably by its author. Three sheets—five and a half days—are excised from it and from King's life. When the excision ends on 14 September we find King praying at his boathouse at Kingsmere, "where I prayed yesterday". The next day he writes, "Joan and I pledged our lives to united effort and service today. God grant we may be given strength to endure." Whatever had happened, it cannot have been so very terrible, for King continues to visit the Pattesons as before. On 16 September he writes, "spent the evening with Joan and Godfrey. . . . Joan and I talked in front of an open fire in the living room. . . . I read aloud to her Wordsworth's 'Ode to Duty', and 'the Happy Warrior'. We spoke of the fight we would make together for what is best for both of us. The supreme effort to make our lives count in human service. . . . It was one of the happiest evenings we have ever shared together."

Early in 1921 the diary is still reflecting emotional tension, but by the spring the situation seems to be approaching equilibrium. On 21 May King records "a very happy talk with Joan" which throws some light on the September crisis:

> She was quite sad when I met her first. She spoke of her fondness for me, and of having to give me up.—It was plain the largeness of the life of the past day or two* had touched her imagination. Too, she feels that a great struggle has been come thro successfully — she said she felt she had nursed me thro' a great illness for wh. she had been partly responsible — How true. She spoke of the anxiety she has suffered for months. Her sorrow & tears were a reaction now that the struggle was over—dear little soul—she would have been an ideal wife — if we only could have met years

*Political activity, including what King considered a successful speech by himself in the House of Commons on 19 May.

ago. Her tender simple loving nature is what mine needs &
craves. She has great intellectual forces & infinite charm as
well. . . .

The autumn of 1921 brings the first general election campaign in which King leads his party. The Patteson household
played a passive part, but one of the greatest importance for
King. Mark his record of 6 November: "Glad, oh so glad, to
reach Ottawa again this morning, to speak with Joan over the
phone and later at 11 to have breakfast with her and Godfroy, I
was very tired all thro' the day, almost exhausted in fact, but Joan
let me rest quietly. . . a very happy day. . . . She has done everything to please me, everything to make me happy. . . . " Indeed,
she made a great sacrifice. Some time before there had been a
tiff between them when King's puritanism (or something) led
him to criticize Joan for playing bridge.[13] Now she announced
that she had given up bridge for good. On 22 November King,
out on the campaign trail, got a telegram from Joan; he had been
writing to her. On the 27th he was in Ottawa again, glad to be
back, and again having breakfast with Joan and Godfroy.

On 2 December (four days before polling day) King was in
Toronto. He went to Ryrie's, the jewellers, and bought for Joan a
bracelet, for which he paid $125; a large sum in 1921, and a
particularly large sum for King, who was a careful man. In
search of a suitable quotation, he visited the book department of
Eaton's store and looked at two favourite poems, *The Happy
Warrior* and *The Holy Grail*. In the latter one, as so often, he
found what he wanted. In the end the bracelet bore this inscrip-
tion:[14]

M.J.P. from W.L.M.K.
A strength was in us from the vision
*The Campaign of 1921*

Early in the morning of the 6th (election day) King was back in

Ottawa and "knelt in prayer before dear mother's picture". "Joan and Godfroy," he wrote, "had beautiful flowers in my room. I went to breakfast with them and later gave to Joan the bracelet I brought her from Toronto. She was greatly pleased with it — she has been very true, very good, very kind, & very loving, has helped me greatly through this whole campaign. . . ." On 7 December, when it was clear that King was going to realize the ambition he had announced to his mother in 1901, and telegrams of congratulations were pouring in upon the Prime-Minister-elect, King recorded, "Tonight I had dinner with Joan & Godfroy, and a little music after."

It is evident that Mackenzie King considered that Joan Patteson had played a very significant part in making him Prime Minister of Canada—a passive and private part, but not the less important for that. And, King being the man he was, perhaps we should not dismiss the idea as being merely absurd. One thinks back to what he had written when contemplating a return to politics: "I cannot live that cruel life without a home & someone to love & to be loved by." Perhaps King had not consciously realized it, but he was finding that home in the Patteson house-hold. There he got the support he so much needed, the ever-available private refuge, the close circle of confidence, and, if not love, sincere and reliable affection. No doubt Joan Patteson, who as we have seen was somewhat older than King, was a substitute for the mother he had lost, and the Patteson apartment was a substitute for the family house in Toronto, the loss of which he had much regretted.* In any case, at the beginning of King's career as party leader and Prime Minister his private life had fallen into a new pattern, a pattern that would persist until his death. What the effect of these new domestic arrangements was upon the unexampled success which King enjoyed in politics is something that cannot be calculated. But I feel certain that

---

*"But father has gone, and our home in Toronto is gone" (Diary, 4 April 1917, the second anniversary of his sister Bell's death).

anyone arguing that they had no effect would be making a very serious mistake.

Obviously, one could write a whole book about King and the Pattesons. Their relationship lasted an entire generation. Here we must strive to be brief.

The Pattesons were the partners of King's personal life. And when one says "the Pattesons" one means, of course, mainly Joan. Thanks to her, King enjoyed for thirty years many of the advantages of a home, while being spared most of its responsibilities. The Patteson home — in the Roxborough, or later at 202 Elgin Street and then at 30 Cooper Street—was always open to him, and he continued to drop in there regularly for a late-evening talk with Joan. Frequently he was to be found there "unwinding", to use a modernism, after a night session of the House of Commons. Conversation, reading aloud (in the way King had always loved), and music, often including the singing of hymns, were the occupations of these visits. Their taste in literature (no doubt mainly influenced by King) was serious; Morley's life of Oliver Cromwell is a good example.[15] Religious books were numerous. After the advent of spiritualism in King's life, books on the occult were also prominent. There was a new bond here; Joan became the partner of King's explorations beyond the veil, and after table rapping began in 1933 their informal *séances* often took place at the Pattesons'.

What was Godfroy's attitude; what did he think about it all? It is very hard to say, for the diary tells us very little. He is always there, but he is a background figure. It seems clear that he and King were not intimate friends. On the other hand, there is no hint of an armed-neutrality relationship such as had existed with Dr. Herridge in the earlier triangle. One has the impression that Joan's husband accepted the situation and tolerated it, but that in the early years that was all. One would very much like to know what was in those five and a half days of diary entries for

September 1920 that King destroyed. What would Godfroy have said, one wonders, if he could have read what King wrote in his diary after a social occasion in 1923: "I never saw Joan look more beautiful. She was a very distinguished lady in appearance, manner, and in all respects sweet and lovely. I felt very proud of her. All the party talked till after midnight then I walked home with Godfroy & Joan and stayed on there another hour and half, having one of the most beautiful talks I have ever had with Joan."[16] King, one feels sure, was more tactful and much less proprietorial in his dealings with Godfroy.

How important Kingsmere was to the Prime Minister we have already seen. The Pattesons become an integral part of the Kingsmere story. We saw them staying with him at his cottage above the lake in 1920. As he steadily extended his holdings, better quarters were available for them. In 1922 he listed grandiloquently among the year's achievements (along with rendering the cause of world peace "a lasting service by the stand taken on the Near East Question") "an estate at Kingsmere created".[17] This reflected the acquisition of a few more acres. In 1924 something more important happened. After the death of Mrs. Herridge he negotiated with her son Bill the purchase of the "large solitary house" where Marjorie had spent the summers with her children (the price was $3000). "Joan & Godfroy," he reflected, "will make a beautiful spot of it." On 19 September King and Bill and Joan inspected the property: "As Joan said, the owner, the former owner & the tenant." Thus the woman who had succeeded to the place Marjorie had once held in King's heart succeeded also to Marjorie's summer home. King had now decided to call the house "Moorside".[18]

In 1927 the prime-ministerial estate was dramatically enlarged. King clearly had a deep desire to be a gentleman farmer. ("How I delight in these rural & pastoral pursuits," he wrote.) He now bought, for $4000, the McGillivray property ("the old Fleury homestead"), close to the land he already owned. Thus, he says, "I become owner of house, barns, woods and another 100+ acres of land within 12 miles of Ottawa." To go with these he acquired a flock of sheep. He also bought a house and lot adjoining for $1400. This, he thought, was important in order to prevent "a sale to Jews, who have a desire to get in at Kingsmere & who would ruin the whole place".[19] From these transactions emerge "The Farm", the house which King subsequently considerably enlarged and in which he died, and the nearby cottage (the $1400 item) to which he gave the name "Shady Hill". (This was the name of his eminent friend Professor Norton's house at Cambridge, which King had been very proud to occupy in the summer of 1898.)[20] In due course "Shady Hill", much improved, succeeded "Moorside" as the Patteson summer home. This continued to the end; on Christmas Eve 1948 King is found writing to Joan extending to her and Godfroy "the use of the cottage at Shady Hill rent free during 1949". Still the careful man, he limited his generosity to a year at a time. His career as a farmer was short; he found that business expensive and worrisome. But the estate, and his pride in it, continued to grow.

King's time in opposition (1930–35) saw the beginning of one of the features of the Kingsmere estate which casual visitors today find most curious: the artificial ruins. King, of course, was not the only romantic-minded person who has indulged his fantasies in this particular way; Horace Walpole did it in the eighteenth century; but it has not been a common eccentricity in Canada.

This part of the Kingsmere story seems to have begun in 1934 as a result of discussions concerning William Lyon Mackenzie's house on Bond Street in Toronto. The house was threatened with demolition. King was not particularly interested in preserving it in its proper setting; but he thought of moving it to Kingsmere. When this immediately emerged as a very expensive proposition, he turned to an alternative: "secure what was required as the house was being demolished and take it by motor truck to Kingsmere and build again the ruin there." The reference is biblical: "I will return, and will build again the tabernacle of David, which is fallen down; and I will build again the ruins thereof, and I will set it up" (Acts 15: 16). What King thought of doing was acquiring the Historic Sites and Monuments Board commemorative plaque from the front wall of the house along with enough of the bricks to make a setting for it. Very fortunately, however, the house was saved for Toronto. In 1935, King told a correspondent who asked him for a donation to help purchase it as a home for the local historical society, "Were I a man of means, nothing would give me greater satisfaction than to be able to purchase the house and present it to the York Pioneer and Historical Society"; not being a man of means, he offered nothing but good advice.* Citizens of Toronto rescued the building, no thanks to Mackenzie's grandson.[21]

In the spring of 1935 another chance offered to "build again the ruins" at Kingsmere. Driving along Daly Avenue in Ottawa, King saw an imposing house being torn down to make way for an apartment house. It turned out to be the Parent family dwelling (Simon-Napoléon Parent had once been Premier of Quebec). King fell in love with a striking semi-circular stone window, which he thought would make "a marvellous ruin". "It is like the Acropolis at Athens," he wrote. (Perhaps he saw a remote resemblance to pictures of the Porch of the Maidens.) On the spot he agreed to pay the developer $50 for it and proceeded to make arrangements to move it to Kingsmere and re-erect it on a hillock where it would be a picturesque object when seen from a distance and would offer romantic views through its openings to a person standing close by. On Victoria Day he and Mrs. Patte-

---

*The letter must have infuriated the recipient, the more so as King, only too characteristically, managed to mis-spell his name. King never understood the sound political principle laid down by Sir John A. Macdonald, that there is nothing people resent more than having their names spelled wrong.

son saw the last stone put in place; the effect was "quite entranc-ing".[22]

The developer now offered King, free of charge, the stone necessary to complete a building incorporating the window. King thought the chance too good to miss. He would put up "something in the nature of a chapel, or library, or hall, or all combined". He quickly recruited an Ottawa architect, J. Albert Ewart, took him to Kingsmere, and told him "what was wanted was a combination of the Parthenon at Athens — [with] a cathedral or Abbey (Westminster) — Westminster Hall at the Silver Jubilee". This extraordinary concept must surely have shaken Ewart a trifle. Rather fortunately, King had second thoughts overnight. He decided to utilize Ewart's services to "do over the farm house" and to "leave the stone structure 'a ruin' for the present". The "vision of the chapel — or library etc." could be realized at some later time.[23] It never was.

King, however, went on collecting stones from various sources and placing them on the hillock adjacent to the Parent window. He called the grouping there "the Temple" or "the Abbey Ruin", or sometimes "the Cloisters". He obtained some pieces from the old centre block of the Parliament Buildings in Ottawa, which had been burned in 1916. When in England in 1936, he got from the British Houses of Parliament some weathered stones which were being replaced. And in 1941, when news came that the Palace of Westminster had been bombed, he strained Mike Pearson's sense of humour by cabling Canada House in London, "Secret and Most Immediate", asking that steps be taken to acquire for him some stone from the wreck of Westminster Hall. The harried British authorities duly produced it. Pieces from other demolished Ottawa buildings, including the Bank of British North America, were erected on separate sites adjacent to "Moorside".[24]

At about the time when he became Prime Minister, King acquired a relatively luxurious residence in the city of Ottawa. Lady Laurier died in 1921, bequeathing to him the large house on Laurier Avenue East where she and Sir Wilfrid had lived. It was in poor condition, and King's first reaction was that he had a white elephant on his hands. But Liberal friends rallied round. Peter Larkin (who had largely financed King's political campaign in North York in 1917) organized a group of well-wishers — Larkin himself being the largest contributor — who totally renovated and refurnished the house.[25] Thereafter King's pride in it was unbounded.*

Laurier House required a staff; and from the time he moved in, in 1923, King was plagued by the servant problem. At times the diary is full of this.[26] It seemed impossible for the Prime Minister to find and keep a butler, a cook, and a couple of maids who were loyal and efficient enough to meet his exacting standards. The turnover of staff at Laurier House was tremendous. Servants imported from England were as unsatisfactory as the local product. The fact is that King was a difficult and sometimes an unpleasant person to work for; in the words of one of his biographers, "he insisted on his own convenience and the private life of his servants was not allowed to interfere."[27] With his secretaries the story was precisely the same. Throughout his life he complained of the impossibility of finding adequate secretarial help. The secretaries he had were regularly represented in the diary as inefficient and selfish people who, instead of subordinating themselves properly to King, were apt to develop concern for their own affairs at critical moments.[28]

---

*Larkin had his reward — the appointment of High Commissioner for Canada in London. On 10 December 1921 King told Larkin he could have the high-commissionership if he wanted it. Later in the same conversation Larkin produced the idea of the Laurier House fund. On 2 February 1922 King told Sir Lomer Gouin, who had campaigned for Sir Charles Gordon for the London appointment, that it was going to Larkin. King wrote in his diary, "it gives me immense satisfaction to see these wealthy selfish men put in their place." Larkin was wealthy — but obviously not selfish.

Obviously, the Laurier House establishment was expensive to maintain. For this, too, Larkin made provision. In 1925 he launched a fund for King's benefit with a deposit of $25,000. By 1928 he and his friends had raised the total to $177,500, which was deposited, presumably for reasons of privacy, not in Canada but in the Old Colony Trust Company in Boston. The ultimate sum was $225,000. The fund was not directly connected with Laurier House; it was for King's personal benefit and incidentally to enable him to maintain the house in a proper manner. King wrote at the end of 1927, "Larkin has been goodness itself. He has secured me financially for the rest of my life. I have no longer reason to be anxious on that score, that means everything." His own savings, he calculated, amounted to about the same as the Larkin fund at that time (that is, $177,500), in addition to his life insurance, the amount of which he did not specify. With his official salary as Prime Minister over and above all this, he was now very comfortably situated.[29]

Mrs. Patteson's relation to the social life of Laurier House is difficult to define. Mr. Neatby has written, "When King was entertaining at Laurier House, she would discuss the menu with the cook, advise on the seating plan, check the table settings, arrange the flowers, and often act as hostess at formal dinner parties."[30] The only doubtful statement here is the last one. No doubt there were formal occasions when Joan acted as hostess, but they were certainly rare. Careful examination of King's diary for 1927, a year in which it was kept with care and in which there was a great deal of entertaining, does not reveal a single case in which she is mentioned as hostess. There are references to Joan (though usually not Godfroy) being present at dinner parties, but not to her acting as hostess.[31] She was present at a large party which King gave for Colonel Charles A. Lindbergh at Laurier House, and at a large dinner in Lindbergh's honour at the Country Club, but it seems that she attended as an ordinary guest.[32] She helped with arrangements for King's reception for

Members of Parliament to meet Lord and Lady Willingdon, the new Governor General and his wife, but apparently merely came in for "a few minutes when the reception was over".[33] When King entertained the Willingdons at dinner, Joan was not present, but when the party was over he "went to talk over the night with Joan — returned to bed at 2".[34] At Kingsmere things were more informal. On an occasion in 1929 when there were visitors, "Joan poured tea & it was real work." But when Mr. and Mrs. Stanley Baldwin visited King there, we read merely that he "had Joan & Godfroy come down & join us" for tea.[35]

The Pattesons' association with King did them no harm in Ottawa society, and indeed probably brought them a certain amount of attention they would not otherwise have had. Lady Willingdon, sitting in the gallery of the House of Commons, invited King's sister Jennie (Mrs. H. M. Lay) and Mrs. Patteson to join her. Some months later the Pattesons dined with the Willingdons at Government House. King was not present; he spent the evening dictating letters, doubtless to a highly displeased secretary. (Almost inevitably, Joan and Godfroy came to Laurier House "for a few minutes after".)[36] But it is clear that Joan felt a certain embarrassment, particularly where the vice-regal family was concerned. In 1941 the then Governor General, Lord Athlone, and his wife, Princess Alice, had tea and dinner at Kingsmere. King recorded, "Joan phoned . . . about being all used up — thought she had grip — could not come for walk or to do flowers. . . . I might have assumed as much — it is terrible how almost invariably she gets these 'inferiority' attacks. . . . She is however going to come, but later. . . . It may have been her way of not wishing 'to receive' with me." Joan did come over later — there is no mention of Godfroy — and "H. E. sat on the verandah" with her, "enjoying very much a talk in the cool of the evening". On this occasion she seems to have been actually ill — temperature 103½ next day — but King's comment, on a subject he seldom touches so directly, is revealing.[37] The implication seems to be that King would have been glad to have Joan "receive" with him more frequently, but that she was reluctant.

Clearly their association was not "clandestine"; many people in Ottawa knew about it; but it never became public, in the sense of being mentioned in the newspapers. Arthur Meighen and R. B. Bennett were not merely King's political opponents; he hated them cordially, as many, many references in the diary show, and they returned the feeling; but neither they nor any other political rival ever sought to make capital out of his relationship with Mrs. Patteson. King took no particular precautions to keep the connection secret, but he would certainly have resented any publicity. Even after his retirement, when an Ottawa newspaperman, Reginald Hardy, showed him the draft of a biography he had written (later published as *Mackenzie King of Canada*), King asked him to delete a passage about Mrs. Patteson, and he did.[38]

The association with Joan by no means put a stop to King's talk of finding a wife, a matter which in fact he often discussed with her, apparently without too much regard for her feelings. Writing of his social problems in 1926, he said, "It all comes down to this living alone business, of which I have spoken a good deal to Joan of late. She has come to see that it is better for me to marry if I can find the right one and she has bravely said she will do her part. She thinks I should marry someone young enough to have children. I would like a son and daughter if they were to be strong and noble characters." Five years later, when he is almost fifty-seven, he describes an afternoon at Kingsmere and speaks of marriage less as a present possibility than as a might-have-been. Joan's two grandchildren came over with their nurse, and everybody sang hymns: "a fire was burning in the fire place, little Pat was moving about wagging his tail. Joan played the piano. I had afternoon tea at a little table—It was a very pretty scene and a very happy half hour. They are dear little children full of love and tenderness and I am very fond of each of them, and their love for me is something sweet to behold. The great mistake I have made in my life is not having married, and having a family; I would have loved to have children growing up around me, bringing me joy & new thoughts into my home and life. It would have developed me more & brought me more into touch with the people around me. As it is I am becoming a very solitary and at times lonely man, living in the past, and hard to move into any environment other than the one I am in."[39] These, of course, are the musings of a reluctant Leader of the Opposition; restored to power, King might take a rosier view of things.

The "very solitary man" continued in fact to enjoy the society of women as he always had, both old friends and new. Julia Grant, the Princess Cantacuzene, whom he had met briefly at Newport in 1899 at the moment of her marriage, now reappears in his life and adds at least a pleasant titillation to the last twenty years of it. They had an accidental meeting in Paris in 1928, and by 1932 they were in correspondence, a development which it is evident Julia welcomed. King also found it agreeable; Julia clearly met those implied criteria of wealth and position so evident in the years when King was actively seeking a wife (perhaps her social conscience was less apparent, but perhaps King was now less inclined to insist on this). In another respect she was eminently acceptable; King was now a convinced spiritualist, and Julia was quite prepared to explore the spirit world with him.[40] In Washington in 1935 Julia and King (he was "Rex" to her, as to other intimates) had a "sitting" in which her grandfather, General—and President—Ulysses S. Grant, spoke to them.[41]

It seems clear that both Julia and Rex were prepared to consider marriage, at least as a remote possibility (Julia finally divorced her husband in 1934). But King, needless to say, had doubts, and more than doubts. He cannot have failed to realize, whenever he reflected calmly about it, how extraordinary such a connection would be considered in Canada, and how much harm it would do him politically. Soon after writing to her in very

warm terms in 1932, he said in the diary that he was resolved to
end the correspondence. However, it did not end, though it
became more cautious in tone.[42] In the summer of 1939 the
Princess visited Canada and stayed at Kingsmere as King's guest.
The Prime Minister took the opportunity to say to her, "I
doubted if I should ever marry, that I was now 65 & that if I did it
would not be out of Canada." (During this visit, incidentally,
Joan Patteson clearly acted as hostess and chaperone, which
must have been "trying" for her — the word is King's.)[43] Even
now the correspondence with Julia went on — the fact is that
King delighted in exchanging letters with all his old flames. Less
than a fortnight before he died he wrote a letter[44] to the Princess
"by hand".*

Looking at the whole thirty years of their close association with
Mackenzie King, one finds oneself asking, what did it mean for
Joan and Godfroy Patteson? What did they "get out of it"?

In a material way, the answer seems to be, not a great deal.
They obtained a pleasant summer home at Kingsmere, which, in
later years at least, was rent-free. They got incidental benefits
such as frequent transportation in the Prime Minister's motor
car. Occasionally there were special treats. At Easter of 1923
Joan and Godfroy shared with King a short vacation at Montauk,
the eastern point of Long Island, in which his private railway car
evidently served as a hotel. This excursion was repeated in 1928,
at greater length.† In 1937 Joan and her daughter-in-law got

*The Princess Cantacuzene died 5 October 1975, at the age of ninety-
nine.[45]

† On this occasion King took considerable precautions (including having his
car placed next the engine) to avoid having the trip come to public notice.
On Easter Monday (9 April) the party left Montauk. The Pattesons went
off to Philadelphia, and King spent the day in New York. There he met,
quite accidentally and separately, not one but two members of his Cabinet
—Lapointe walking on Fifth Avenue, and Rinfret in an elevator at Macy's!
The Prime Minister observed ruefully that this showed "how little one can
get away unobserved anywhere".

seats in Westminster Abbey, courtesy of the Canadian government, for the Coronation of King George VI.[46] And at the end King remembered the Pattesons very generously—by his standards, at any rate—in his will. He left to "my friends, Mr. and Mrs. Godfroy B. Patteson" a joint annuity of $2500, to be continued to the last survivor.[47]

It is fair to assume that it was not considerations of this sort that kept the Pattesons loyal to King all those years. Joan had a deep affection for King; no one who reads her letters to Violet Markham after his death can doubt this. In the beginning perhaps she was in love with him. And it seems likely that it gave both Joan and Godfroy a good deal of satisfaction to be the uniquely confidential friends of the Prime Minister, even though that friendship was never declared to the world. Godfroy, whatever his feelings may have been earlier, seems to have had a warm regard for King in later years. But he and Joan must often have been aware of disadvantages. The association was decidedly one-sided. The Pattesons were always at King's call, he was never at theirs. He could go off across the country or the world on political or public business and count upon their being there to welcome him when he returned, upon their home being open to him on any day and at any hour. In 1939 his debt to them in connection with the visit of Julia Grant moved King to record his appreciation of the Pattesons: "both are always so considerate, they never take undue advantage in any way of our friendship, or presume upon it."[48] From King's point of view this was important. It was their readiness to subordinate their lives to his that made the relationship so successful. A few days after King died Joan wrote, "Godfroy and I are like two creatures of stone...for the one who gave us the very essence of our life, has been taken from us."[49] No doubt there was emotional exaggeration here, but there was certainly much sincerity also.

King, it is to be feared, often took Joan Patteson for granted, but when he thought seriously about her he realized that she was the most important woman in his life after his mother. In 1928, making one of his numerous complaints about the mistake of not having had a wife, he went on to say that of all the women he had cared for there was not one whom he now wished he had married. He added, however, "Had Joan been free I would have been very happy with her." That same year, crossing the Atlantic to fulfil official engagements in Europe, he set down in his diary one of those sentences, so rare with him, in which there was a touch of poetry: "I think much of Kingsmere, the lighted house on the hill, Joan at the door."[50]

This did not mean that King felt a compulsion to be faithful to Joan. On the contrary, this summer of 1928 witnessed an episode that recalls his discovery of Lily Hendrie at the height of his affair with Marjorie Herridge in 1902 (above, page 94). In Paris we suddenly find him calling on a "Mrs. Robb", taking her for a drive, and recording "a delightful talk together". Next day he calls again, to say good-bye before leaving for Geneva. But two days later he is calling on Mrs. Robb again—in Geneva. They met frequently during the next few days. We subsequently find them in Evian-les-Bains, across the Lake of Geneva, where King takes the lady to dinner more than once. Back in Paris, it is dinner again, and the Opéra. This was the beginning of a warm friendship that lasted until the end of King's life. Beatrix Henderson Robb — the name she used after her divorce from Nathaniel Thayer Robb, which seems to have been recent in 1928—was a New Yorker, "a resident also of Murray Bay, Que.". After 1928 King almost invariably dined with her when visiting New York. During the Second World War she was active in organizing entertainment for Canadian and other Allied servicemen in the United States. She died in 1957.[51]

In spite of that summer idyll of 1928, Joan Patteson was really much more important to Mackenzie King than Beatrix Robb was. One must quote his final word on Joan, written less then a month before he died: "So helpful and cheerful. Godfroy equally so. I can never repay all their kindness. She has filled the place of my mother in my heart over the years."[52]

To his personal life she meant much. What of his political life? We have already suggested that she gave him, in effect, that home and home life which he felt were so vital to a public man. She ministered to that fundamental insecurity in him to which the whole diary is a monument. He had believed that she helped to make him Prime Minister in 1921, and he would certainly have said that her support contributed largely to his remarkable record of successes thereafter. Perhaps, if justice were done, the Liberal party of Canada should raise, in some secluded corner at Kingsmere, an appropriately modest memorial to Mary Joan Patteson, one of the founders of its fortunes.

# LITTLE ANGEL DOGS

In 1924 the Pattesons gave King a dog, an Irish terrier named Pat. At the same time they themselves acquired one from the same litter, which they called Derry. Something new and important thus came into King's life.

Pat arrived at one of those moments when the diary was temporarily in abeyance, so the transaction is not documented. One speculates, however, that the Pattesons felt that their bachelor friend would be the better for having a household pet to provide affection and companionship. The idea succeeded, I suspect, beyond their dreams.

The first references to Pat when the diary resumes are rather tentative; animals do not seem to have meant very much to King until now. "Little dog Pat glad to see me back" is the first note, and next day, "A little dog Pat getting to know me well & obey me better."[1] It is not surprising however that Pat soon made his way. Dogs are notoriously flatterers of the human ego, and King had a considerable ego to flatter. By 1931 Pat had risen beyond normal dogdom. King tells how, when he was kneeling in prayer before his mother's portrait, "little Pat came up from the bedroom and licked my feet,—dear little soul, he is almost human. I sometimes think he is a comforter dear mother has sent to me, he is filled with her spirit of patience, and tenderness & love."[2] Pat becomes more and more linked with King's mother in his mind, and more and more he treats the animal as if it were in fact human. In 1934 Derry is sick, and King writes, "I knelt at the side of the arm chair in which dear mother died, with little Pat on his knees to pray for 'his little brudder, Derry' who is very ill and to ask God to send his good angel Dr. Pasteur to direct the hand & mind of the Doctor Vet[er]inary to what will heal the little fellow."[3] (At this point, we shall see, King was in the most extreme phase of his spiritualistic excitement.)

On the day in 1939 that Great Britain and France declared war on Germany, King, at Kingsmere, met Joan Patteson while walking Pat. "Little Pat," he wrote, "always seems to me a sort of symbol of my mother, as J. in her tender way also makes me think very often of her. When she spoke it was as though my mother, through her, was giving me assurance of being at my side at this most critical of all the moments. . . . " The dog was now fifteen years old, and could not be expected to live a great deal longer. Reluctantly recognizing this, King wrote the following spring, "He is a little 'angel dog' that some day will be a little 'dog angel'." The reference was to a modest bit of Can Lit that Joan had given him:[4]

> High up in the courts of Heaven to-day
>   A little dog-angel waits,
> With the other angels he will not play,
>   But he sits alone at the gates;
> "For I know that my master will come,"
>   says he:
> "And when he comes, he will call for me". . . .

Pat in fact lived to be seventeen, until the summer of 1941. The poor little animal was sick, deaf, and nearly blind, but presumably nobody ventured to tell the Prime Minister that the time had come to release him. The end came in July, just after King returned from a trip to the West Coast. He reached Ottawa on the morning of the 12th, and after doing some business in the city he got to Kingsmere about four in the afternoon. He found Pat very ill. Immediately he began to draw parallels with his mother's last illness in 1917. "I cried very hard as I realized it could not be long before his little spirit, his brave, noble spirit would have taken its flight, but my tears were mostly of gratitude for God's mercy in so guiding my steps as to bring me home in time. I thought of dear Mother, and how I had come too late, had stayed too long at North York,—the night of my defeat.* It seemed to me to be [an] answer to my prayer not to be defeated this time in triumphing over all else in reaching my little loved one in time." The diary goes on, "I was very tired, did not go over to see Joan, felt Pat was more to me than all else in the world, & wished to be alone with him. Dear Joan came over, as I hoped she would, but I was too overcome to speak to her. . . . "⁵

The record continues in great detail, with the painful clinical details of poor Pat's condition (the reader of the diary is indeed reminded of 1917). It never occurs to King that the time has come for euthanasia, any more than he would have thought of it for his mother. He does begin to wonder whether he is not responsible for Pat's state; might he not have lived if his master had got to Kingsmere earlier on the 12th? If he had not indulged so much during the western trip? What about the "few drinks of Scotch" at Harrison Hot Springs? Or the parties at Vancouver and Winnipeg? He might have arrived at Ottawa fresher, and got to Kingsmere sooner. The vet was wrong to give Pat stimulants. "I felt it was all meant for me, a part of God's plan, to have me renounce for ever† the use of alcohol."⁶

On the morning of 14 July King went into Ottawa, did some business, instructed the Secretary to the Cabinet to postpone

---

*In the general election of 17 December 1917.

†Of course, this did not happen. I remember King in Normandy in 1946 doing at least moderate justice to the fine wines produced at a dinner tendered by the government of France. Nevertheless, it seems to be the case that he seldom touched alcohol while the war lasted.

until the next day a meeting of the Cabinet War Committee that had been scheduled for that afternoon, and hastened back to Kingsmere.[7] Early the following morning Pat died. King described the night at great length in his painful longhand (normally at this period the diary was dictated, but private passages like this were not for even the most confidential secretary). He took the dog in his arms. "During this time I sang aloud to him— first 'Safe in the arms of Jesus'—looking at dear mother's picture as I sang — was amazed how calm & peaceful I felt. . . . " As morning approached, King felt the end was near. When he had bent down to pat his little friend when he first met him on his return on the 12th, his watch had fallen out of his pocket. He was now sure that Pat would die "at either 10 to 5 (the time at which my watch fell from my pocket) (as Pat slipped from my hands) or at 10 past 5, the hour at which it stopped. . . . * Morning was just beginning to break—I kissed the little fellow as he lay there, told him of his having been faithful and true, of his having saved my soul, and being like God—thought of how I felt as I knelt at dear Mother's side in her last illness. . . . "

The business was now nearly over. "I sang more hymns, held him to me, his little body warm, legs not cold his little heart got very weak, almost imperceptible. When 10 past 5 came I sang again 'God be with you till we meet again. . .' It was at that moment . . . that we crossed the bar. . . . My little friend, the truest friend I have had—or man ever had—had gone to be with Derry and the other loved ones. I had given him messages of love to take to father, mother, Bell, Max, Sir Wilfrid & Lady Laurier, Mr. and Mrs. Larkin & the grand-parents." King adds, "I felt a great peace when all was ended."[8]

The most extraordinary thing about this maudlin and, I fear one must say, rather repulsive record is that it was set down by the Prime Minister of a country engaged in a desperate war.

*Here King was in fact wrong. At the time he recorded that the watch stopped at 5:25.

Here, surely, we have a prime example of King's double life, his capacity for keeping his curious private affairs separate from his public career. On the afternoon of 15 July, between Pat's death and his burial that evening at the "Abbey Ruin" at Kingsmere, King presided at the meeting of the Cabinet War Committee that had been put off from the day before. He seems to have performed with his customary efficiency, warning his colleagues in his best (or, if you prefer, his worst) manner against the dangers of enlarging the Army by mobilizing a 6th Division as recommended by the Minister of National Defence.[9]

Later in 1941 King acquired another dog. The Pattesons, one speculates, had had a contingency plan to fill the void that Pat's obviously impending death would leave in their friend's life. Having lost their own Derry,* they found another Irish terrier and named him Pat. In the diary of King's dog's last illness, this one figures as "the other Pat". When the first shock of his loss was over, the Pattesons appear to have transferred the new Pat to King, who, of course, already knew him and was known to him. He probably never quite replaced the first dog, but he made a special place for himself. King came to call him "the Little Saint".[11] One gets a hint of the reason on Christmas Eve 1944, when King writes, "Before going to bed I had a little talk with Pat, in his basket. We spoke together of the Christ-child and the animals in the crib." Most people talk to their animals, but few go as far as this.

The regard King came to have for Pat II had one of its strangest manifestations in October 1947, when King George VI offered the Prime Minister membership in the Order of Merit, a most distinguished honour, since the Order never has more than twenty-four members and no other Canadian had ever been appointed to it. King, the great opponent of titles and

*The report of Pat's death reached the newspapers, and in spite of a request by King the Ottawa *Journal* printed a reference to Derry. Joan, King recorded, was "a little hurt", though the Pattesons were not mentioned.[10]

distinctions, had a severe internal struggle, fully described in the diary, over the question of whether or not to accept. Pat II had lately died. And King wrote in part, "I can honestly say. . . that my thoughts, singular as it may appear, went later [more] to my little dog Pat II than anything else. I felt that that little creature deserved an O.M. a thousand times more than I do myself and then came the thought of the other little Pat who also merited more than I do, and the loyalty of his nature, fidelity and all that counts for most."[12] Nevertheless, King did accept the O.M. and did not recommend that it should be conferred posthumously upon his dog instead.

Pat II did not live as long as Pat I. He died on 11 August 1947. His last illness was for King an episode only less tragic than that of Pat I. But there was a difference. Pat II had cancer, and was "put away" to spare him further pain, his master sadly assenting. He was buried near what King called the "Bethel Stone" at Kingsmere. The Prime Minister reflected that Pat II was nobler, stronger, "truly greater" than himself, and wrote, "God grant I may be worthy of him."[13]

At the beginning of 1948 King was dogless, but his memories of his animal friends were lively. On 20 January he wrote, "The little dogs have been very near to me all day. When I went to my room tonight, I felt I could talk to them as if they were again jumping over my bed in their joyous ways. They are very near to me in times like these." (The reference perhaps is to the stress of economic troubles and consequent tensions in the Cabinet.) Predictably, the Prime Minister got another Irish terrier. This one was the gift of the Handy family (J. E. Handy was the valued confidential secretary to whom King dictated his diary). But Pat III, perhaps because time was short, never achieved the position of his predecessors. King wrote on his own birthday in 1949, "I thought much of old Pat No. 1 & dear Derry boy & Pat II, the little Saint. Pat III may become so but is not yet."[14] In the last months of King's life diary references to the dog are comparatively few.

# PART III
# THINGS IN HEAVEN
# AND EARTH

Mackenzie King was obsessively devoted to his family, and above all to his mother. When his sister Bell, his father, and his mother all died within three years in 1915–17 the effect upon him was traumatic. This, it seems clear, is the origin of the spiritualism that came to play such an important part in his life in later years.

When King left the family house on Beverley Street, Toronto, in 1896 to go to the University of Chicago, he left for good, in the sense that he never lived with his family again. But he visited them frequently; he always spoke of the successive homes they occupied in Toronto as "our house"; his mother, we have seen, often visited him in Ottawa, and after he acquired his Kingsmere cottage both she and his father came there in the summer. The family circle remained unbroken.

I suggested that his discovery of his political grandfather made his mother more important to him, and that the affair with Mathilde Grossert in 1898 left him more devoted to Mrs. King than ever. His declaration at that time, "I must work now for all at home, keep them before me...." (above, page 69), was no idle statement, for he did precisely what he said. The ability to give financial help to his father, whose affairs were so disordered, was an element in his accepting the well-paid civil service job in Ottawa in 1900; and as soon as he began to draw his pay he likewise began to send money home to pay off his father's debts. In the first eighteen months he spent $1200 in this way, chiefly in taking over at his father's request a chattel mortgage on the family's household goods. Mackenzie King was a thorough believer in what people today like to call the Protestant work ethic. If it had not been for him John King would certainly have died a debtor and have had nothing to leave his family. As it was, Willie was able to reflect with satisfaction, in reviewing his father's affairs after his death (18 October 1916), that with his own assistance he had "not only cleared off honourably every obligation, but left ample provision for mother as well after all expenses at the end had been met."

In his last years John King was blind. The benchers at Osgoode Hall were about to replace him in his lectureship, but were prevailed upon (presumably by his son) to continue him in it for one more year, and thereafter to give him an emeritus appointment with partial salary. In the final year of his life he had a Carnegie pension, doubtless also obtained for him by Willie. This provided a degree of ease at the end of an existence which, in the son's words, had been "lived ever on the margin".

# SIX CANDLES ON THE CAKE

As we have seen, there are large gaps in King's diary at this period, and it is a curious fact that it actually records none of the three deaths of 1915–17. Perhaps readers should be grateful for this, for as we know King's accounts of such matters can be painful. His sister Bell died on 4 April 1915, "Easter Day"—the words are on the stone. King had loved her dearly. Perhaps he loved her even more when she was gone, for there are many poignant references to her in the diary later. She had apparently given him *Daily Strength for Daily Needs,* one of the devotional "little books" which he read every morning of his life.[1] She was buried in the plot near the north wall of Toronto's Mount Pleasant Cemetery, where in due time the King family circle would be reunited. Her father joined her there before a stone could be placed above her. He died on 30 August 1916, only a few weeks after Willie had moved his parents into the new house on Avenue Road (above, page 69).[2] "Our home in Toronto" was now broken up.

Placing a family stone on the plot in Mount Pleasant now became one of King's special cares. His father had wished to do this, and there was money enough in his estate to pay for it; but Willie made the arrangements. The stone was to be "an exact reproduction in outline & proportion of the St. Martin's Cross at Iona". King wrote, "While others are forging links of Empire with shell & steel I have forged this link which unites the birth-place of Christianity in Scotland with the British Dominions [in] the New World." In the autumn King went to see it in place, and thought it "absolute perfection"; it brought "a great happiness" to his heart:[3]

> Poor old father. It seemed impossible that his mortal remains could be lying there. To me the spiritual presence of both Bell & himself was far more real than their graves which my eyes were witnessing. I stood with one hand on the side of the cross by father's grave, the sun from the West came out from behind a silver cloud in great brightness and lighted all the side of the cross symbolical of immortality. As I turned around the shadow of the cross stretched far behind, and my shadow stretched across father's grave. It was apparent there could have been no shadow but for the light & the objects between. Here was the whole parable of life, the individual & the cross, the material things left behind in shadow, the immortal relieved in light. There was great comfort in the thought & the incident, and I left the grave ere the sun again disappeared behind the cloud. There was just such an occurrence at the unveiling of the Harper monument.* This may be all chance, but to the eye of Faith there is no such thing as Chance, and Faith is the first and the last of the realities.

King's mother was still with him. For a time she stayed with his married sister Jennie in Walkerton, Ontario, but King was anxious that she should live with him, and late in 1916 he took her into his small apartment at the Roxborough in Ottawa. (In the autumn of 1917, when they returned from the annual sojourn at Kingsmere, he rented an extra room.) The old lady was now extremely ill, and King nursed her with the help of a woman who

*Above, page 83.

might be called today a "practical nurse". From the beginning of 1917 the diary is full of painful passages describing her symptoms and discussions with the doctors. Obviously she ought to have been in a hospital or a nursing home, but such institutions were less used in those days and it is questionable whether her son would have countenanced any such idea.[4]

This is a tragic episode in King's life, and the reader of the diary is likely to feel a (perhaps unwonted) sympathy for him. The present writer, however, experienced an ebbing of sympathy when he reached 6 February 1917, Mrs. King's seventy-fourth and last birthday, and read the enormously long account King wrote of the observances with which he marked the occasion. The affair cannot be omitted here, but I shall treat it more briefly than King did.

The day began auspiciously with a telegram from Max, King's brother. Max was a doctor, and as already mentioned he had moved with his family to Denver in the hope of recovering from tuberculosis. He had now written a book about that disease, *The Battle with Tuberculosis and How to Win It*; and Willie, on the advice of Dr. Simon Flexner of the Rockefeller Institute, had had it submitted to Lippincott, the Philadelphia publisher. Now Max reported that Lippincott had accepted the book and would pay him a 10-per-cent royalty. Willie was delighted: "How wonderful. It was on little Bell's birthday anniversary, that in remembrance of her beautiful Christian spirit, & to continue her service, I went and spoke to Dr. Flexner about Max's writing.... Now on mother's birthday 2½ months later, the word comes to cheer her heart and mine, to make us all rejoice. Dear little Bell —her birthday gift to mother—*Yes, somewhere near by she watches and helps to plan & arrange*."*

Time faileth to tell of all the telegrams and letters and presents, and the flowers that poured in until the rooms looked

---

*The italics have been added.

"more like a conservatory than aught else". King's own present was a brooch: "I told her the black centre was in remembrance of dear father and little Bell, who were near us today and the gold band around it, spoke of the glory in which they dwelt." The birthday cake had "six lighted candles, one for each of our family". Father and Bell were still present.

The climax came in the afternoon. King, it is evident, had been carrying on some historical research:

> When it was near 4 o'clock I asked mother if she knew what time of the day she was born. She replied No. Then I told her it was around 4 o'clock in the afternoon. The midwife's certificate shows this, — Born on Chambers St. New York — her father at the time serving as actuary at the New York Mechanics Institute — he in exile — the family so poor as not to be able to afford a physician other than a midwife who could only make her mark not sign her name — It was honourable poverty, everything sacrificed to principle in the great struggle for freedom — self government — But speak of the Romance of life — of the ways of God — there were a few things with which the family never parted, — amongst others bits of valuable china. One or two of these pieces mother still has in her possession. It was on one of these plates that I put the birthday cake for today, and it was on her lap when she cut it. — Then when I had told her it was about 4 in the afternoon when she was born 74 years ago, I began to give her a kiss for the years that had gone by since then, and so I kissed her 74 times, and at the end thanked God for her and her mother. I gave her a few more kisses for the years to come — To return to the romance of life, Is there not romance here. That little 7 months' delicate infant, born in exile, amid conditions of penury, spared thro' long life to receive on her 74th birthday anniversary word from one son that the leading publishing house (of medical

books) in America had accepted and was about to pay him a royalty on a treatise... which may be the means of saving many lives, and her other son, a member of the Privy Council of Canada, who has helped somewhat to improve conditions for labour and to avert some of the loss that comes thro' strikes and lockouts & other forms of industrial strife —loss of life possibly, loss of happiness certainly, & who can say what else: — there if anywhere is verified the truth that God chooses 'the weak things of the world to confound the strong' — and the end is not yet.

The conscientious reader will realize that he has seen something very like this before — far back in 1895, when King was discovering William Lyon Mackenzie (above, page 67). What the diary told us in 1895 it tells us again in 1917, in almost the same words. We are in the presence of a man of destiny, entrusted from on high with a mission to carry on the work of his grandfather.

The great birthday party was followed almost at once by a change of doctors. Dr. Thomas Gibson had long been a close personal friend of King's. Now, however, he was discharged from the case and replaced by a Dr. McCarthy. The diary makes it evident that Dr. Gibson had committed, in King's eyes, four sins. First, he had given his mother a morphine pill. King, who apparently considered himself as competent as the doctors to decide treatment, disapproved of this. Secondly, and this perhaps was the worst offence, Gibson had said that the old lady could not recover. When King complained of this, Gibson told him that he was being irrational: "if I wanted a man who wouldn't tell me the truth, well & good". Mrs. King lived through the summer, which led her son to conclude that he had been right and Gibson wrong. But she died before Christmas, so perhaps it was not the doctor who was mistaken.

Dr. Gibson's third crime was that neither he nor his wife "sent mother a flower or a greeting of any kind" on her birthday. This in turn may have grown out of King's fourth complaint. He was sure the Gibsons were trying to marry him to one of their female relatives, and he had told Mrs. Gibson he had "no thoughts of" the lady. The rift was not purely professional.[5]

As this grim winter drags to its close, with his mother fighting her losing battle for life, phrases familiar long ago appear again in King's diary. "The past two weeks have been poorly lived. I have worse than wasted much of the time...." "Worse than wasted": King has gone back to the girls of the streets. On the second anniversary of Bell's death, he walks on the Driveway in the sunset, and writes afterwards, "I should never complain, I would not but for the loneliness of plugging along alone, with the endless battle of spirit against the flesh."[6] King is forty-two now, an ex-Minister, very well known in Ottawa, a place where even today everybody knows everybody else. One pictures the distracted man slipping along the street in the April darkness on his private errand, hoping he does not meet an acquaintance.

One of the expeditions into the sub-world gave King a most painful shock. The day's entry in the diary begins, "From today I begin a new chapter in my life. God has mercifully spared me an affliction the most terrible I could ever know and one I have secretly dreaded for many years, — that when Mother might be in a critical condition I might be away from her, and possibly selfishly indulging, when I should be at her side." He had started the day by reading Bell's book, "with its lesson for the day to flee from temptation, not to let the shadow of it come nigh"; but that was not the way things went. During the day he "became impatient", fell into "a restless mood". "It was half past 7 when I got back & as soon as dinner was over I went out again, hardly more than kissing her good-bye—when I came back the doctor was at the telephone in my hall trying to get me at the Club, and I learned that mother had just been through a terrible ordeal which might easily have cost her her life. She had found it impossible almost to get her breath. . . ." King's helper Miss Petrie had got the doctor, and "but for his coming at that late hour, she would probably have been gone ere my return, and my life for ever after blighted. I knew I was not doing right in going out and following a path of pleasure, when one of duty was so plainly mine. It was as if God had wished to say to me How long! . . . I can only feel the goodness of God in sparing her life, and by her side I consecrated my life anew to purer living and nobler service."

These events took place on Easter Monday, 9 April 1917. The date may strike the reader as familiar. That morning the Canadian Corps had stormed Vimy Ridge.

The sequel to the story is anticlimactic. As is usually the case with good resolutions, King's came to naught. Before the end of the month he is again reproaching himself. "I am amazed at myself and my apparent apathy to duty." "I have. . . . allowed myself to give way to inclination & desire in a manner which is wholly wrong. I prayed God would forgive me. . . ." "Certainly I am not living as I ought. . . . Truly a double minded man is unstable in all his ways."[7]

Mrs. King's illness had interfered with her son's Rockefeller work, interfered too with progress upon the book *Industry and Humanity*. Now politics obtruded itself, in the form of the general election of 1917. In his mother's last days, his campaign in North York kept him from her side. The diary does not tell us a great deal, but we know that on 29 November he was called back from Sutton to Ottawa because she was worse. The situation was now such that even King's optimism was overcome; he made arrangements at the undertaker's.[8] He was still in Ottawa when the diary ends for the year on 2 December. It does not begin again until 1 February 1918, but some later references give us glimpses. One of King's anniversary days was 9 December, "the last day I saw dear mother alive"; this presumably was the date of his return to his constituency.[9] (He apparently left his sister

Jennie in charge.) And in 1929, at a dinner party for Ramsay MacDonald, he talked to Sir Robert Borden and others of how his mother told him that Sir Wilfrid Laurier "was an old man & needed my help, that he had been good to me when I was a young man, to go & help him, tho' she was dying, not to mind her".[10] Polling day was 17 December; it was also King's birthday. He shared in the general Liberal *débâcle*. And on the 18th Mrs. King died. We have already seen Willie, in 1941, at the time of Pat's death, recalling how he came too late, "had stayed too long at North York". That anguish twenty-four years later makes one glad that he made no record at the time.

Something of his misery can be gathered from the diary entry carrying the date of his birthday the next year (17 December 1918), which was actually written on the 5th of the following January: "A year ago today I was defeated in North York, though nearer the top on the Liberal side, than most of the other candidates. A year ago tomorrow dear mother died. A year has gone by and it has been lonely, lonely without her. What would I not give to see her but for an hour. . . . Mother lives, yes, and is powerful in the Kingdom of God — Her love still guards and protects me and will save me in the end—her love and the love of God revealed in Christ."

After seeing his mother buried in the shadow of the Iona Cross in Toronto, King seems to have gone into seclusion for a time. When the diary begins again, he speaks on 2 February 1918 of going to Government House to skate: "It is the first of people I have seen since dear mother's death." Shortly afterwards he thought he had contact with her in a dream. "Last night I dreamt that I saw dear mother's face in death. . . . I said to her —as though talking to her spirit apart—you promised mother— which she did—to tell me from the other world if you were still alive & near me, & when I said this her lips opened and she said 'I am alive', but it seemed as tho' it was forbidden her to say more. I felt she had told me all she could—All day the dream has been with me."[11] Many years later King makes another reference to having discussed with her the question of communication after death; it is Christmas 1930: "I spent the most of the morning seeking to commune with dear Mother's spirit and the spirits of the loved ones in the Great Beyond. How could Mother guide me, how send the word I long to have—The Bible is the medium of which we spoke—." He proceeds to read the Bible and quote passages.[12] Nevertheless the time of direct communication with his mother had not yet come.

In 1922 Max followed his parents and his sister. Soon after becoming Prime Minister Willie travelled to Denver to see him. He writes, "we had a good talk about his book* and about my nervous condition, the latter he thinks arises from a psycho neurotic condition, some complex due to suppressed emotions. He assures me some things I had believed to be real are not such but wholly due to effect of thought & will." King had lately written, "I find the psycho-analysis literature Max has recommended helpful." (It is a pity the Prime Minister does not tell us more about these problems of his.) Three days later a long and painful passage describes the two brothers' farewell interview; Max is clearly dying. The Prime Minister tells us that in his compartment on the train afterwards he "cried like a child".[13] Max died on 18 March. Willie brought his body back to Toronto to be buried in the family plot, where he was commemorated by a new monument adjacent to the Iona Cross. It was modelled upon the tomb of Louis Pasteur, one of King's great humanitarian heroes. Max had been a good friend to his brother, not least in that he was a candid critic of his performances. In September 1921, for instance, he had written him a long letter commenting on the fact that he had used alleged poor health as an excuse for making an inferior speech. There was no one to succeed him in this role, and King's biographer Dawson is probably right in

*A new book, *Nerves and Personal Power*, published in this year, 1922.

thinking that Max's death removed what would have been a valuable influence on his later career.[14] Max left two sons, one of whom, "young Lyon", named after the Prime Minister, followed his father into the medical profession and was killed in action while serving at sea in 1943.[15]

With Max gone there remained only two of the six members of the family who had been represented by the candles on Mrs. King's birthday cake: Willie himself and his married sister Jennie, Mrs. H. M. Lay, who in the end survived him. His relations with Jennie and her family (including her stepson, Horatio Nelson Lay, who in due course, very suitably, rose to high rank in the Navy) were always friendly, but Jennie was not close by and had her own concerns. King was very much alone, and it was his great good fortune that at this point in his life he had found Joan Patteson.

In his mind, however, there were still six candles on the cake. He continued to be convinced that his parents and his brother and sister were "somewhere near by" and watching over him. Scores of entries in the diary over the years affirm this. A notable example is King's record of the final stage of the Liberal convention that elected him leader in August 1919. That morning he had read Bell's little book and the page for the day had told him, "Nothing shall be impossible unto you." Thereafter he was sure that it was the will of God he should be chosen:

> The majority was better than I had anticipated. I was too heavy of heart and soul to appreciate the tumult of applause, my thoughts were of dear mother & father & little Bell all of whom I felt to be very close to me, of grandfather & Sir Wilfrid also. I thought: it is right, it is the call of duty. I have sought nothing, it has come. It has come from God. The dear loved ones know and are about, they are alive and with me in this great everlasting Now and Here. It is to His work I am called, and to it I dedicate my life.[16]

The man of destiny was on his way to completing his grand-father's work (whatever that might be) with the aid of his dead loved ones and Sir Wilfrid Laurier, who from this point seems to have been virtually adopted into the King family. And the divine origin of Mackenzie King's mission is again made amply clear.

Just one later instance of King's belief that his family were still about him may be given: a rather peculiar one. In May 1923 the Liberal parliamentary caucus tendered King a testimonial dinner. It is perhaps evidence of the fact that his status in the party was still somewhat shaky that it was held in the notoriously inexpensive Parliamentary Restaurant. But King was pleased with his own speech: "Through the providence of God, I was permitted to be at my best." And afterwards he had a remarkable experience: "as I stood alone on the stairs looking out to the front of the prlt. Bldgs. I found myself whistling 'By Cool Siloam's Shady Rill'. It was as tho dear father & mother wished to make their presence known to me, to give me a message from the world beyond. As I read the lines of this hymn anew, its reference to childhood, to subsequent years of sorrow & passion, then manhood etc., I cannot but believe it was a real revelation." What he read was,

> Lo, such the child whose early feet
>   The paths of peace have trod;
> Whose secret heart with influence sweet
>   Is upward drawn to God. . . .
>
> O Thou, Whose infant feet were found
>   Within Thy Father's shrine,
> Whose years, with changeless virtue crowned,
>   Were all alike divine;
>
> Dependent on Thy bounteous breath,
>   We seek Thy grace alone,
> In childhood, manhood, age, and death,
>   To keep us still Thine own.

The next day he read the hymn again, and wrote, "I feel sure that so far as it is possible for those who have passed into the Great Beyond to send a word or guidance to us here, it was the spirit of dear father & mother speaking or communing with mine when I felt the moment of great rest and peace and joy and a sort of sacred light round about as I stopped on the stairs of the building. . . . " It all seems a little strange, but many years later King gives us a further hint as to how it happened; "By Cool Siloam's Shady Rill", he says, was "one of my father's favourite hymns".[17]

# MOVING INTO SPIRITUALISM

It is clear that Mackenzie King was a "religious" man, to the extent that the name of God, if not always on his lips, was very frequently in his diary.* The line between religion and superstition is hard to draw, and it is particularly hard in King's case. From the beginning of the diary, one encounters passages that seem superstitious rather than religious. Notably, we find the young man following the ancient practice of getting guidance by opening the Bible at random. He gets "the most wonderful revelation I have ever known"; on seven successive nights the book opens at verses that proclaim it his destiny to be a minister of the gospel.[1] Many passages of the diary reflect a violently emotional religiosity, doubtless largely the result of family background. At a communion service in 1894, "I could not keep from crying as usual during the singing of the XXXV pharaphrase [sic]." A few weeks later he heard a "beautiful" sermon by an eminent visiting preacher: "I was simply entranced. When

*Denominational religion, however, seems to have meant very little to him. Religion was a matter between King and God; the clergy of any church, including the Presbyterian one which he attended, were not particularly important. It was important to him that Jean Greer was a "Christian woman" (above, page 112); that she was an Episcopalian seems to have had no great significance. King was certainly conscious of the fact that she was a bishop's daughter. Perhaps, however, this was important to him in a temporal rather than a spiritual sense.

the organ played & the people sang 'Blest be the tie that binds' I had to leave the church. I cried very hard." Nevertheless, he recovered in time to introduce himself to the eminent preacher.[2]

As time passes, specific obsessions develop. We have seen a good deal already of King's cult of anniversaries — birthdays, death-days, and others. He was a trifle taken aback in 1934 when the *Ottawa Journal* called attention to one he had forgotten—the twenty-fifth anniversary of his being sworn in as a Cabinet minister. "I am now convinced," he wrote, "it was dear mother who had arranged all this to let me know on this anniversary she was near me."[3] In 1918 something new appears—the concern with the position of the hands of the clock. King begins to note moments when the hands are both together—as at twelve o'clock — or in a straight line — as at six o'clock. In his later years — notably during the Second World War and afterwards — the diary sometimes refers to the hands of the clock several times a day. On 2 November 1944, when recording the fateful advice of the Army Council that the voluntary system of recruiting had failed, he writes, "As I look at the clock from where I am standing as I dictate this sentence, the hands are both together at 5 to 11." The meaning of all this has rather stumped his biographers. Dawson wrote, "What significance he attached to the occurrences is difficult to determine; there is no key to his interpretation." In fact, there is something like a key in King's record of a conversation with Violet Markham in 1944 in which he was speaking of Pat's death. "As I. . . . went to take the watch out of my pocket, to show her how the face had been broken,* I looked at it and the two hands were exactly at 10 to 10. I mentioned it to her as an illustration of my belief that some presence was making itself known to me. That I was on the right line, and that the thought was a true one which I was expressing."[4]

"Mystical numbers" are increasingly in evidence as the years

---

*Above, page 142.

pass. Here is a fairly early example (1926): "This morning I dreamt of dear Mother, thought I was giving her an old one dollar bill. I was ashamed of its appearance.—She took a 2 and a 5 from the number I had, smiling so sweetly and I thought, this is the *mystical number*—7, that is why it is a sign, and I awoke. I truly believe, dear Mother is near me & guiding me." At the outbreak of war in 1939, Parliament is called to meet on 7 September to approve Canada's declaration of war on Germany; "I like the '7'," wrote King.[5] As we shall see, there were other mystical numbers to which the Prime Minister was devoted. Since his birthday was 17 December, the number 17 always had a special significance. Pat I was 17 when he died; "that number is his and mine" was King's reflection.[6]

All this suggests a mind that might well turn to spiritualism, whether one regards spiritualism as superstition or as something higher. In fact, however, Mackenzie King's advance into spiritualism was slow and gradual, and he cannot be said to have embraced it fully until he was fifty-eight.

There is some evidence that in his young days King was actually very hostile to spiritualism. In a memorandum of "Books read during 1901" we find the note, "Chambers—'Life after Death' — read 30 pages Feby. 9th with Mrs. Herridge. Threw book away to prevent further blasphemy."[7] *Our Life After Death*, by the Reverend Arthur Chambers, an Anglican clergyman,[8] was scarcely a spiritualistic work, but it tended that way. It argued that on leaving the "earth life" people entered an "Intermediate, or Hades-life", and that they continued to live as "conscious personalities" and could "recognize" those they had known on earth. Chambers made a good deal of the episode in the First Book of Samuel (Chap. 28) in which the witch of En-dor "brought up" the ghost of Samuel to confront Saul.

At the time when King rejected these ideas so violently he had not suffered the tragic series of bereavements that fell upon him in 1915–17 and left him eager for comforting contact with those he had lost. It seems likely that most people who have become spiritualists have been moved by yearning for the loved and the lost. This was clearly the case with Mackenzie King.

In 1925 he was faced with a general election whose outcome was very doubtful. He was extremely worried. However, he wrote, "I believe dear mother & father & Max & Bell are near and about me and Sir Wilfrid as well. Their spirits will guide and protect me."[9] The campaign brought him to Kingston, and there he consulted, apparently for the first time, a fortune-teller named Mrs. L. Bleaney. (She was not his first fortune-teller; as long ago as 1896 one had told him "some strange truths".)[10] He had a long conversation with Mrs. Bleaney; he called it afterwards "one of the most remarkable—if not the most remarkable interview I have ever had". She described the members of his family and what had become of them—this was perhaps hardly surprising, since the facts were common knowledge; she said he would marry a widow ("of real worth, good blood"); she told him he would win the election; but the thing that probably most impressed King at the moment was this: "Let me tell you something else, I see two flags, take [?] two persons in uniform, you are between them, some one comes up and puts flags in their hands, — the British & the American. You will be asked 'which flag', it will be called out to you, it will be done to embarrass you. You will pause for a moment, but will give an answer from your heart which will make clear you are British, that while you respect the American flag, the British flag is yours. . . ."

That evening during King's meeting in a Kingston theatre something very like this happened. King described it: "there was a Canadian flag over the table & one over the [stage?] box, I was standing between the two—I spoke once of the flag, and someone in the back of the hall under the gallery called out 'which flag'? [I] paused for a moment, — it was an exact fulfilment of what Mrs. Bleaney had said would happen. I came back with an answer expressing surprise that anyone in Kingston of all cities would wonder under which flag his allegiance & interest lay and I went after the heckler in strong fashion. In fact, I let myself out in strong form on the Empire & the flag and made I believe what on the whole was the best speech I have made in the campaign." The incident is not really so very remarkable, for it is pretty evident that King, with his mind full of Mrs. Bleaney's prophecy, brought it on by his reference to the flag. But it helped to make this visit to Kingston, in his view, a unique experience. He wrote afterwards, "The influence of the talk with that little woman is strange, it has brought me very near to the dear ones in the Great Beyond, what seems now more like the Great Omnipresent, Here & Now. I can never not believe in spiritualism so-called after today's experience."[11]

This was not a final conversion. Being King, he shortly began to develop doubts. Ten days later, after the election with its unsatisfactory result (above, page 24), he wrote, "My nature & reason revolt against 'spiritualism' & all the ilk, — but not against the things of the spirit, — the belief in spiritual guidance, — thro' institutions. It is the material manifestations I feel charry [*sic*] about, — on the other hand when in faith & prayer I have asked for them, and they come in such an unmistakable manner, are they not to be accepted in all faith & humility — just at this time when guidance from on High is needed. . . ."[12]

There was no doubt about the direction in which King was moving, however crablike the progress. He continued at intervals to consult Mrs. Bleaney. And when he was in London for the Imperial Conference in the autumn of 1926 he evidently decided to ask advice of high authority. Attached to his diary there is a memorandum[13] (regrettably, unfinished) of an interview with Sir Oliver Lodge, the eminent scientist and spiritualist, and Lord and Lady Grey of Fallodon. Grey was a Liberal elder statesman, long retired, for whom King had a very special regard. King described his interviews with Mrs. Bleaney and gave some account of his mother and Max (his memorandum makes no mention of the flag incident, and perhaps he was now disposed to discount it). Lodge and the Greys expressed much interest, and King recorded that Sir Oliver said, "The extent of the ordering and planning of our lives by those who are beyond, is much greater than we imagine. . . . that this little woman was able to tell you what she did was due in part to her own powers, but also to your own faith; both are needed."

Unfortunately there is no diary text at this point, so we do not know how King arranged for this discussion or what his reflections on it may have been. It is clear, however, that it did not result in his plunging at once into spiritualistic activity. In the months that follow he continues to see his mother in dreams,[14] and occasionally there is a special manifestation. In October 1927 he went to the University of Toronto for the inauguration of the carillon in the Soldiers' Tower. The old scenes stirred family memories. As the ceremony proceeded, King saw two birds flying overhead, in "full flight, strong & free". They seemed to him, he wrote, "the embodiment of the spirits of dear father & mother, as certainly a symbol sent by them to me, that I might know they were both very near at that moment."[15]

In the summer of 1928 King set out for Europe, to lead the Canadian delegation at the League of Nations (Canada had been elected to the Council) and to sign the Kellogg Peace Pact. If there were any passengers in cabins adjacent to that occupied by the Prime Minister of Canada on the *Ile de France*, they must have been surprised the night before the ship reached Plymouth, for at midnight, solitary in his stateroom, he "began to sing hymns for each of the loved ones". For his father, "Dear Father, Art Thou Weary?"; for Bell, "O Love That Wilt Not Let Me Go"; for Max, "Fight the Good Fight" (*that* came direct from the sitting with Mrs. Bleaney on 20 October 1925),* and finally, for

---

*"He [Max] tells me to tell you to go on. It is worthwhile, to keep up the fight, 'fight the good fight' is what he says. . . . "

Mother, "Lead, Kindly Light"—which ends, it may be remembered, with the lines:

> And with the morn those angel faces smile
> Which I have loved long since, and lost awhile.

"All brought to me assurance," wrote King, "of the loved ones round guiding & protecting my life at this moment."[16]

The autumn of 1929 brought the Wall Street crash, followed by the onset of the Depression. The immediate sequel was political disaster. On 6 August 1930 Mackenzie King ceased to be Prime Minister. For more than five years thereafter he was in the wilderness. During this period, with time on his hands, he finally gave himself over to a wild obsession with the other world which —very privately—became for a time the main interest of his life.

It would seem that under the influence of defeat and relative idleness King found himself longing for the companionship of his dead more than he had before. He has a dream "in which I heard dear Mother's voice". "I have longed & prayed to feel dear mother's presence and nearness to me and guidance. I believe it will come back to me. I pray God it may." On the thirteenth anniversary of her death he writes, "Time makes no difference in the feeling of loss which I have." We have already seen him on Christmas Day of 1930 (above, page 156), "seeking to commune with dear Mother's spirit and the spirits of the loved ones in the Great Beyond. How could Mother guide me, how send the word I long to have. . . . "[17] In September 1931 he has "a most important spiritual experience". As he reads the sixth chapter of Revelation ("and I heard, as it were the noise of thunder") a great thunderstorm duly comes up. "It seemed to me this chapter had a special meaning for me, was the word from dear mother of which I am in so great need at present as I enter again on my strictly political work."[18]

At the beginning of 1931 King had confided to his former secretary Norman Rogers, now a professor at Queen's University, that he had a "feeling of isolation—& inadequacy to present tasks". That summer he went to Kingston and Mrs. Bleaney "gave him a reading" at Rogers's house. There seems to have been a certain reserve between them now, the result of the fact that the fortune-teller had prophesied that King would win the 1930 election. She told him again that he would marry, next year. In spite of doubts, King still seems to have found comfort in consulting her. A little later he makes the incidental remark, "my purpose in seeing her has always been to have her as a sort of medium through whom dear mother sends her messages to me".[19]

In recent years King had become increasingly friendly with the Fulford family of Brockville. King was particularly fond of Mrs. Fulford, the widow of the senator who had died in 1905. Visiting the family in August 1931, he paid her the ultimate tribute: "I know no one who is more like mother in many ways."[20] It came to light in due course that Mrs. Fulford was a spiritualist; and in February 1932 King was invited to a *séance* at the family house, Fulford Place. He accepted eagerly; in the midst of the Beauharnois scandal (above, page 26) he felt an urgent need for support and guidance. This appears to be the first time he ever attended a *séance* properly so-called.[21]

The medium was a woman from Detroit, Mrs. Etta (Henrietta) Wriedt, noted in spiritualistic circles on both sides of the Atlantic. When King was introduced to her she mentioned being acquainted with "Lord Grey & Lady Glenconnor [*sic*]* & Sir

*Lady Glenconner, after the death of her husband, married Lord Grey of Fallodon as his second wife. She was the Lady Grey whom King met in London in 1926. She died in 1928. Mrs. Wriedt told King (14 April 1933) that Lord Grey "was not interested in spiritualism". It was Lady Grey who was the spiritualist. See her article, "Some Aspects of the Higher Spiritualism", in *Fortnightly Review*, October 1922. King spelled Mrs. Wriedt's name both Wriedt and Wreidt; but her signature on a letter in the King Papers indicates that the former is correct. See also her obituary in the *New York Times* (16 Sept. 1942), and a reference to her in Sir Arthur Conan Doyle's *History of Spiritualism* (2 vols., London, 1926).

Oliver Lodge". King was shown the record of the first *séance* Mrs. Fulford had had with her at Fulford Place, "some 20 years ago". She was a sweet-faced old lady whom it would be difficult to think of as a charlatan. King's records show that she was comparatively poor, and she certainly made no effort to make money out of him. In connection with the many *séances* she held for him in the years that followed she was glad to accept the modest sums he paid her and never seems to have asked for more.[22]

During King's visit to Brockville (21-22 February) there were at least four *séances* with Mrs. Wriedt. He made careful records of them (which are not available). He does not describe them in the diary. It is quite clear, however, that he considered them extraordinary. He invited Mrs. Wriedt and Mrs. Fulford to lunch with him in Ottawa later the same week, and obtained their permission to invite Joan Patteson. After lunch on 24 February at Laurier House they had a long *séance*; King says, "It was if anything even more remarkable than what took place at Brockville." Joan "was full of the wonder & mystery of today". It is quite evident that King was convinced he had had the long-hoped-for contact with his mother. He had been reading the Book of Ruth, and on the 25th he writes in the diary, " 'Where thou diest I will die, & there I will be buried'—my grave plot is at her side at Mount Pleasant, already so arranged." That day there is another *séance,* short "but quite wonderful, mother, Isabel, Max, grandfather all appearing & talking much with Joan". The following day there is a variation: "Joan waited in the library while I had 'conversations' with dear mother & Max, Senator Cox,* Sir Wilfrid & grandfather, then Joan came in & the talks were with Isabel, Joan's little girl Nancy, her mother." That evening there were further "wonderful" conversations. Among the spirits who spoke were King's mother and father and Bert Harper.[23]

*George A. Cox, 1840–1914, capitalist and Liberal senator. The connection is not evident.

A new phase of Mackenzie King's life had begun. That June Mrs. Wriedt came to Kingsmere and there was another series of *séances*, at some of which Norman Rogers and King's college friend Thomas Eakin, Principal of Knox College, Toronto, were present. (Rogers is reported to have been "impressed", Eakin "skeptical".) King wrote into his diary a passionate declaration of his faith in the genuineness of the experience:

> There can be *no doubt whatever* that the persons I have been talking with were the loved ones & others I have known and who have passed away. It *was the spirits of the departed*. There is no other way on earth of accounting for what we have all experienced this week. Just because it is so *self-evident*, it seems hard to believe. It is like those who had Christ with them in His day. Because it was all so simple, so natural, they would not believe & sought to destroy. I *know* whereof I speak, that nothing but the presence [of] those who have departed this life, but not this world, or vice versa could account for the week's experiences.[24]

In September King went to Detroit and had further *séances* with Mrs. Wriedt there. Back at Laurier House he felt, he wrote, "a new joy in my home with the feeling of absolute possession and privacy, which was afforded me by the 'conversations'".[25]

Mrs. Wriedt was a "direct voice" medium, that is, the actual voices of the spirits who were assumed to speak through her were heard during her *séances*. And though King had made some attempt at ensuring privacy, they were heard by people who were not intended to hear them. He wrote after the Kingsmere *séances*, "The 'conversations' in many cases have been so loud, so clear, etc. that I have felt great embarrassment at the servants in other parts of the house, hearing what was said, as I am sure they have."[26]

King also tried a different form of communication. He made another visit to Brockville and Mrs. Fulford introduced him to a woman who used a ouija board for conversations with those in the Beyond. King's mother, Sir Wilfrid Laurier, and Senator Fulford were among those who, supposedly, spoke. But King thought most of it came out of the lady's own mind. "I confess the proceeding made little or no impression, it was quite different than [*sic*] the direct voice."[27]

For Mackenzie King, following up the new revelations of 1932, the year 1933 was a time of great excitement. He made more visits to Mrs. Wriedt in Detroit, and she made further visits to Ottawa.[28] On all these occasions there were *séances*, usually but not invariably "wonderful" in their results. In August, King, on a western trip, spent some time in Winnipeg with Dr. T. Glen Hamilton, a well-known spiritualist. Hamilton described the psychic experiences his group had had, including the taking of spirit photographs and the obtaining of new writings by Robert Louis Stevenson, supposedly dictated by the author. King was delighted. "The afternoon was quite the most remarkable one— save the direct voice experiences with Mrs. Wriedt—I have had in my life. . . . I believe absolutely in all that Hamilton & his wife & daughter have told me."[29]

This year 1933 also witnessed, however, an important new development in King's own spiritualistic activity. He discovered what he believed to be a means of direct communication with the spirit world without the intervention of a medium.

# THE LITTLE TABLE

On 13 November 1933 Mackenzie King had a small dinner party at Laurier House. His guests were his old friend the Dominion Archivist, Dr. (later Sir) A. G. Doughty, Mrs. Doughty, and "Mde. Pouliot". (Godfroy and Joan Patteson were on a trip to the United States.) King writes: "We had an amazing evening. The first time I have seen table wrapping [*sic*] & having messages come thro' to me from father, mother, Max & Bella. There can be no shadow of doubt as to their genuineness." King does not say which guest introduced the table rapping, but his further remark, "Doughty is a dear soul and I am very fond of him," seems to leave little doubt that it was the Archivist.

No sooner had the Pattesons returned than King and Joan began to experiment with the new system of communication. Here is King's description of the first evening:

> At 10.30 Dr. Eakin arrived from Toronto. Joan and I had started to see if we could get results from placing our hands on the small table. It had spelt out the word "Godfroy" & was under way with other words when we had to stop for Eakin, he joined us & the first word he [*sic*] spelled when he came in was "Eak" — later we got quite a number of messages.

It was, King thought, "amazingly successful". "I was delighted to find Joan and I had the power."[1] There was no need to call on Doughty or any other helper. It is doubtful whether Doughty—if indeed it was Doughty—ever knew just what he had started on that November evening.

He had in fact started a great deal. The "little table" plays a large part in King's life from this moment. Only a week or so after that first experiment, it lent excitement to the celebration of Joan's birthday: "After dinner we spent most of the evening in the sun room with little table serving as the means of communication with those beyond. They came trooping in with their love and birthday greetings. Joan's family & mine, many friends, members of prlt. & others. . . . It was a truly amazing evening."[2]

Readers of King's diary will find it hard to discover from it just how he and Joan worked the little table. He seems to have left no description of their technique. But they evidently followed, in the beginning at least, the procedures familiar in spiritualistic literature.[3] They placed their hands on the table and questioned the spirits, and the spirits replied by "responsive raps". Two raps meant Yes (we know this much from a note by King)[4] and one presumably No. Where detail was required the table "spelled out" the answer in code; the method usually accepted seems to have been that one rap meant A, two meant B, and so on through the alphabet. No doubt Rex and Joan used this system, though I have not found specific confirmation of it. Obviously it was a slow and cumbersome procedure.

In the early weeks after 13 November 1933 King's records show that the spirits were brief, replying to questions with one or two words.[5] This is consistent with use of the alphabetical code. Soon, however, the spirit communications become longer and more complicated; King writes down extended speeches, sometimes covering a good part of a page; and we occasionally encounter records of chatty exchanges such as this rather comic one with William Lyon Mackenzie after the abdication crisis of 1936:[6]

Mackenzie    ... *You were predestined to be Prime Minister at*
             *this time ...*
             *The fate of Canada is in your hands,*
             *The fate of Great Britain depends on Canada,*
             *The fate of Europe depends on Great Britain ...*
K.           Go on Mackenzie   (Joan laughs)
J.           Go on Mr. Mackenzie
Mackenzie    *Mrs. Patteson is more polite than you are.*
K.           I was speaking historically.

It is rather hard to imagine this sort of thing being laboriously
spelled out letter by letter. Is it possible that King had turned
himself into a medium and believed himself to be receiving, in
his head, messages which he repeated aloud for the benefit of
Joan Patteson and then wrote down? There are references in
1934 to names being "spelt out" when the phrase is not used in
any other connection.[7] Perhaps the spelling technique continued to be used for identification, whereas the body of messages came in another way.* It is possible that thorough examination of all the papers, including those still closed, would make
more definite conclusions possible. In any case, the matter of
technique is not of primary importance. What matters is that
Mackenzie King was convinced that he was receiving communications from the Beyond, and that he made a full record of those
communications on paper.

From King's point of view it was obviously a splendid thing
that he could now communicate with his family, and other people, in the spirit world, without the aid of Mrs. Wriedt or some
other medium. He continued, it is true, to have *séances* with Mrs.
Wriedt, for whom he had a deep regard; but it was now possible

---

*There is an account in Myers's *Human Personality and Its Survival of Bodily
Death* of a spiritualist who, finding the rapping too cumbersome, passed on
into automatic writing (below, page 180). This clearly did not happen with
King.

to have contact with the loved ones at any time, given only privacy, a table, and a sympathetic partner. The partner was usually Joan Patteson, but there were others. We have already seen King having a successful sitting with Julia Grant (above, page 134); and in the spring of 1934, when visiting the artist Homer Watson at Doon, Ontario, he "tried the table with Watson & got some splendid results". About the same time he refers hopefully to the possibility of being able to "operate" the table alone.[8] This aspiration seems to have been realizable only on great occasions. On 12 May 1937, Coronation Day, in London, King went back to his hotel when all the ceremonial was over and —evidently alone—"tried the little table". He recorded, "What I got was Mackenzie — also Mother — Love from all here."

The reader is at liberty to believe, if he wishes, that King's messages actually came from the spirit world. My own opinion, I regret to say, is that they came subconsciously out of King's own head. (How the rapping was produced I do not pretend to explain; doubtless there was some form of "unconscious pressure".) My opinion is strengthened by the manner in which the "spirits" told King what he most wanted to hear. One striking example may be mentioned. At the end of the year 1933 King casts his usual annual balance and reflects that he is entering on a new phase of "the old old battle"—"plutocracy vs. the people & their rights": "I go into it with my life consecrated as never before to the cause, and with the knowledge that I am not alone but have great forces fighting with me. . . . I do not want power unless it is given me to use it for the good of my fellow men. I pray God that my life may be worthily devoted to their service, and that I may be able, under divine guidance, & through the power of the spirit to help to better conditions in this country & the world — to make thy kingdom come Thy will be done on earth as it is in heaven."[9] With King's mind working along these lines, no one need be surprised that less than a month later

King's spiritual guide "Meyers"* revealed to him that he, King, had received a special favour from God:[10]

> What he told me. . . was. . . wonderful. . .—a consecration to God's service in the service of Humanity — God['s] grace having saved me from my sins and His love chosen me to help to work out his will "on earth as it is in Heaven"—The supreme prayer of my life heard, and answered with the assurance of God's strength & vision being vouchsafed in time of need. There have been forecastings of this all along the way, but nothing so direct & immediate and now that it has come, I can hardly believe it. The time chosen is that which above all others I would have, — just before the important speech on the address which opens the real work of the session.

Once again we see King as the chosen of God. The combination of simple-mindedness and egotism required to produce this result leaves one slightly breathless.

After reading widely in the records of Mackenzie King's adventuring in the spirit world, one feels driven to attempt some assessment of the man's intellect, and the assessment I fear can only be unfavourable. He had five "earned" university degrees. His political success was unparalleled, and his political shrewdness no one can doubt. But his spiritual activities give one pause. The mere fact of his being a spiritualist scarcely makes him a simpleton, though some would argue so. It is the extraordinary crudity of the manifestations of his spiritualism, the shattering

---

*As usual, King was having trouble spelling names. Frederic W. H. Myers, a respected Cambridge scholar, critic, and poet, was the author of a two-volume work, *Human Personality and Its Survival of Bodily Death,* published after his death in 1901. There are many indications that both King and Mrs. Patteson thought of Myers's spirit as commanding particular authority, and as charged with special responsibility concerning communication between the spirit world and those on earth.

naïveté of his judgements in these matters, that leave one with the ineradicable impression of a limited intelligence. At times, it is simply impossible to take him seriously. Perhaps advancing age had dimmed his intellectual powers—after all, he was sixty in 1934. But I find myself wondering whether, back in the 1890s, when the University of Toronto invited him out, and Harvard invited him in and gave him the very best it had, the Canadian institution did not show the sounder judgement.

The year 1934 is perhaps the moment in King's life when he came closest to losing contact with reality. King was still in opposition, and had plenty of time for the spirit world. His diary for that year is an utterly extraordinary document. It devotes untold thousands of words to King's various "spiritual" experiences. For the first half of the year he kept separate records for the spiritual and the temporal, keeping the journal of his dreams and his *séances* apart from that of more mundane matters; but the two departments kept getting mixed up together and at the end of June he abandoned the attempt.

  Though the "little table" dominates the year, the ex-Prime Minister got revelations in other ways, ways which will impress some people, I fear, as mere superstition. Numerology—the cult of "mystical numbers"—now reaches its peak. At one stage, King becomes obsessed with the numbers 30 and 10. He sees 30 everywhere. The loose-leaf paper for the diary has three holes in it, round holes: 3–0; thirty. King noted that the word *radio* was significant because the number 10 was concealed in it (i–o); and suddenly he began to hear the word on every side.[11] Looking across the House of Commons, he found both magic numbers much in evidence:[12]

> Looking at the front benches, I thought I am looking for the last time at Guthrie, Bennett and Perley in this H. of C. I thought it is the last day they will be sitting together, 3–0—I

looked further along & there were Manion and a vacant seat (Stevens). I thought that means 1 – 0. Stevens will not be again in H. of C. — other front benches were empty thro three absentees, Rhodes, Matthews & Cahan—here again I thought this is significant, 3 – 0. . . .

The occupants of the government front bench would have been surprised had they known what was going on behind the impassive features of the Leader of the Opposition.

Then there was teacup reading. Joan Patteson seems to have had a sense of humour, which if given freer rein might have curbed King's extravagances. She was inclined to laugh when, in a session over the table about the majority in a forthcoming by-election, Sir Wilfrid Laurier told King, "What you saw in the tea cup is correct. Glad you believe in this medium of transmission." But King, who as we know had no sense of humour at all, explained to her seriously that "it was from the higher realm . . . one of the very many media",[13] and he went on seeking enlightenment among the tea-leaves. Though he was glad of professional help when he could get it, he did his own interpretations, sometimes with curious results. On one occasion he was able to explain most of the objects presented in the leaves, but could make nothing of one — an obvious bear. He solved it, however: "I came to see it related to mother 'bearing' me."[14]

But the central fact of King's personal life at this point was the little table, and it was worked very hard. In the summer of 1934 there was an occurrence that indicates how important it had become, though the incident also reveals devils of doubt in the minds of Rex and Joan.

In 1933 the government of R. B. Bennett revived the practice of recommending Canadians to the Crown for the honour of knighthood. This had been in abeyance since 1919, when a resolution of the House of Commons asked the King to refrain from conferring titles of honour on Canadians.[15] Mackenzie

King reacted violently against Bennett's action, issuing a strong statement attacking it at the New Year of 1934.[16] As the King's birthday (3 June) drew near, he evinced an almost pathological interest in the matter of who were to be knighted, and sought information from the spirits over the table. On 13 May his father's spirit gave him a long list, including Bill Herridge (who had become a close associate of Bennett and had married his sister, and who was now Canadian Minister in Washington), H. J. Cody, Vincent Massey, and Herbert Marler.[17] On 3 June King wrote, "I believe in what I have been told and believe it will be verified.* It will be 6 o'clock before the Canadian press will be permitted to give out anything — then will come the names of those who have been carried away by false standards — poor weak vain creatures." In due time the announcement came. There were only two knighthoods. And they had gone to people whom nobody in the King family, living or dead, had thought of: two admirable men of science, Charles Saunders, the originator of Marquis wheat, and Frederick Banting, one of the discoverers of insulin.[18]

King was bowled over. All the prophecies he had received from the spirits now seemed called in question. (They had told him, among other things, that there was going to be a general election in the autumn of 1934, and that R. B. Bennett was going to be married; neither event took place.) He began to think that "a lying spirit" had been at work. But he found comfort in the tea-leaves. In his cup he saw "quite distinctly" the letter "I". After a time he felt that this had "a real significance, that it meant July 1". The real honours list — the one about which the spirits had informed him — would be published on Dominion Day. The Saunders and Banting knighthoods had been "only a blind", "to throw the public further off its guard".[19]

On 24 June King asked Sir Wilfrid Laurier, over the table, for

---

*One wonders whether the defiant phrasing does not indicate that King actually had doubts about the revelation.

information about knighthoods on 1 July. Sir Wilfrid replied, "Glad you asked me this—Herridge, Marler, Massey, Ferguson, Bruce, Roy, Longley will be knighted. Look out for elections in September." On 1 July itself Sir Wilfrid repeated the list, adding two more names — those of H. J. Cody and Edward Beatty. "They know about it now," he said. King was struck by the use of the word *now*: "I had felt all along if Sir W. told us that there could be no mistakes, for he could see all current happenings etc. even if [there is] doubt about prophecy." But alas, there was no honours list on Dominion Day.[20]

King's last hope was to assume that the list had been put off until the end of the parliamentary session, which fell on 3 July. But by the 5th he had to admit that he had been misled. That morning Joan thought she spoke to Sir Wilfrid and Mr. Myers, and they told her that "an evil spirit" had given the misinformation. Joan proceeded to demonstrate that she had at least a somewhat firmer grasp of reality than King. She told King "that she thought the mediums the best way to get information, as they were usually ignorant people—their minds a blank—that with our minds so strong & feelings etc. entering as we wrote, and especially saying we would call so and so to tell us, Laurier & the like, we were not getting the right source, we were either using our own subconscious thoughts, or an evil spirit was creeping in. ... She believed what we got through Mrs. Wriedt."[21]

King proceeded to review the disaster in his own mind. He accepted the "evil spirit" theory, and added, "with it goes by the board completely all that may be said of a definite character re events, times, seasons etc. and prophecy, — save as may be evidenced in other ways." Real guidance was to be found elsewhere: "It comes back to the celestial and immortal voice of conscience — to the revelation that comes through the Scriptures, to much told truly by those we love & who love us, to mother & father & Bell & Max, & especially grandfather, as continuing to shape my life. Sir Wilfrid also yes—but not to the degree of my own parents and grandparents, home, etc. I come back to the highest spirituality being the real power." He was doubtless remembering that Sir Wilfrid was an agnostic. The next day he added, "As to the table, I think it well to use it sparingly, and as dear mother said to let God send who will, not for us to call those we want. I think it brings both truth & error.... "[22] A few weeks later Mrs. Wriedt came again to Kingsmere for *séances*.[23]

It is tempting to say that from the time of these disturbing events the "little table" was in decline, but it is doubtful whether this was really the case. King may have relied less upon it for prophecy, but it continued to have a central place in his life, and he and Joan spent hours over it, frequently at the Patteson establishment at 202 Elgin Street. (It seems evident that any table would serve their purposes; there was no one particular table that had special virtues.) In the autumn of 1934 King made a trip to Europe, and while there he made new spiritualistic contacts. He spoke to Lady Aberdeen (the "Governess General" of Canada, 1893–98), whose husband had died a few months before. King recorded, "she told me of having had evidence of Lord Aberdeen's cont'd existence from automatic writing & I told her of what I got from him by the table." Lady Aberdeen arranged a series of automatic writing sittings for King with a medium in London.[24] (Automatic writing, it may be explained, is a procedure in which the medium conveys messages from the other world by writing, sometimes while in a trance.) He did not have such good fortune with the son of another eminent Victorian. He met Lord and Lady Gladstone of Hawarden in Paris. "I told them both," he wrote, "about having talked with Mr. Gladstone, — via Mrs. Wreidt & also by the table & of his speaking of the Queen shaking her finger at him.... 'It is all very strange' was Lord Gladstone's remark, it seemed to nonplus each of them a little & I wondered afterwards if I should have told them what I did, but something seemed to prompt me.... "[25]

Back home in Ottawa, King rushed for the little table. The broadening influence of travel is reflected in the guest list; Leonardo da Vinci and Lorenzo de' Medici appear, as does Louis Pasteur, at whose tomb King had prayed in Paris. Pasteur prescribed for the dog Pat's heart condition.[26] King again makes the acquaintance of Philip, a character of biblical times, perhaps Philip the Apostle, to whom Mrs. Hester Dowden, the automatic-writing medium in London, had introduced him. For some time Philip acts as a control, introducing other spirits.[27] But what was perhaps the table's supreme triumph was reserved for 17 December 1934, King's sixtieth birthday. Joan and Godfroy came to dinner. Thereafter Joan and Rex had "an hour with the little table". Only King's own words could do justice to the occasion: "It was beautiful the manner in which one after the other of the loved ones 'came trouping [sic] in', and how the number included the Leaders of Liberalism in the old world and this." The order of their appearance, he thought, clearly reflected "planning and design to the last detail": "Max & Bell had not a chance to speak last night. They were the first tonight . . . Godfroy's, Mr. Patteson & Joan's family . . . then Mr. Larkin also missed last night but first to come after the family—the inclusion of Mrs. Larkin characteristic of him, then more love from Mother & Father (wishing to speak on the day itself, but waiting till the others who could not come last night got their chance)— then Sir Wilfrid and Lady Laurier ditto. — Then Marjory [sic] Herridge, [Andrew] Haydon & Harper —, close personal friends."*

But it was the parade of politicians that was really impressive:

Then passing to the old world. Love from London — the great political leaders, Grey of Falloden [sic] — whom I

*The inclusion of Haydon is interesting. King had, in effect, thrown this loyal Liberal fund-raiser to the wolves at the time of the Beauharnois investigation.[28] Haydon had been a personal friend, but certainly not in a class with Marjorie Herridge and Bert Harper. One suspects that King was salving his conscience by being good to Senator Haydon after he was dead.

dearly loved, Lord Oxford, Gladstone, McLean [Sir Donald Maclean], Roseberry [sic]—Campbell-Bannerman—a marvellous group—Then the Canadian Liberal Leaders, Alexander Mackenzie, Edward Blake & "the whole lot of us"—a typical political expression—Then "try to speak to Toronto's first Mayor"—How beautifully associating . . . with the [Toronto] Centennial celebration and linking grandfather with my present and future, giving him the joy of saying what is to come — how rejoiced he must be to see this vindication of his life & work—the Prime Ministership—my part to draw England & Canada closer together—a marvellous completion of his aims & work—The grandson of the one whom [sic] the Tories said was "disloyal" seeking to save & secure the British Empire as the greatest agency of peace & good-will in secular affairs—the concluding word with Sir Wilfrid, & his word of kindly counsel, — all linked up with Bengough's little poem, written when I became Leader & making clear the guidance all along the way.

J. W. Bengough's "little poem", "The Spirit of William Lyon Mackenzie to his Grandson", written in sham-Scots at the time of the 1919 convention,[29] certainly well expressed the sense of "guidance all along the way" that King had felt so often. It is not surprising that he had cherished it for fifteen years:

> Rise, then, ma laddie, a' is fine,
> Wi' eager party noo in line,
> In Laurier's name, aye, an' in mine,
>    Charge on the foe;
> Lies canna' last, Truth's aye divine,
>    The Wrong maun go!

It was cheering doctrine for a tarnished party on the morrow of Beauharnois, with a general election looming ahead. And what could be more encouraging to an insecure political personality than that muster of great men, summoned up to do honour to him on his birthday? Once more one stands in awe before the ego that could produce such a tribute to itself out of its own viscera.

There had been a sitting on 9 March 1934 which strengthens my belief that the relationship between King and Mrs. Patteson was entirely platonic, even if King sometimes wished that it was something more. A "Hindoo" priest of ancient times, "Koramura", spoke, and at the end of a long rigmarole said, "Hail God who has ordained that you should love each other," and more to the same effect. King recorded, "Joan at once protested. . . . She took her hands off the table and shook them away from her as if to protect herself. . . . " King wished to go on and for a time they did. But next morning he decided that Koramura was "a pagan spirit that I do not want to have around". No more was heard of him.

October 1935 brought the general election which Sir Wilfrid Laurier (or an evil spirit substituting for him) had foretold for September 1934. The Chosen of God charged on the foe, constantly advised and inspired over the little table. In January his grandfather told him, "You will be Prime Minister this year in June. Get ready for the long struggle . . . go to bed early whenever you can, eat lightly, drink no spirits or wine, try to pray all you can, prayer ascends to God. . . . " As polling-day drew near, the spirits became more excited. On 6 October at Laurier House, a distinguished company spoke over the table on the theme of God's intention that William Lyon Mackenzie King should rule: Laurier, Gladstone, Lord Morley, Lord Oxford, Lord Grey of Fallodon, the two Mackenzies, St. Luke, St. John, Mother, Father. St. John said, "Love to Mrs. Patteson and you. Long ago I wanted to tell you that God had chosen you to shew men & nations how they should live."

A week later, on the night before the vote, a similar group of spirits dwelt (rather surprisingly, it must be said) on King's

mission to restore peace to an increasingly troubled world. Witness Lord Grey:

> *Long ago I saw that you would be a peace-maker. . . .*
> *Long ago I tried to end war.*
> *Long ago I failed to achieve that end. You will succeed.*
> *God has chosen you for that purpose. . . .*

King's brother Max struck an individual note:

> *Long ago I tried to help you to see that God wanted you to do his work*
> *among men and Nations. . . .*
> *Long ago he told me that you would help the people out of their*
> *distress. . . .*
> *Long may you reign, Long may Joan reign with you. . . .*

When King asked for information about the outcome of the
election, Laurier gave it through King's father:

> *Sir Wilfrid says that you will win handsomely* [he did].
> *He thinks that you will carry the country from East to West.*
> *He says that you will have a majority of about 45* [it was 97].
> *He says that Bennett will lose his own seat* [he didn't].
> *He says that Stevens will be defeated in Kootenay* [he wasn't].
> *He says that Woodsworth will lose his seat* [he didn't]. . . . [30]

Apart from the basic fact of the great victory (and in view of the
catastrophic unpopularity of R. B. Bennett's government nobody could have prophesied anything else), Sir Wilfrid could
hardly have been more wrong. But in the hour of triumph this
was evidently forgotten.

Most Canadians, if they had been confronted with the document just quoted, would have said that the Liberal leader was out
of his head. Fortunately for him, however, the electorate had no
knowledge of what went on behind the doors of Laurier House.
The day after King wrote these curious lines, the Canadian
people made him Prime Minister for the third time.

The pressures on a Prime Minister are heavier than those on a Leader of the Opposition, and it is probably true that mere shortage of time increasingly reduced Mackenzie King's attention to spiritualism from 1935 onwards. But the decline was certainly gradual. The diary becomes less and less a record of personal experience and more a record of public business efficiently transacted, a change remarkable enough in itself; but we continue to read of "sittings", both with mediums and over the little table. It did not even occur to King that it might be politic for the Prime Minister of Canada to curb his spiritualistic activities when in a foreign country. In December 1935, when he made one of his periodical visits to Baltimore for medical treatment, he spent a day in New York and had a long sitting with a medium ("Mrs. G."). Then, hearing that there were good teacup readings at a tearoom on Fifth Avenue called "the Gypsy Tent", he went there for another long session. Extended notes of both conversations are in his papers. The day ended with dinner with Beatrix Robb at her apartment.[31]

There were numerous sittings over the table in the summer of 1936. Harper came and said, "Mrs. Herridge is beside me." (She sent her love but did not herself speak.)[32] King appealed to his family for support: "Please help me, father, I am beginning to feel unequal to these tasks — help me to realize that there is power from beyond and above." Father in reply, like Grandfather earlier, advises him to eat less, take no wine, and pray. Frederic Myers gives a disquisition on mystical numbers. He explains that 7 and 10 are mystical numbers for King, Joan, and Godfroy: "This means that the important events of your life have a relationship to those numbers."[33] In August Mrs. Wriedt came to Kingsmere for a series of *séances*. The international situation was causing more and more disquiet. King asked Peter Larkin's spirit if he had anything to suggest. "Larkin: Preparedness."[34] On this question there was disagreement between John King and William Lyon Mackenzie. John King reported, "I would let them [the Europeans] fight among themselves. He claims we ought to be prepared."[35] Here we doubtless have a reflection of conflict in King's own mind. I speculate that King had been discussing his problems with Mrs. Wriedt, and that, perhaps subconsciously, she brought them into the *séances*. The Cabinet Defence Committee had just been set up, and King was now facing its first meeting with the Chiefs of Staff to discuss a rearmament program.

In the autumn of 1936 King again goes to Europe. At Geneva for League of Nations sessions, he forms an unexpected new contact. He meets the Duchess of Hamilton, at her invitation. She turns out to be a spiritualist, and he has "an amazingly interesting day" with her. He moves on to London, where of course he has the obligatory interviews with King Edward VIII and with the Prime Minister (Stanley Baldwin). More privately he has talks with a number of the spiritualistic fraternity and visits the London Spiritualist Alliance.[36] Soon after returning to Canada he is faced with the crisis over the King's abdication. This brings another distinguished visitor to the little table: the late King George V.[37]

The year 1937 took King across the Atlantic again, for the coronation of King George VI and the Imperial Conference. Joan and Godfroy Patteson travelled in the same ship. In England King visited the Duchess of Hamilton, at Salisbury (where he again met Sir Oliver Lodge, now eighty-six) and in London.[38] Subsequently he made what may be called his one serious attempt at living up to the spirits' estimate of him as a peacemaker, when he visited Hitler* and warned him that the British Empire would be united in case of war (above, page 27). Obviously it was not effective (Hitler might well have said to himself, "How many divisions has Mackenzie King?"), but King thought, or tried to convince himself, that it was a stroke of statesmanship.

*It appears that he had considered doing this in 1936, but had been dissuaded by his adviser O. D. Skelton.[39]

At Christmas he wrote of "this marvellous and *miraculous year*": "clearly the purpose of God is related to my securing the good will of Germany & the Brit. Empire, working with Hitler towards this end, and saving France thereby & much else."[40]

Influenced no doubt by Hitler's polite reception of him, he continued to see him in a favourable light. It is evident too that this interpretation was coloured by King's beliefs and experience. He wrote on 27 March 1938:

> I am convinced he is a spiritualist — that he has a vision to which he is being true . . . his devotion to his mother — that Mother's spirit is I am certain his guide. . . . I believe the world will yet come to see a very great man — mystic, in Hitler. . . . much I cannot abide in Nazism — the regimentation — cruelty — oppression of Jews . . . but Hitler him[self], the peasant — will rank some day with Joan of Arc among the deliverers of his people, & if he is only careful may yet be the deliverer of Europe. . . .

It all seems extraordinarily naive today. But in fairness to King it seems in order to quote the comment of a recent German biographer of Hitler: "If Hitler had succumbed to an assassination or an accident at the end of 1938, few would hesitate to call him one of the greatest of German statesmen, the consummator of Germany's history."[41]

Through this year 1938, while the world slid down the slope towards war, King contrived to combine his official responsibilities with considerable spiritualistic activity. The little table was frequently in use;[42] and early in the year Mrs. Wriedt made a visit. She was now seventy-five or seventy-six, and wanted King's help in disposing of certain possessions she particularly valued. One was a ring given her by Lord Dudley. Another, more important, was a watch given her by W. T. Stead, recognizing the fact that through her mediumship the voice of Queen Victoria was supposedly heard in London in July 1911, a decade after the

Queen's death; King's version is that she won it "as the best of all mediums". The watch was said to have been presented to a much earlier medium by Queen Victoria herself in 1846. Mrs. Wriedt wanted the watch to go to the Queen Victoria collection at the South Kensington Museum. King spent considerable time arranging to send these items to Canada House, London, in the Department of External Affairs official bag. The ring went back to the Dudley family. King apparently thought the watch should go by way of the reigning Queen, the consort of King George VI; luckily, however, he did not send it direct, but confided it to the Duchess of Hamilton to be passed on. The Duchess consulted the Mistress of the Robes, who presumably scotched the idea.[43] The watch went not to Buckingham Palace and South Kensington but to the London Spiritualist Alliance, where Blair Fraser saw it on a blue velvet cushion in 1951.*

This series of *séances* with Mrs. Wriedt was remarkable for an innovation: Godfroy Patteson took part. He had evidently held aloof on earlier occasions, but now, to the "amazement & delight" of Joan and Rex, he came in. Through Mrs. Wriedt he heard the voices of a number of his old friends of the banking world. We later catch a glimpse of him at a session over the little table; but it must be said that he is dividing his time between the spirits and a broadcast of a boxing match.[44]

Late in the year a rather special *séance* with the table touched on public events.[45] The impending tour of Canada by King George VI and Queen Elizabeth produced another visit by King George V, who assured the Prime Minister, "The visit is due to their affection for you", while King's father told him that the late King would be with the visitors on their tour "and will guide

---

*Fraser's article "The Secret Life of Mackenzie King, Spiritualist" (*Maclean's*, 15 Dec. 1951) contains some errors but on the whole is accurate. Note, however, that it is almost entirely based on interviews with King's spiritualist friends in London. Of King's do-it-yourself spiritualism with the little table Fraser knew nothing.

you as well as them". New Canadian–American and Anglo-
American trade agreements were about to be signed. Sir Wilfrid
Laurier said these were a great victory, and added, "The President [Roosevelt] is very fond of you. He will treat you like a
Prince." Perhaps the most extraordinary feature of this session,
however, is the appearance of the late Sir Robert Borden to deny
a statement in his recently published memoirs to the effect that
King would have liked a portfolio in Borden's wartime Union
Government. Borden says the statement is untrue, that he did
not have time to revise the book before he died, and that he will
"make amends by helping you all I can". The statement, as
published, does in fact seem to be unfounded.[46] King made a
public denial, but needless to say did not mention that Borden
had apologized to him from the spirit world.

# WAR: THE PRIME MINISTER
# SWEARS OFF

The autumn of 1939 brought the war which Canadian politicians, remembering the desperate domestic crisis of 1917, had had particular reason to hope might be averted. The outbreak had a special consequence for Mackenzie King. In effect, he swore off spiritualism for the duration.

On 1 September Hitler, no longer "careful", invaded Poland. On the evening of the 2nd, King and Joan Patteson held at Kingsmere what turned out to be the craziest of all their sessions with the little table.[1] It began with King's father announcing that Hitler was dead: "He was shot by a Pole." King's mother, Laurier, Gladstone, and Max King followed; and William Lyon Mackenzie drew a parallel between himself in 1837 and the German dictator:

> *I did not want to shed a drop of blood*
> *I was driven to desperation*
> *Hitler did not want to have war*
> *He has become desperate.*

At this point there was an interruption. It was 11 p.m. O. D. Skelton telephoned to say that at midnight (London time) the British Cabinet had decided to have Sir Nevile Henderson, the British Ambassador in Berlin, deliver an ultimatum to Germany demanding the withdrawal of German troops from Poland, failing which there would be immediate war. King and Skelton agreed that the British should have allowed more time. King then returned to the table. His father's spirit still asserted that Hitler was dead, and said, "The French and British will agree to a conference when they hear of Hitler's death." King asked, "Are you sure this is not all subconscious thought and desire asserting itself?", but the spirits insisted, and the sitting ended with his mother declaring, "War will be averted."

This very peculiar personal problem added to King's anxieties at this desperate moment. He wrote in his diary:[2]

> ... The real issue: — Christ vs. anti-Christ. I felt strongly tonight, after conversation J. and I had, that there are some things that [as?] Asquith said which we were not meant to know in the sense of attempting to know them by the senses, but which could be known only to Faith. In other words, that the spiritual things must be spiritually discerned; that we must not hope to get the profound spiritual experiences and truths through material agencies. Least of all, must we seek to convince ourselves as to courses of conduct in great decisions by occult means. The Roman Catholic church, I believe, is right in recognizing the existence of phenomena of the kind, but in recognizing its [sic] dangers. Evil and Good exists [sic] in the Hereafter as well as the here and now. Men may be guided by evil spirits or by good spirits. . . .

On 4 September the Prime Minister added a rather formal note to his memorandum of the *séance* of the 2nd:

> This all makes perfectly clear either that a lying spirit has come in somewhere, or that sub-conscious wishes dictate the words expressed. — I felt terribly exercised at this for I felt at the time it was not truth, however, that it would serve as a guide to future action & belief as to worth of "automatic

writing"—I felt I should perhaps not have sought to use the table to discover the course of events. I had a feeling at the time that it was a sort of betrayal of faith so to do.—Like in Lohengrin.* Elsa determined to know what it was not intended she should know—It is faith one must be guided by and intuition—our guide

WLMK  Sept 4.

Here King seems to be repudiating the little table, while reserving judgement as to automatic writing. From this moment the familiar pencilled memoranda of sittings at the little table vanish from King's diary, and references to the table disappear from the text.

The Prime Minister's motives in abandoning the table at this particular point are interesting to speculate upon. The doubts he records about the genuineness of the information it gave him could have arisen at any time, and in fact they had arisen at the time of the knighthoods affair in 1934, "lying spirit" and all. But war is a more serious business than peace, and the leader of a country at war has reason to be especially cautious about the sources of his information and the influences that bear upon him. What is more, he has particular reason to be cautious about his public image. It would have been highly dangerous to King politically at any time if the Canadian public had been informed of his spiritualistic proclivities; with the country at war, it would have been instantly fatal, and King undoubtedly was well aware of it.

It is interesting that King suggested that the table's messages were a product of "subconscious thought"—his own, of course — (though it was surely very simple-minded to ask the spirits about it). Joan had suggested this in 1934 (above, page 179). I am left wondering whether, for King, the table had finally become a sort of game, which he enjoyed enormously but did not abso-

*King had been seeking for explanations of Hitler in the Wagner operas.

lutely believe in, and which he could give up without serious injury to his life.

It should be added that with the outbreak of war King's tolerance for Hitler was at an end. On 23 January 1940, *à propos* of the refusal of General Hertzog of South Africa to believe in Hitler's desire for world domination, he wrote, "I shared that view myself at the time but I have changed it in the light of what has developed since this war began. Germany could not have developed the military machine she has nor proceeded in any way she did unless she were bent on world domination by terror and violence."

The little table was a highly personal and private operation, and very few people apart from King and the Pattesons knew about it. It is questionable whether his secretaries knew, for his records of the *séances* held across it were written by himself in longhand. The danger of the wrong people coming to know about the table was therefore comparatively slight. *Séances* held with mediums were a different matter. When King consulted a medium he was putting his career in her hands and in those of her associates.* Moreover, in wartime the steps of a Prime Minister were apt to be dogged by the press even more than in peace. In these circumstances it is not surprising that he severed almost all connection with the spiritualistic fraternity in Britain during the war. He made two wartime visits to London, in 1941 and 1944. In striking contrast with his actions earlier and later, during these visits there were no *séances*. Of his spiritualist friends, the only ones he had contact with were the Duchess of Hamilton and some members of her circle; and none of these

---

*I have been assured that many people in Kingston knew of King's consulting a fortune-teller there. But this never reached the newspapers, or if it did it was not published. In spiritualism, as in other matters, King was lucky. The mediums he dealt with were sincere and dedicated people who kept his confidence and were not interested in making money out of him. He would have been an ideal blackmail target, but so far as I know no such attempt was ever made on him.

contacts seems to have been closer than a telephone conversation. In 1941 he did not even manage to speak to the Duchess (she was trying to get him as he left his hotel to return to Canada), but he sent her a farewell telegram. In 1944 he recorded what appears to have been a telephone talk with her: "She is most understanding. She had hoped to have me meet a number of friends. But realized what the situation was."[3]

In the course of these visits King did not darken the doors of the London Spiritualist Alliance, where before and after he was wont to make arrangements for meetings with mediums. In October 1945, when he had revoked his self-denying ordinance against spiritualism, he went back there again to see Miss Mercy Phillimore, the Secretary of the Alliance. "I was amazed," he wrote, "to learn it was nine years since I had last been there or seen her."[4] He had apparently not been there during his 1937 visit.

The general absence of *séances* from King's diary for the years 1939–45 does not mean that it is a dull or conventional document. It is true that it is basically an enormously valuable dictated record of public business, a detailed day-to-day account of the direction of the Canadian war effort, having as its highlights King's memoranda of his conversations with Churchill, Roosevelt, and other great figures of the crisis. But — well representing the double life that King continued to lead — it continues also to be highly eccentric. It describes — often in King's difficult longhand—his psychic experiences, and in particular his dreams, which he normally terms "visions".* Almost every day's diary entry commences with an account of the overnight vision. Frequently, but not always, it stars the deceased members of his family. And frequently King's attempts at in-

---

*"Was surprised to find I had been keeping records of visions from 1934, etc., re future—quite clearly recognising later in the day & often in year the vision coming true—(I recall how mother emphasized these are not dreams, they are visions). . . . " (Diary, 9 Jan. 1938).

terpretation are as curious as the dream. Here, from the early days of the war, is an example taken at random. King records how he felt cold in the night and put an extra quilt on his bed. Then came the vision. He was following a well-known Ottawa lady through the streets of the capital, with an umbrella in his hand. They turned into "a sort of Club or room where a lot of men seemed to be lying in pyjamas. . . . Suddenly the word 'Mac' and 'Max' came very strongly before me, and I felt at once it was my brother the Doctor who was advising me that it was the covering on me which was causing the damage. The men lying in pyjamas stood for lighter form of bed clothing. . . . Once I threw off the brown quilt which I had added for the cold, I began to feel relief of body and mind. . . . " King's final conclusion was, "I am quite certain that those who are nearest to me are watching over me hour by hour, and that this was another evidence of it. . . . "[5]

Also increasingly prominent in these wartime diaries is the old obsession with the position of the hands of the clock. Perhaps this and the dreams are compensating King for the loss of the little table. One could give innumerable examples. One is enough. On 25 August 1943 President Roosevelt visited Ottawa; and King wrote a "Memo re hands of clock" as they were at various times that day, beginning with "Exactly 10 past 8 when I looked at clock on waking — straight line", and including "12 noon when noon day gun fired & I read my welcome to President—together", not to mention "25 to 8 when I was handed in my room a letter from Churchill re supply of whiskey to troops . . .—both together". Occasionally King is still found consulting the tea-leaves, though not, I think, to discover the future course of the war.[6]

It must further be said—and it will probably surprise nobody —that King's rejection of spiritualism for the duration was not total. Like a drinker who has taken the pledge, but secretly resorts at intervals to the bottle, he occasionally returns to the old ways. The death of Pat I in July 1941, an episode of enormous importance to King, resulted in a *séance* over the little table in which King's parents reported Pat's arrival in the Beyond. They did not mention receiving the "messages of love" that King had entrusted to him (above, page 142). But they described his happy reunion with the Pattesons' dog Derry: "They know all about hunting for rabbits and squirrels." (At this point, Joan remarks, "I hope there are no cats in heaven—it would be hell if there were.") Joan, it is to be feared, did not always take the little table quite as seriously as King.

This sitting was closely followed by two more, arising out of King's plan to visit Britain shortly — another very important matter (flying the Atlantic was novel and serious business for an elderly politician in 1941). In one, Sir Wilfrid Laurier tells him to go by bomber plane and adds that the weather will be bad for flying in September; his mother tells him that Churchill will be delighted to see him ("He likes you very much"); and W. E. Gladstone tells him that the war will be over before Christmas, and that the President loves him, and wants to see him before he goes to England. (That did not happen, but King did have a telephone talk with Roosevelt before he took off.) The other sitting consisted mainly of advice about the will that King was making. All three were recorded in the old way, in pencilled memoranda written by King and placed in the diary.[7] This revival of the table seems to have been a brief and isolated incident.

As with the table, so with *séances* with mediums. They were rare, but it cannot be said that there were none. Notably, there was one in Toronto in August 1942. King was visiting the office of his publishers, the Macmillan Company of Canada. Conversation with an official of the company revealed that she was a spiritualist and resulted in a spur-of-the-moment *séance* with a "little medium" that evening before the Prime Minister caught the Ottawa train. A galaxy of talent attended: not only King's relations and Laurier, but Queen Victoria, Florence Nightingale, Anne Boleyn, Sir Frederick Banting, Norman Rogers, and others. King had never seen the medium before.[8] One is amazed by his imprudence in putting his career at the mercy of this unknown young woman. It seems likely that he would not have done so had he had more time to think. As always, he was lucky; the story did not get out. But every such episode must have widened the circle of people who knew about the Prime Minister's peculiarities.

In addition to these recorded incidents, we have to reckon with the possibility that others went unrecorded. Did the secret tippler perhaps hold some sessions at the little table without telling the diary? It may be worth while to note something about the record of the epoch-making sitting of 2 September 1939. Except for the pencilled memorandum of it, there is no direct reference to it in the diary. It may be recalled that the text states that King's doubts arose "after conversation J. and I had". This is certainly the table sitting. Elsewhere the text says, "had J. come over for a little *talk, reading and conversation* together" (the italics are mine). The word *conversation* was sometimes used as a synonym for *séance* or *sitting*. Here it was doubtless used to conceal the real meaning from the secretary to whom King was dictating.* But when we find King writing, for instance, in 1941, "I spent an hour or so with J. in conversation. Had an exceptionally interesting talk,"[9] is this a concealed reference to a session with the table? It is quite conceivable, but it seems impossible to be certain.

The war's interference with King's spiritualistic activities does not seem to have depressed him. There is no return of the morbid desire for contact with his mother that is found in the diary before the first *séances* with Mrs. Wriedt in 1932. He now

---

*King dictated his account of the *séance* in Toronto in August 1942 to J. E. Handy, who thus became aware of the Prime Minister's spiritualistic activities, if he had not been before.

thought he knew what he had wished to know. On 18 December 1943, the anniversary of his mother's death, he recalls in some detail the events of 1917, and how he failed to reach Ottawa in time. He proceeds in terms that can only be called triumphant:

> My mother is nearer to me today than she was in her last day upon earth and I am nearer to her. . . . she has come back to me and I have now the assurance that she is at my side and that we will be together for ever.

At the end of this account of Mackenzie King's involvement with the spirit world, one faces the question, so often asked, Did he conduct the affairs of Canada in accordance with what he believed to be advice from the Beyond? And the answer is quite clearly No.

After King's death, reports of his spiritualistic activities at once began to be published, and his friend the Duchess of Hamilton was quoted in print as saying that he "fully appreciated the spiritual direction of the universe and was always seeking guidance for himself in his work".[10] Joan Patteson, who knew him better than anyone else, was much disturbed. She said nothing publicly, but she wrote to Violet Markham at this time, "*never* did he allow his belief to enter into his public life—or [himself to] be guided by anything he found in his search for Reality, as he put it. He looked forward to re-union & he longed to feel that those who loved him, still loved & watched over him & that death did not end but rather began the real life."[11] Mrs. Patteson knew more about King's private than about his public life, but all the evidence fully supports her. Blair Fraser, assiduously interviewing in 1951 the mediums whom King had consulted in the United Kingdom, came to the same conclusion.[12] Blair Neatby, after years of research in the diary and King's other private papers, saw no reason to differ. The spiritual communications King received, he writes, "did no more than confirm his confidence in his own judgment and strengthen his conviction that he was on the right path". He comments on King's "infinite capacity to rationalize, to accept what he wished to believe and to reject the rest".[13]

My own reading leaves me in no doubt of the soundness of these conclusions. A good deal of the evidence has been presented in the foregoing pages. As throughout his life, Mackenzie King in his spiritualistic period was a worried and insecure individual seeking for support. It was support, strength, not advice, that he asked for and received from the spirits. Mainly, he wanted approval, and by a strange coincidence that was what he usually got. The spirits did not, in general, tell him what to do; they told him that what he had done, or what he had decided to do, was right. Thus they sent him on his way with confidence renewed.

Though requests for help are fairly commonly recorded in the diary or in King's notes of *séances*, there are remarkably few requests for advice. At one point however, in January 1935, he did show a tendency to make such requests. He asked Lord Oxford for advice "as to demanding an election", and Oxford told him to try to force one. A week later he asked Laurier to advise him on how long to speak on the Address in reply to the Speech from the Throne; and Sir Wilfrid said, "Speak for an hour and a half. . . . Speak on trade and labour . . . try to touch the high spots only, give up reading figures, or quotations. Try to be humorous, light touches help to relieve the monotony. . . . "[14] I have no doubt whatever that both these replies actually represented plans already formed in King's mind, and now returned to him by his subconscious self with the stamp of approval of two great, dead Liberals. (Humour was an aspiration only; King had always known that he was not capable of it.)*

What King would have liked to have, apart from general encouragement, was information about future events. (What

*"I cannot be other than earnest. I often wish I could be humourous [*sic*] but I cannot, it is a decided limitation" (Diary, 20 Jan. 1904).

politician, what human being, would not?) We have seen him seeking it, in the comic case of the knighthoods in 1934 and in the episode of the election in 1935. In both, the information he received was wrong. The things King got over the little table, I have suggested, came out of his own head; and there were no revelations about the future to be had from there.

King constantly refers to receiving "guidance"; but these references are normally after the fact. After a successful day in Parliament, he is likely to feel that he has been "guided". The examples early in 1935 just given are isolated. Apart from them it would be difficult to find many instances in which he asked one of his correspondents in the Beyond to tell him what to do in a specific situation.

It would be strange, nevertheless, if the irrationalities of King's private world never boiled over into his other world — the rational world of public business. And I believe that this did in fact happen during the greatest political emergency of his career, the Cabinet crisis over conscription in the autumn of 1944.

King told the Governor-General's secretary, after the crisis was over, that it was "wholly the power from beyond" that had saved the day: "I was a mere instrument in working out a higher will."[15] It was a characteristic phrase, though commoner in the privacy of the diary than in conversation. The detailed record in the diary contains no indication, during that long agony, that King felt he was receiving actual guidance. The "little table", we have seen, was not much in use during the war. But to me, at least, the diary does indicate that at one very important point King acted on a basis of intuition rather than reason.

Sir Wilfrid Laurier, it has been made amply clear, was never far from King's mind. And he went into this supreme crisis in 1944 full of memories of the earlier battle over conscription in 1917 and what it had meant for Sir Wilfrid and the Party. When, on 13 October, he received Colonel Ralston's cable telling him that he was returning from England at once in order to raise grave questions, King wrote: "It is a repetition of the kind of thing that led to the creation of the Union government after Borden's return from England [in May 1917]. That will not take place under me."

When trying to write the history of this episode some years ago, I thought I was faced with an interesting conundrum. Ralston told King that the time had come to adopt overseas conscription, and said that if this was not done he would have to resign. For nearly a fortnight King devoted himself to trying to argue Ralston out of resigning. On 26 October he told the Minister of National Defence that it was his duty as a soldier, and his duty under the oath he had sworn as a Minister of the Crown, to remain at his post. And then, on 1 November, when Ralston was still prepared to go on discussing the problem and to seek a compromise, King suddenly and without warning dismissed him from the Cabinet.[16] This seemed to me a little strange; and I examined the diary with care in an attempt to discover just when and why King changed his mind. I thought, and still think, that I found the turning-point on the evening of 30 October.

By this stage of the controversy nerves were certainly fraying. After a long and trying Cabinet meeting, King found awaiting him at Laurier House a telegram from George Fulford, Liberal Member for Leeds. It demanded universal overseas conscription. King remembered Fulford as a strong opponent of his family allowance ("baby bonus") project in the Liberal caucus. Fulford, moreover, though evidently no spiritualist himself, was a son of one of King's close friends in spiritualism, the lady who had introduced him to Mrs. Wriedt; the name Fulford on any document was perhaps likely to have a rather special impact upon him. At any rate the telegram triggered an extraordinary reaction in King's mind. He suddenly became convinced that there was in the Cabinet a conspiracy against him personally.

This is what he wrote in the diary:

> This, at once, caused me to feel exactly what the conspiracy is, because I believe it has come to be that. It is not merely a question of conscription. The same men who are for conscription are the same identically as those who opposed most strongly the family allowances and other social reforms in the budget: Ilsley, Ralston, Howe, Macdonald, Crerar and Gibson? [sic] It is perfectly plain to me that in pretty much all particulars my position is becoming identical to that of Sir Wilfrid Laurier's [sic] where his supposedly strongest colleagues left him, one by one, and joined their political enemies and became a party for conscription. They will find that at this time they have not the Wartimes Election Act to assist them in a campaign. . . . [17]

From this moment, I think, King was determined to dismiss Ralston, presumably because he thought of him as the kingpin of the conspiracy. The difficulty is that the diary never says so; it continues to talk in terms of Ralston's impending *resignation*. But what King *did*, as distinct from what he *wrote*, gives a different impression. The day after the revelation from the Fulford telegram, he sent for General McNaughton and obtained his promise to take the National Defence portfolio if Ralston "resigned". That afternoon he again recorded his conviction that he was the intended victim of a conspiracy: "As I sat in Council, I thought of [sic] what was happening to me, was exactly the same as had happened to Sir Wilfrid. I can see this whole thing has been worked out as a plot. Some of the men who were incensed at the proposal at the start are now coming round, being fearful."[18] Yet still he says no word indicating that he has a purely personal counterplot, a plan to strike the conspirators before they can strike him. Why? One explanation occurs to me. Edouard Handy, to whom King dictated the diary, was very, very reliable. But there are some risks that no wise politician takes; and this was the deadliest secret of King's career. Unfortunately, there is no private handwritten diary at this point.

Before the Cabinet met on 1 November, King took steps obviously designed to provide against other conscriptionists leaving with Ralston. He telephoned W. P. Mulock and T. A. Crerar asking them not to commit themselves to anything hasty at the meeting. He did not dare approach J. L. Ilsley and Angus L. Macdonald, Ralston's closest associates, but he did make a curious proposal to the Governor General. He suggested that if Ralston, Ilsley, and Macdonald all resigned, His Excellency should accept Ralston's resignation, but not Ilsley's or Macdonald's, at least for the moment. This would surely have been an interesting constitutional innovation. As the Cabinet was actually assembling for the meeting, King told Louis St. Laurent that McNaughton was willing to take National Defence. This politic hint to his Quebec lieutenant was the only word he had spoken on the subject. As he entered the meeting, having told nobody else—nobody at all—what he intended to do, he had on his side one of the most potent of the principles of war — surprise. Late in the afternoon he exploded his mine; and Layton Ralston gathered up his papers and left the Cabinet room — alone.[19]

If it seems strange that King recorded nothing in advance about his intention to dismiss Ralston, it is at least equally strange that later he denied that he had dismissed him at all. He appears to have denied it in the Cabinet on 7 November, before a tableful of men who had seen it happen; and he denied it in the diary that day and again six days later, although this contradicted the detailed account of the dismissal that he had written in the diary at the time. He had apparently convinced himself that Ralston had carried out his threat of resignation, and that was all.[20] It is all very peculiar, and one wonders what King's colleagues thought about it.

The fact is that there was no Cabinet conspiracy against King.

The evidence is now pretty complete — there seems little likelihood that much more will come to light — and none of it supports the conspiracy theory. King himself seems to have recorded no evidence for it. The plot existed only in his mind. It was a product of irrational intuition, in the same class with the information King's dead father gave him about the knighthoods in 1934.* And yet I think it is evident that King made it the basis of a great act of policy. The most remarkable thing about the whole affair is that it turned out so well for King. Not only did he survive the crisis, but it left him stronger than ever. I have suggested elsewhere[21] that, though his strategy was non-existent, his tactics in the Ralston case were flawless and typically deadly. I might have added that he was probably the luckiest tactician who has operated in Canada since General Wolfe.

> *King would not have admitted this. See page 192, above, where he makes a firm distinction between information received over the table and "intuition — our guide".

# PART IV
# THE FINAL YEARS

When the surrender of Japan ended the Second World War, Mackenzie King had less than five years of life remaining to him: rather more than three years as Prime Minister, somewhat less than two years of retirement.

He was over seventy now, and indubitably an elder statesman, recognized as such both at home and abroad. He had always complained that people — even Liberals — failed to perceive in him those sterling merits of which he himself had always been so well aware. Now, if only by the mere effluxion of time, he received at least some of the recognition that he was sure he deserved. The incense smoke curled upward, and the old man's nostrils sniffed it gratefully.

The routine of the Ottawa seasons proceeded. In the winter King continued to live at Laurier House, and continued to visit the Pattesons, who were now living at 30 Cooper Street. Florence Bird, a friendly neighbour, recalls that she and her husband became accustomed to hearing through the wall the Prime Minister's unmelodious voice raised in hymns. Reading, talk, and hymns were again the order, with the little table still in eclipse. Summer, as always, brought the move to Kingsmere, where King in his last years lived at The Farm, while the Pattesons continued to occupy Shady Hill near by. His acres at Kingsmere, and the satisfaction he derived from the thought of leaving them to the nation, were still among his greatest delights.

Delightful, too, was the society of old friends. The Pattesons did not have a complete monopoly of his private life. In particular, he had many meetings in these years with Lily Hendrie, the lady in Hamilton who had so powerfully impressed him far back in 1902 (above, page 94), and with whom he had maintained a warm friendship ever since. She had been a widow since 1924. Speaking to her on the telephone on his birthday in 1947, he reflected that she was "the oldest friend of all" — and then immediately recollected that he had actually known Joan Patteson longer, "having met her first at Woodstock, before she was married, when I was at the University". That, presumably, was even before he started keeping the diary. Early in 1948 Mrs. Hendrie dined twice at Laurier House and King escorted her to the theatre. That autumn she was in London (she had a daughter living there) while King was there for the Prime Ministers' Conference, and they saw each other several times. In March 1949 she was again dining at Laurier House. Unfortunately, this relationship made trouble with Joan Patteson. King, taking her for granted in his deplorable way, had not invited her to meet Lily; and, very naturally, she resented it. King wrote, "J. has been so caustic about Lily that as I told her over the phone. . .she had almost spoiled our friendship. . . . Joan's weakness is her jealousy of anyone that seems to be a close friend of mine other than herself." Fortunately the two ladies met on neutral ground at a tea-party and are reported to have liked each other. At this news King recorded (10 March 1949) experiencing "a great sense of peace, & restoration of early relationship, which has been threatened by the happenings of the past year". Joan may have been jealous; perhaps she was also troubled by the possibility of her distinguished friend making a fool of himself at the age of seventy-four.*

With other women friends of the days of his prime King continued to correspond. As we have already seen, he was in touch with Julia Grant, the Princess Cantacuzene, to the very end, as he was also with Violet Markham and with Mathilde Grossert (Mrs. George Barchet), an even older friend than Lily Hendrie. At Christmas 1949, his last Christmas, these and other friends received from him copies of Reginald Hardy's book *Mackenzie King of Canada*.

*Elizabeth Ann (Lily) (Brown) Hendrie died on 11 August 1975 at the age of ninety-eight.

# THE MEDIUMS OF ENGLAND

In each of his last four years in office Mackenzie King visited England. In 1945 there were atomic energy and Soviet espionage to discuss; in 1946 there was a conference of Commonwealth leaders, as well as an international conference in Paris; in 1947 there was Princess Elizabeth's wedding; and in 1948 there was a full-dress Prime Ministers' Conference.[1] In spite of much that has been said, and some things that he said himself, King was very fond of England (to say nothing of his sentimental atavistic regard for Scotland), and he greatly enjoyed London. He had some particularly dear personal friends there. Of Violet Markham we have already said a good deal. In 1937 he met for the first time the painter Frank O. Salisbury, and from that time Salisbury and his wife Maude had a special place in his heart and a great deal of attention in the diary. In 1944 he wrote, "They have given me in larger measure than any persons excepting J. and G., their affection and devoted friendship."[2]

There was something else about England. There, more than anywhere else in these last years, King could satisfy his craving for spiritualistic contact with his loved ones and other friends in the Beyond. The little table which had given him so much satisfaction seems to have remained in abeyance, largely if not absolutely. Mrs. Wriedt, "the best of all mediums", had died in

1942, much regretted,[3] and there was no replacement for her west of the Atlantic. But in the active and friendly spiritualistic community in London King was very welcome. He had denied himself the pleasures it offered during the war, but now he was prepared to enjoy them once more.

During his visit in the autumn of 1945 he plunged back in. His friend Miss Phillimore at the London Spiritualist Alliance arranged sittings for him. One was with Mrs. Dowden, the automatic-writing medium; another, involving a visit to Tankerton, was with Mrs. Gladys Osborne Leonard.* He saw the Duchess of Hamilton. In 1946 he had similar experiences, though a sitting with a new and inexperienced medium was "not successful".[4]

The visit in 1947 yielded particularly intriguing results. Once the royal wedding was over King evidently felt free to indulge himself. Miss Phillimore again made arrangements for him. On the morning of 22 November he had a sitting with a Mrs. Sharplin; he had already had one with her the year before. President Roosevelt (who had died in 1945) "took up most of the morning", but King's mother and father were also heard from. In the afternoon he went to Miss E. B. Gibbes's house for a session with her associate Miss Geraldine Cummins, an Anglo-Irish lady with a long list of psychical and other publications after her name in *Who's Who*. Miss Gibbes told him "about the extraordinary surprise they had when a propos of nothing, President Roosevelt sent word direct that he knew I was in London. Most anxious to have a talk with me. Was most urgent as he was concerned about something I had in mind to do. . . ."

Miss Cummins, after merely greeting King (both parties agree that she had no idea who he was) went into a trance and pro-

---

*Mrs. Leonard was the author of *My Life in Two Worlds* (London [1931]), which has a foreword by Sir Oliver Lodge. The autographed copy which she gave King is in the National Library of Canada.

duced automatic writing.* King sat beside her and watched closely. Sir Wilfrid Laurier was the first "communicator". In the course of his remarks he made incidental references to his Cabinet colleagues Oliver Mowat and W. S. Fielding. He urged King not to retire as he had considered doing: "You alone can manage the various conflicting interests." Then came Roosevelt. He likewise begged King not to retire; he, said the President, had the wisdom that Winston Churchill lacked, also "the caution and that integral honesty that holds a country together". "I beg of you at whatever cost to continue in public life." Later, Roosevelt says, "You have that slow Scotch way with you, you *are not clever*, you are wise. That is why I want you to hold on. . . . I saw you wanted to get out. Don't. Don't. . . ." And Roosevelt promises help: "When you sleep we will put suggestions into your mind."[5]

The similarity of these messages to those that King so often received over the little table is striking. Again the spirits are telling him what he wanted to hear; for it cannot be doubted that he did not want to retire if only his health would hold out. The extravagant praise, so soothing to his ego, is equally familiar. But all this is coming now, not over the little table, and presumably from King's mind, but from Geraldine Cummins. And one is faced with the question: where did the references to Mowat and Fielding come from? Miss Cummins could hardly have heard of these people. The only explanation I can offer is that thought-transference in some form took place between King and the medium. It is much easier to believe in this happening between living people than to believe in communication between the dead and the living. With King concentrating eagerly on Miss Cummins as she wrote, the conditions for thought-transference were surely as favourable as they could ever be. Miss Cummins,

*I am most grateful to my colleague Graeme Patterson for giving me copies of the two automatic-writing scripts produced by Geraldine Cummins for King in 1947 and 1948. The originals are in the Cummins Papers in the Archives of County Cork.

indeed, recognized later the possibility, at least, that the script she wrote reflected "the remarkable manner in which Mr. MacKenzie [*sic*] King's subliminal self communicated; his subliminal mind fusing with my mind".[6] If this was really the case, then Miss Cummins's automatic-writing script on this occasion is precisely parallel to King's own records of sittings over the table; and the fulsome praise of King from Laurier and Roosevelt, and their conjurations to him not to retire, came from King's own head and from nowhere else.

Soon after King returned to Ottawa there was a bizarre crisis in the Cabinet. His colleagues, in his absence, not regarding the matter as one of great importance, had agreed to Canada's accepting membership in a United Nations Temporary Commission on Korea. King now blew up, asserting that this was a dangerous commitment, insisting on the acceptance being withdrawn, and carrying the matter to the point where three important members of the Cabinet, including his ultimate successor, Louis St. Laurent, might have been forced to resign. It has been suggested[7] that King's extraordinarily exaggerated reaction here was the result of a warning received from Roosevelt during the session with Geraldine Cummins in London. If this were true, it would provide an uncharacteristic and unprecedented case of King allowing what he thought was advice from the spirit world to influence his action in a matter of national policy.

The story however is quite unfounded. Miss Cummins's script of 22 November 1947 contains no reference whatever to Korea, the Far East, or any related matter. It was during her sitting with King in the following year (23 October 1948) that "Roosevelt" warned King not to forget Asia (Korea, as such, is not mentioned in either script).[8] King's diary does not mention advice from Roosevelt on Asiatic problems in connection with either the sitting of 22 November 1947 or the Cabinet meeting of 18 December 1947 when he exploded about Korea. What he does say is that he told the Cabinet that President *Truman* had warned him of danger in the Far East during the Trumans' visit to Ottawa in June.* Whatever the origin of King's curious outburst, it was not the Cummins sitting. King's record of not allowing the spirits to influence him in matters of public affairs remains unblemished. Incidentally, Geraldine Cummins reports that King said to her in 1948 that "he made it a rule to ignore advice volunteered at sittings: he trusted solely to his own and his advisers' judgement."[9]

King did, however, let his excitement over the Cummins sitting in 1947 lead him into a foolish action. On 25 November he told Churchill about the sitting, saying that Roosevelt had asked him (King) to give messages to Churchill (a statement the script does not support). Churchill asked to see the document, which King had carried away with him, and King duly sent it to him (perhaps forgetting the remark in it that King had the wisdom Churchill lacked). Churchill returned it, says King, "with a most significant little note".[10] Thus one more person — and a very important one—came to know of the Canadian Prime Minister's peculiarities. What, I wonder, did Churchill say, and how many people did he tell?

By the time of King's visit to London in 1948 his situation had changed. He had beaten Walpole's record for political longevity; he had announced his impending retirement; and with his successor as party leader already chosen, attending the Prime Ministers' Conference would be a distinguished finale to his political career.

In fact, however, he did not get to the Conference. Arriving in London after a visit to Paris for the General Assembly of the United Nations, he found himself unwell. He consulted Lord Moran, Churchill's physician, who called in Sir John Parkinson.

*In a book review in the Toronto *Globe and Mail*, 14 October 1961, Louis St. Laurent said that King "stated Mr. Roosevelt had told him Korea was going to be a trouble spot and had warned him against becoming involved in Far Eastern turmoil." "Roosevelt" is pretty obviously a mistake for "Truman".

They found "evidence of considerable heart strain" and ordered him to bed. Louis St. Laurent was hurriedly brought from Canada to take his place at the Conference, and King kept to his rooms at the Dorchester Hotel. But the situation had its compensations. The elder statesman now had his apotheosis. The King came to call. So did everybody else who was anyone at all. Clement Attlee (the Prime Minister), Churchill, Nehru, Ernest Bevin, Harold Macmillan, and many others "came trooping in": it was almost like one of King's best sessions over the little table, but these people were living and breathing realities. The personal friends came too. Violet Markham was there more than once, as was Lily Hendrie (she had lunch with King before he embarked for Canada on 30 October). Once Lily and Maude Salisbury were present at the same time "and the three of us had an enjoyable talk". The University of London conferred an honorary degree on King in a ceremony in his suite.[11]

And then there were the mediums. King had got in touch with Miss Phillimore as soon as he reached London, and she undertook to try to arrange sittings "with some of the best mediums". This program went ahead in spite of King's illness. It seems very unlikely that his doctors knew about it; surely the excitement of a *séance* must be very bad for a heart patient. But the mediums came to the Dorchester and the *séances* proceeded. King records that Mrs. Thomson, a medium from Glasgow, was "in a trance for just over an hour": "she got Mackenzie quite clearly". Mrs. Gladys Leonard made "just a friendly call", but she too went "into a deep trance"; this, King wrote, was "in every way the best of all the sittings I have had". Yet he had had a very remarkable one three days before, when Geraldine Cummins and Beatrice Gibbes came to his suite and Miss Cummins had another session of automatic writing similar to that of the previous year.[12]

This time King's mother spoke for a considerable time. She used phrases not found in the little table records ("My own dearest Boy. My pride and joy. Best of sons.") but went on, in a manner quite familiar from the table sessions, to urge King to take care of his health. Then she introduced Franklin Roosevelt ("Frank as I call him"). This time the President told King that he must take a real rest, "knock off for at least a year": "What I want to tell you is that three years from now is the critical time. That is when you will be wanted for advice." He also said that it was very vital that King should write his memoirs, including "the important chapter, your firm faith in a future life, that you have evidence of it". He proceeded to comment on the international situation, ending with the warning, already mentioned, not to forget Asia.[13]

Within a fortnight of returning to Canada from this trip King resigned as Prime Minister. He never crossed the Atlantic again. Of the many observances that marked his retirement, one he particularly appreciated came on his seventy-fourth birthday, 17 December 1948. The Governor General, Field Marshal Lord Alexander, gave a dinner in his honour. With the courtesy for which he is so well remembered, "Alex" invited Joan Patteson; and the Alexanders and their staff made a point of paying her special attention. (Godfroy was undoubtedly invited, but his health precluded his attending; King and Joan told him all about it later that night, and he was "immensely pleased with the account of the evening".) King was enchanted. "I have never seen Joan happier. She really looked lovely. . . . I think I derived my greatest happiness through her pleasure. She has been self [ef]facing all her life."

His first year of retirement was a time of quiet non-achievement. He did a lot of thinking about the memoirs, concerning which Roosevelt's spirit had been so solicitous. Many possible helpers were discussed (even the author of this book was mentioned once); but no writing of any note got done. The ideas for the plan of the work which King set down in his diary during the return voyage from England in November 1948 make one feel that perhaps we are not much the poorer for the fact that King was not spared to write it.[14]

Deprived of the political concerns that had been the central fact of his life for so long, the old man tended to be at a loss. On 12 February 1949 he records that Joan Patteson came to dinner: "I can see she feels real concern about my loneliness & depression for such it is becoming . . . we had the little table for a short time." Here, presumably, is the explanation of the partial revival of the little table at this period. Joan doubtless felt that King needed the support it could give him. Not only his family but many old associates, including Mrs. Wriedt, Peter Larkin, and O. D. Skelton, spoke to him.[15] Of messages received during a sitting on 7 April King wrote, "These words were comforting."

# THE LAST SUMMER

Perhaps King overdid things at Christmas of 1949. At any rate, it seems evident that he had a heart attack on the night of 26-27 December. He dictated his diary for the 27th (until then it had been handwritten): "Joan was very concerned. Determined to get a nurse and will arrange for the same during the day. I really was alarmed. Felt I might die during the night without Will made or any disposition of property, possessions, etc. Nothing done on reminiscences. It is a frightful situation to face. Have never felt more up against complete possibility of collapse than last night." On New Year's Day 1950, on his physician's advice, he did not attend the Governor General's Levee; he reflected that, if his memory was accurate, it was the first time he had missed it since his arrival in Ottawa in 1900.

From this time on, King's health and his symptoms are a main concern of the diary. He worked on his will, and on 28 February, under some pressure from his friend and associate Fred McGregor (who had been retained to help with arranging his papers, and who pretty clearly feared that King might die without completing the disposition of his property), he signed it, evidently fully expecting to make further changes in it from time to time. He did add a codicil on 24 June. He devoted much thought to a project of many, many years' standing — arrangements for the writing of a biography of his grandfather, William

Lyon Mackenzie.* The will provided that this should be done by a Scottish lady, Miss Catherine Macdonald Maclean, whose writing King admired. (He had been particularly struck by her life of Dorothy Wordsworth, which he and Joan Patteson had read together.) He had invited Miss Maclean to dinner in London in 1944 and been much impressed. Joan suggested that Mrs. Skelton, the biographer of Thomas D'Arcy McGee, might be a suitable biographer for Mackenzie also. Perhaps it had occurred to her that it was desirable that the task should be given to a Canadian. But King dissented: "Catherine McLean [*sic*] has the Scotch Presbyterian background and faith."[1] In the very last days of his life he was corresponding on the project, through Fred McGregor, with the intended publishers, the Macmillan Company of Canada.[2] But the book, alas, never appeared. Miss Maclean accepted the assignment and made at least one visit to Canada in connection with it. But she died before the book was quite finished, and it is reported that the manuscript was destroyed. Thus a plan very close to King's heart was ultimately frustrated.

Always worried about his health, and sometimes "lonely and depressed", King might be; but there were still moments of apotheosis. They were chiefly provided by overseas visitors; for Canadians, even now, seemed a bit unwilling to apotheosize Mackenzie King. The Duke of Windsor came to call at Laurier House, and King's description of the call takes up seven pages in his diary. "How I pray," he wrote, "I may be spared to write my Memoirs as I should like to write them, and as they ought to be written." (His 1948 plan had included a chapter entitled "Rela-

---

*An interesting essay could be written about King's concern for his grandfather's historical reputation. In 1906 he exerted himself successfully to obtain the suppression of a biography of Mackenzie that had been written by W. D. LeSueur. About the same time he suggested to William Wilfred Campbell, the poet, that the two of them should collaborate on a book about Mackenzie and his times, emphasizing "psychological forces", etc. (Diary, 3, 8, 12 Jan., 1906).

tionship with Sovereigns of Britain".) Recently he had received Churchill's volume *The Grand Alliance*, which only discouraged him, making him realize, he said, "how next to impossible it is going to be to ever complete my Memoirs in a way I should like to have been able to manage them".[3] He never attempted to put into practice the infallible formula for writing a book recommended by Sinclair Lewis: "Apply the seat of the pants to the seat of the chair." In any case, it was now much, much too late.

Representatives of the countries of the wartime alliance came to decorate the old statesman who had played his part in those great days. France had offered him the highest class of the Legion of Honour when he was in Paris in 1948. He had begged leave to decline because he was still in office, but in October 1949 he received it at the hands of M. Robert Schuman at the French Embassy in Ottawa. In 1950 the Belgian Ambassador came to Laurier House to confer upon him the Grand Cross of the Order of Leopold; he received the same class of the Grand Ducal Order of the Crown of Oak of Luxembourg; and the Prince of the Netherlands made a visit to invest him with the Grand Cross of the Order of the Netherlands Lion. This was an important day. King complained to the diary that he had not expected to have to make a speech, but when Prince Bernhard made one, reading the royal decree conferring the order, he contrived to improvise remarks to his own satisfaction. They showed that he had changed very little; for he mentioned that he "had noticed the date of the decree — Feb. 6th — which was that of my mother's birthday". The Prince, perhaps, knew enough about King to avoid being surprised. King wrote in the diary, "What pleased me most of all was that the day's events seemed to bring me back into that spiritual nearness with those who have gone which, up to the present, I have found it so difficult to recover. Also the actuality of the spiritual realm."[4]

Human vanity does not decline with age. Certainly King's didn't. One of the features of the improvement of Ottawa that was then in progress was a new bridge across the Rideau Canal in the centre of the city. It was planned to name it after Colonel John By, founder of Ottawa and builder of the canal. On 20 May 1950 Solon Low, leader of the Social Credit group in the House of Commons, suggested in a newspaper interview that it should be named instead after Mackenzie King, in recognition of his contribution to the beautification of Ottawa. King thought this an excellent idea, and he at once launched an active underground campaign in favour of the change. He sent out Fred McGregor to talk to the right people; and on 30 May he asked his former secretary J. W. Pickersgill to let the new Prime Minister know "that that was something I would really value for historic reasons". In the eyes of any Canadian politician, and particularly of any Liberal, poor By already had three strikes on him: he was a soldier, he was an Englishman, and he was dead. On 10 June the change of name was announced.[5] So the Mackenzie King Bridge stands in the middle of the Capital, a monument both to King's interest in Ottawa and to his considerable ego.

On 26 June King made the last of his annual moves from Laurier House to Kingsmere, the Pattesons moving also. The Korean War had just begun, and the ex-Prime Minister reflected grimly that everything had turned out pretty much as he had prophesied in 1947. On 30 June the Governor General and Lady Alexander drove out from Ottawa to see him, choosing for the visit the day of the prorogation of Parliament, when the old man was particularly likely to be lonely. King read them his diary for December 1947, when he had made such a row in the Cabinet about Korea. Later he recorded, "The more I think over the whole situation, the more I believe ... that the U. S. foreign policy at bottom is to bring Canada into as many situations affecting themselves as possible with a view to leading ultimately to the annexation of our two countries. . . ."[6]

In these last months the consolations of spiritualism were denied him. Apart from all other considerations, he probably did not feel equal to the exertions of the little table (back in 1934 he had remarked, "the table is exhausting").[7] He missed these things now, for he had written on 2 April, "what I have regretted most is my feeling of remoteness from those I love who have passed away." But he continued to derive satisfaction from the position of the hands of the clock ("I cannot believe there is not some real significance behind it") and he still read the "little books", with their comforting scriptural quotations.[8]

There was one other great comfort: Joan Patteson. King had written just at the moment of moving to Kingsmere, "She has been amazingly kind. Has come every evening to read or talk since the beginning of the year."[9] Joan herself was now eighty, and apart from providing companionship for King she had an ailing husband to look after; Godfroy, long retired, had been in poor health for years. It is not surprising that she had to limit herself in the main to evening visits.

King was no longer able to walk far, but he contrived to get around the estate, which continued to give him enormous pleasure. The woodland goddess still wove her spell for him. On 15 July he drove with Joan to Moorside and his ruins, and wrote happily, "I walked about quite a bit at Moorside and greatly enjoyed the view." One evening he recorded, "One of the joys of today was to see a little doe run across the lawn while I was at dinner."[10] Kingsmere, however swept and garnished, was still on the edge of the wilderness.

At the beginning of July, King admitted in a letter to Violet Markham that, though he had had some "remarkably good" days, others unfortunately "continue to occasion a good deal of disappointment". Apart from the difficulty of walking, he complained of sleeping badly. It is pretty evident that the doctors now felt that he could not last much longer. On 7 July a consulting physician suggested that he should go into a hospital "for observation". The old man made it quite clear that he intended to do no such thing. "I said that my own feeling was that my last hope lay in the summer at Kingsmere. . . . if now my condition was such that the summer at Kingsmere would not improve matters, I would rather end my days in the country in the Summer-time than wait over for examination in some Hospital. . . ."[11] And at Kingsmere, in the summer, the end came.

After fifty-seven years, the diary's last day was 19 July 1950. It is largely concerned with difficulty in getting attention during the night: "It was terrible to think of the kind of service one receives from some quarters when one is helpless." The last sentences are, "Then went downstairs for dinner, at quarter to eight, dictating diary to date. Very very sorry to have kept Lafleur all that time." (Rolland Lafleur was a new member of the staff to whom King dictated the diary in Handy's absence on holiday.) But a letter from Joan Patteson to Violet Markham tells us what happened the next day:

> Thursday, the 20th, was a sunny day. At lunch time, Dr. [Campbell] Laidlaw & Rex drove in to our cottage & told us they had been to see the ruin & Moorside. It was the Dr's 70th birthday, & Rex was as ever anxious to make it a happy day. After they left & we had lunch I felt a desire to go to see how he was for his color was strange. To my joy I found him enjoying his lunch & he said, "My appetite is coming back". I said "Kingsmere!"

The mail arrived, bringing a letter from Violet Markham, and a packet from a publisher including an article on Wordsworth by Catherine Maclean. Now King decided to rest. He slept for two hours, then got up and had "a violent chill". It was the hand of death, in the form of sudden acute pneumonia. Joan continues: "He wanted me & Camille* came down to get me—that was after 5 o'clock—the doctor got out [from Ottawa] at 7 o'clock & gave him morphine. The two hours [between] were the worst I ever went thro'. I did not think he could endure the pain much longer

*Camille Cleroux, chauffeur, another fairly new member of King's staff.

& the terrible effort to get a breath — nor could he have, the Doctor said. So the morphine gave him relief & he became unconscious & never spoke again. While we were enduring those last conscious hours, he was so sweet & kept praying that God would let him live to finish his work, thanked me for what I had done, but I don't think he realized that it was the very final attack. . . . "

The rest was watching and waiting. The Reverend Ian Burnett, who now occupied the pulpit at St. Andrew's in which Dr. Herridge had once preached, twice came and held "a little service" at King's bedside. The minister bent over him, says Joan, "& perhaps some words may have reached him". His nephews arrived—Jennie's and Max's sons. "Godfroy went up the hill & climbed the stairs to bid him good bye but he broke down & could not stay longer." The end came on the 22nd. Joan wrote, "At 9.42 Saturday night it was over and we were alone. It was a lovely evening but just at the moment he died thunder & lightning & torrents of rain came without any warning. So many have remarked it—for the rain fell only at Kingsmere—not Ottawa even. The rest you know. The country took charge & he was out of our care. . . . "[12]

Was there sentience in him during those hours when they watched by his bed? It is hard not to wonder what thoughts might have passed through his mind at the latter end of those seventy-five remarkable years. Did it dwell on politics, statecraft, and war? Did he think perhaps of his "great friend" Roosevelt? Or of his reluctant admiration for Churchill, who he had once thought would die of drink before the war was over, but who was now perversely outliving King? Or perhaps of Lord Byng, possibly his closest friend among Governors General until the wretched man lost his head?

Somehow it seems more likely that his mind would turn to the friends of his other world. Bert Harper, whose place had never been filled. And the extraordinary succession of women whom he had known since the day in 1893 when he gave Mrs. Browning's poems to Mab Moss. Mathilde, Mathilde. Kitty Riordan. Shamefaced adventures in the sub-world here and there. Beatrice Burbidge, whom he had called "the little Queen". Nurse Cooper. The Child, reading Matthew Arnold with him in Mrs. McMinn's Kingsmere boarding-house so long ago. Lady Ruby. Dorothy, and Aileen, and Lily. Miss Greer, whom he had never called Jean, and who had not answered his letter. Beatrix Robb, and that halcyon European summer of 1928. The Princess, who had sometimes seemed a bit too anxious. Violet, dear woman. All the women whom he had thought of marrying, and hadn't. Joan. Joan, the partner of his spiritual adventures. Joan, who had "filled the place of his mother in his heart". His mother. Dear Mother. He had the assurance, they would be together forever. There had been so many women, but at the last there was really only one. So one imagines him thinking, if thought was still permitted him. And then the storm burst, and Mackenzie King went home.

# MACKENZIE KING'S PERSONAL FORTUNE AND HIS WILL

The disclosure after Mackenzie King's death that he had been a wealthy man surprised most people, for he had consistently presented to the world a picture of himself as a person of very modest means. If we can credit the diary, he even believed this himself. On 31 March 1949 (in the first year of his retirement), working on his 1948 tax return, he wrote, "to my amazement I found that my investments had been so carefully husbanded that they were really about double of what I had believed them to be. . . . I had not realized that my investment mainly in Dominion Bonds & a few private Co shares had reached proportions that would not be understood by the public. . . . I can honestly say I would almost prefer to be without more than a mere subsistence, could I be sure of this to the end of my life. I would not like my life's record of service to be overshadowed by anything savouring of wealth, and that is what I have now come to possess, [while] believing in fact, that I was none too well off, for one living out of office and [without] a calling of any kind. . . . " One of his secretaries pointed out, however, that his income and expenditure for 1948 "exactly balanced". With his two establishments, Laurier House and Kingsmere, and a considerable household staff, he was in fact living on a fairly lavish scale.

If he successfully concealed his wealth even from himself, it was not surprising that those nearest to him did not know of it.

Joan Patteson made a gentle complaint to Violet Markham in a
letter dated 17 December 1950. "The estate you know about —
but to me it is unexplainable — because he could have given
himself more & made himself more comfortable. We always
tho't that he had *very* little to look forward to when he retired. I
think one reason may have been that he did not want any
severance from the ordinary men & women — which capitalism
would have made, and the dread of long illness & needs at the
end, doubtless preyed on him. . . . Dear soul, it only increases my
tenderest affection & the wish that he had confided in us." Joan
seems to have undervalued the scale on which King lived, and
perhaps she had an inflated idea of the emoluments of a Prime
Minister.

On 8 August 1950 King's executors issued a statement valuing
his estate at "something over $750,000".[1] The actual probated
value recorded in the Carleton County Court House in Ottawa
was $681,252.00.[2] This did not include the Kingsmere estate,
situated in the Province of Quebec. Laurier House was valued at
$29,925.00. The largest item was Bonds, $547,432.48. Others
were Cash in Bank, $22,043.26; Life Insurance, $22,464.88;
Household Goods and Furniture, $29,681.00; Bank Stocks and
other Stocks, $25,678.00; Automobiles, $3,400.00. It is hardly
necessary to say that these figures were more impressive in 1950
than they are a quarter of a century later.

Where did the money come from? There is no mystery about
it at all. King started with nothing; the Kings, we have seen, lived
in genteel poverty. From the time he came to Ottawa in 1900 he
drew a respectable civil service salary and in general was careful
of his money. When he became a Minister (1909) he acquired an
official income of $7,000 a year. As Prime Minister he was draw-
ing, at the time of his retirement in 1948, pay and allowances
totalling $19,000.[3] The largest income he ever made was that
from his work as an industrial consultant in the United States
during the First World War; his income in 1918 was $22,000, a

very large sum at that time.[4] This episode certainly laid the foundations of his private fortune. In 1928 he spoke in the diary of "my own savings to date, about 200,000 for the interest is over 10,000".[5] (It seems evident that even then he did not know precisely the amount of his capital.) It would appear that his savings did not increase very much after that date. The size of his estate was largely due to three gifts that were made to him: the fund of $225,000 collected by Peter Larkin to enable him to live in a manner befitting the owner of Laurier House; $50,000 left him by Sir William Mulock on his death in 1944;[6] and $100,000 given him by John D. Rockefeller, Jr., his friend of so many years, on King's seventy-fourth birthday in 1948, with a view to easing (in the words of King's will) "any financial problem I might have in the years that lay ahead". This was in addition to provision made by the Rockefeller Foundation to assist in the preparation of King's memoirs.

It is interesting that although King's will refers at some length, and in almost fulsome terms, to the Larkin and Rockefeller gifts, it makes no mention of Sir William Mulock. King's attitude towards Sir William was peculiar. He was unwilling to admit the debt he owed to Mulock, who had done so much to give him his start in life. When Sir William died, King listened to a broadcast eulogy of him by Canon H. J. Cody, and thought it admirable except for one matter. He wrote in his diary, "He referred to Sir Wm bringing me into public life in Canada and my being his *protegé*. This last I resent. I owe what I am to my parents & their parents before them. My coming into department of Labour to my suggestions, & planning. My coming into Parliament to my own decision. Sir Wm had left Ottawa 3 years before. It was Laurier who took me into the Ministry."[7]

In his will[8] King left Laurier House to the nation in the belief that there would be "increasing interest and pride", as the years passed, in a house occupied by two prime ministers, and in the hope that it might be used for historical study and research (it hasn't been, not being well suited to those purposes). To assist in maintaining the house, King also left to the nation the $225,000 of the Larkin fund, upon the principal of which he had never drawn. He directed that the income from the $100,000 Rockefeller gift should be used to establish travelling scholarships for Canadian university graduates wishing to engage in graduate study in international relations or industrial relations in the United States or the United Kingdom. The residue of the estate, after provision had been made for a large number of legacies to relatives and friends (including that to the Pattesons, above, page 136), was to be used to set up other scholarships for graduate study.

Laurier House is not precisely as King left it, but it contains many of his household goods and memorabilia. (Much of his library, rather unfortunately, has been transferred to the National Library.) It also contains many items associated with Sir Wilfrid Laurier. The house is open to the public and attracts many visitors. A curious recent decision has consecrated one room in the building to a third prime minister, Lester B. Pearson, who had no connection whatever with Laurier House. King, one feels, would have been extremely displeased.

The Kingsmere estate, as King had always intended, was likewise left "to the Government of Canada as a public park in trust for the citizens of Canada". He hoped that part of the property might be set aside "as a country home for the holder of the office of Prime Minister of Canada". This has not been done, his successors having found a place considered more suitable at Harrington Lake. The Farm, the house where King died, has become an official residence for the Speaker of the House of Commons. King's original cottage above the lake still stands — one wonders, for how long. Shady Hill, where the Pattesons lived, has been torn down. But on fine summer days the citizens of Canada visit the estate in throngs; queuing up at Moorside, once the Herridges' house, which is now a tea-room, and gazing at the Abbey Ruin and speculating about the strange man who built it.

# REFERENCES

Notes consisting merely of dates are references to the Mackenzie King Diaries.

## INTRODUCTION: THE MASTER POLITICIAN

1. R. MacGregor Dawson, *William Lyon Mackenzie King: A Political Biography, 1874–1923* (Toronto, 1958), 30.
2. *Ibid.*, Chaps. 3 and 4. King Diary for the period. Examples of the King–Mulock family friendship, 15-16 Oct. 1894.
3. 17 Dec. 1900.
4. 8 and 10 Feb. 1902.
5. Violet Markham, *Return Passage: The Autobiography of Violet R. Markham, C.H.* (London, 1953), 82.
6. 2 Sept. 1901. See Dawson, 113.
7. Dawson, Chap. 6.
8. *Ibid.*, Chaps. 8 and 9.
9. 25 Aug. 1900, 18-22 Feb. 1919.
10. Dawson, 306-10.
11. *Ibid.*, Chap. 13. J. Murray Beck, *Pendulum of Power: Canada's Federal Elections* (Scarborough, Ont., 1968), 149-62.
12. C. P. Stacey, "From Meighen to King: The Reversal of Canadian External Policies, 1921-1923", *Transactions of the Royal Society of Canada*, 1969.

13. H. Blair Neatby, *William Lyon Mackenzie King, 1924–1932: The Lonely Heights* (Toronto, 1963), 149.
14. *Ibid.*, Chap. 9. Beck, 177-90.
15. Neatby, Chaps. 16 and 18. Beck, 191-222.
16. C. P. Stacey, ed., *The Arts of War and Peace*, Historical Documents of Canada, Vol. 5 (Toronto, 1972), 437.
17. James Eayrs, *In Defence of Canada: Appeasement and Rearmament* (Toronto, 1965), Chap. 3.
18. *Ibid.*, Document 3.
19. Stacey, *The Arts of War and Peace*, 494-6 (27 March 1939).
20. Beck, 223-40. J. L. Granatstein, *Canada's War: The Politics of the Mackenzie King Government, 1939–1945* (Toronto, 1975), Chap. 3. C. P. Stacey, *Arms, Men and Governments: The War Policies of Canada, 1939–1945* (Ottawa, 1970), Part 1.
21. Granatstein, Chaps. 6 and 9. Stacey, *Arms, Men and Governments*, Part 7.
22. Stacey, *Arms, Men and Governments*, Parts 4 and 6. J. W. Pickersgill and D. F. Forster, *The Mackenzie King Record*, 4 vols. (Toronto, 1960-70), Vol. 3, 219; Vol. 4, 269.
23. Beck, 241-58. Granatstein, Chap. 10. Stacey, *Arms, Men and Governments*, 64-5. Stacey, *The Arts of War and Peace*, 173-8.
24. *The Mackenzie King Record*, Vol. 4.

PART I: THE BOY AND THE GIRLS

*The Blushing Young Ladies*

1. E. M. Chadwick, *Ontarian Families*, 2 vols. (Toronto, 1894–98), Vol. 2, 46. *The Times* (London), 21 Sept. 1895.
2. 27 and 29 Dec., 1893. *University of Toronto, Official Class and Prize Lists, 1895*, 29 (King usually misspells her name as Sherridan).
3. 14 Dec. 1893; cf. 26 Oct. 1893.
4. 7 Dec. 1893.
5. 22 Feb. 1895.

6.  16 Oct. 1894.

7.  15 Sept. 1893.

8.  6 Sept. 1895.

9.  27 Aug. 1895. On the Douglases and Highlands I., Lake Rosseau, information from Dr. Harcourt Brown.

10.  30 Aug. *et seq.* 1895.

11.  27 Dec. 1893. References to letters, 15 and 19 Nov., 1893, 10 Jan. and 1 Apr. 1894.

12.  31 Dec. 1893.

13.  15 Mar. 1894; cf. 5, 11, and 16 Mar., 22 Apr., and 6 May, 1894, and 5 May 1895.

14.  24 Aug. 1895; cf. 24 Mar. 1895.

15.  7 Nov. 1916.

16.  See Dawson, 38-9. Cf. Diary, e.g., 24 Dec. 1893, 3 June 1894. King uses the word "service" for his ministrations.

17.  24 and 31 Mar., 7 and 14 Apr., 7 July, and 13 and 20 Oct., 1895.

*Strolls in the Sub-World*

1.  C. S. Clark, *Of Toronto the Good. A Social Study. The Queen City of Canada as it is.* (Montreal, 1898; reprint, Toronto, 1970).

2.  7 Sept., 9 and 26 Oct., 1893. *Class and Prize Lists, 1895*, 36 ff.

3.  1 and 2 Feb., 6 Apr., 1894.

4.  7 Jan., 6, 8, and 10 Feb., 1894.

5.  15 and 20 Feb., 5 June, 2-3 Oct., 1894.

6.  2 and 5 Oct., 1894.

7.  19-21 Oct., 6, 11, and 23 Dec., 1894.

8.  5 June, 11 Oct., 1894. 11 July 1894, quoted in Dawson, 45. On the student strike, see Dawson, 33-6.

9.  6 Dec. 1896.

10.  6 Jan. 1897.

11.  21 and 23 Apr., 1897.

12.  8-27 March, 13 June, 1897; Appendix II to 1897 Diary (letter dated 27 July 1897); 15 Jan. 1898.

13.  13 and 15 May, 1897.

14. 23 and 24 May, 12 June, 1897.
15. 7 and 25 Aug., 6 Sept., 1897.
16. 28 Sept. 1897.
17. 20 and 30 Oct., 1897.

*Mathilde Grossert*

1. 3-4 Jan. 1898.
2. 13 Feb. 1898.
3. 16 Oct. 1914.
4. 29 Dec. 1897.
5. 24, 25, and 26 Feb., 1898. Dawson, 79. On Professor Norton, *ibid.*, 75-6.
6. 6 March 1898.
7. 10, 14, and 18 March, 1898. Parts of letter copied into back of 1898 Diary.
8. 25, 28, and 29 March, 1898.
9. 30 March 1898.
10. 31 March, 3, 4, and 6-7 April, 1898. Dawson, 79-80.
11. 7 April 1898.
12. 19-21 April 1898.
13. 23 and 24 April, 1898.
14. 7 May 1898.
15. 7, 8, 10, and 26 June, 1898.
16. 27 and 31 July, 5, 11, 12, and 13 Aug., 1898.
17. 16 Aug. 1898.
18. 17, 20, and 21 Aug., 1898.
19. 23 Aug., 3 Sept., 9 and 10 Oct., 1898; 20 and 25 Jan., 1899.
20. 11 July, 21 May, 1898.
21. 23 Dec. 1898; 15 and 19 March, 1899.
22. 19, 20, and 21 Aug., 1898.
23. 8 and 15 Dec., 1900.
24. 29 Mar., 10 Apr., 1901. Re intention of destroying copies of Mathilde's letters, 11 Jan. 1902.
25. 5 Nov. 1916; 29 Feb., 7 March, 1932.

*Mother*

1. 17 and 22 June, 18 July, 1895.
2. See Dawson's account of her, 24-8.
3. 29 Sept. 1898.
4. Dawson, 82. 4 Sept. 1900 (transcript).
5. Quoted in Dawson, 83. 25 Aug. 1899.
6. 17 Nov. 1904; 22 June 1916. *Toronto City Directory, 1902-05.*
7. 21 Feb. 1904.


PART II: THREE FRIENDS

*Bert Harper: "The Loss Was Irreparable"*

1. 6 Jan., 24 July, 1899.
2. E.g., 5 Dec. 1937, 14 July 1941.
3. 13 Aug.-22 Sept., 1899. Especially 12, 8, and 9 Sept.
4. 17 Feb. 1899.
5. 4 May 1900.
6. 10 Oct. 1901. *Citizen* (Ottawa), 11 Oct. 1901.
7. 6-9 Sept. 1895. 8 Mar. 1898.
8. 12 Aug., 20 Sept., 14-15 Oct., 1900. On title of Harper's appointment, see the obituary notice, undoubtedly by King, in *Labour Gazette*, December 1901. King, in *The Secret of Heroism* (see note 17 below), says Harper accepted the position in November 1900; the Diary makes it evident he was working with King in October.
9. *Of Toronto the Good*, 90.
10. H. A. Burbidge to Wilfred Davis, Secretary to Hon. Colin Gibson, 24 Apr. 1944, King Papers, J 1, Vol. 360, pages 312142-3.
11. 8 and 25 Jan., 1901.
12. 2 March 1901.
13. 24 Oct. 1900.
14. 30 Aug. 1901.

15. 24 July 1900.
16. 5-6 Jan. 1901.
17. W. L. Mackenzie King, *The Secret of Heroism: A Memoir of Henry Albert Harper* (New York, 1906), 151-60.
18. *Evening Citizen* (Ottawa), 11 Aug. 1950. Dawson, 116. I have not found the "Memorandum on Kingsmere" cited by Dawson. This episode is not in the Diary.
19. 17 June, 7, 8, and 10 Aug. (etc.), 1901. "Cash Account" (back of Diary), Aug. and Sept., 1901.
20. *Morning Citizen* (Ottawa), 7 Dec. 1901. King, *The Secret of Heroism*, 9-11.
21. *Morning Citizen* 9 and 10 Dec., 1901.
22. *Ibid.*, 10 and 11 Dec., 1901.
23. 7 Jan. 1902 (conversation with Hon. Sidney Fisher).
24. King, *The Secret of Heroism*, 13.
25. 4 Nov. 1905.
26. King, *The Secret of Heroism*, 13-18. *Morning Citizen* (Ottawa), 20 Nov. 1905. There is no entry in the Diary, which is very thin for 1905.
27. Dawson, 131.
28. *Ibid.*, 119-20.

*Marjorie Herridge: "Happiness and Pain"*

1. *University of Toronto, Official Class and Prize Lists, 1895*, 1.
2. Obituary of Very Rev. W. T. Herridge and appreciation by R. E. Knowles, *Toronto Daily Star*, 18 Nov. 1929. Obituary of Mrs. Herridge, *Citizen* (Ottawa), 24 March 1924. Herridge tombstone, Beechwood Cemetery, Ottawa.
3. 10 Feb. 1901.
4. 10 March 1901.
5. Dawson, 24.
6. 17 June, 7, 10, 16, and 23 Aug., 2 Sept., 1901.
7. The body of Arnold's writings is enormous, as is the body of

writing about him. For an introduction one may cite John Bryson, ed., *Matthew Arnold: Poetry and Prose* (London, 1954), and a book by a Canadian scholar who became, briefly, a member of King's staff: E. K. Brown, *Matthew Arnold: A Study in Conflict* (Chicago, 1948).

8. 7 and 8 Sept., 1901.
9. 8 Sept. 1901.
10. 11 and 15 Sept., 13 Oct., 1901.
11. "Equality" in *Mixed Essays* (in Bryson, pages 586-7).
12. 7 Oct. 1901.
13. 1 Jan. 1902.
14. 2 and 6 Jan., 9, 18, and 26 Feb., 1902.
15. 2 March 1902.
16. Cash account, July (there is no cash account for August).
17. *Gazette* (Montreal), 6 Sept. 1902 (p. 4).
18. 21 Sept. 1902.
19. 24 and 25 Sept., 1902.
20. 16 Jan. 1903.
21. 23 April 1903.
22. 20 Jan. 1904.
23. 12 and 18 Sept. ff., 1904.
24. 27 July 1907.
25. 31 July, 1 Aug., 1907.
26. Letters, W. D. Herridge to W. L. M. King, 1907–11, King Papers, MG 26, J 1, pages 6118-23, 7993-4, 10686-9, 15776-81.
27. 1, 11, and 15 Feb., 1904. Letter to Mrs. Cheney, 27 Nov. 1904.
28. 9, 11, and 12 Jan., 1904.
29. 26 and 30 Jan., 1904.
30. 13 Nov. 1904.
31. 29 Aug. 1907.
32. 25-28 Aug. 1907.

33. Markham, *Return Passage*, 83.

34. F. A. McGregor, *The Fall & Rise of Mackenzie King* (Toronto, 1962), 68.

35. 23 Oct. 1911. Letter of 30 Dec. 1911, Dawson, 224. See also Diary (Mission to the Orient), 30 Dec. 1908.

36. 1-6 Jan. 1914.

37. 13 May 1914.

38. Article on Violet Markham by Lady Tweedsmuir, *Dictionary of National Biography, 1951-1960*, 692-3.

39. Violet Markham, *Friendship's Harvest* (London, 1956), 162. 6 Oct. 1934.

40. Dawson, 224.

41. 13 Jan. 1912.

42. 26 April 1914.

43. 11 Aug., 12 Oct., 1914.

44. 16 Oct. 1916.

45. 6 Feb. 1917.

46. *Toronto Daily Star*, 18 Nov. 1929. Diary, 22 March 1924.

47. 25 March, 13 April 1924.

48. 1 July 1934.

49. 30 Oct. 1908.

*Searching for a Wife*

1. 25 Jan. – 1 Feb., 1911. On Thomas P. Fowler, *Who Was Who in America*, I, *1897-1942*, and Obituary, *New York Times*, 13 Oct. 1915. Neither gives any family information.

2. 28-30 Jan., 3 Feb., 1911.

3. 4 Feb. 1911.

4. 24 Sept. 1911.

5. 31 Dec. 1911.

6. 1, 9, and 17 Jan., 1912. On Strathcona and the Grenfell Mission, see J. Lennox Kerr, *Wilfred Grenfell, His Life and Work* (Toronto, 1959), 106-7, 206, 210.

7. 20, 21, and 17 Jan., 1912. Cf. McGregor, 85-8.

8. *Burke's Peerage, 1963*, under "Strathcona". *Who Was Who in America*, I, *1897-1942*, under "McCook, John James".
9. 7, 11, and 12 May, 1914. *Who Was Who in America*, I, under "Mather, Samuel".
10. 13 May 1914. Various dates, e.g. in 1919. Kerr, 197-8, 202.
11. 9, 10, and 31 March, 1 April, 1917.
12. 24 Feb. 1918.
13. Obituary, *New York Times*, 20 May 1919. [Bishop] Charles Lewis Slattery, *David Hummell Greer, Eighth Bishop of New York* (New York, 1921) is not very helpful.
14. 20 Feb. 1918.
15. 21 Feb. 1918.
16. 24 Feb. 1918.
17. 21 Feb. 1918.
18. 28 Feb. 1918.
19. *Who Was Who in America*, IV, *1961-1968*.
20. 13 April 1918.
21. March 1918.
22. King Papers, MG 26, J 1, Vol. 45, pages 39556-7. *New York Times*, 24 July 1919.
23. 11 Aug., 7 May, 1917.
24. *New York Times*, 24 July 1919.
25. *Ibid.*, 27 Sept. 1919.

*Joan Patteson: "She Has Filled the Place of My Mother in My Heart"*

1. 1-14 Jan. 1919.
2. *New York Times*, 5 Oct. 1945. Re Miss Stirling, information from Mrs. J. R. Mallory. 6 Jan. 1949; 3 Jan. 1948; 21 Nov., 8 Dec., 1933; 6 Feb. 1934. Information from Richard Alway. Death notice of L. Aileen Larkin, *Globe and Mail* (Toronto), 14 Jan. 1967.
3. 21 Sept. 1918.
4. 2 Oct. 1918.
5. Patteson tombstones, Park Lawn Cemetery, Toronto. *Ot-*

*tawa City Directory*, 1920. Reference to John MacWhirter, 21 Dec. 1930.

6. 29 Aug. 1919. *What's Past Is Prologue: The Memoirs of the Right Honourable Vincent Massey, C.H.* (Toronto, 1963), 504.
7. 20 Oct., 2 Nov., 1919.
8. 8 May 1920.
9. 22 July 1920.
10. 30 Aug., 4 Sept., 1920.
11. See particularly Neatby, *The Lonely Heights*, 199.
12. 30 Aug., 6 and 7 Sept., 1920.
13. 11 July 1920.
14. 2 Dec. 1921.
15. 6 Sept. 1931.
16. 4 Aug. 1923.
17. 31 Dec. 1922.
18. 30 Mar., 20 Apr., 19 Sept., 10 Aug., 1924.
19. 30 Dec. 1926. 12, 14, 18, and 3 April, 1927.
20. Dawson, 75.
21. 12 May 1934. King to J. R. Nason [incorrectly spelled Nanson], 4 April 1935, in "Mr. King Was Unable to Subscribe", *York Pioneer* (Toronto), 1959, 16-18.
22. 9, 10, 12, and 24 May, 1935.
23. 24, 25, and 26 May, 1935.
24. 27 Oct. 1936. *Mike: The Memoirs of the Right Honourable Lester B. Pearson*, I (Toronto, 1972), 187-8. 16 July 1936. National Capital Commission brochure, "Moorside, in the Beautiful Gatineau Park".
25. Dawson, 398-9. Cf. 268 on the 1917 campaign.
26. Many periods, but see particularly 1927–28.
27. Neatby, 200.
28. Diary, *passim*.
29. King's survey of the history of the fund, Diary, 8 Jan. 1928; 31 Dec. 1927.
30. Neatby, *The Lonely Heights*, 198.

31. 20 April, 3 Dec., 1927.
32. 2 and 3 July, 1927.
33. 5 and 9 Feb., 1927.
34. 17 Jan. 1927.
35. 16 Sept. 1929; 4 Aug. 1927.
36. 8 Feb., 2 Dec., 1927.
37. 21 and 22 July, 1941.
38. 15 Jan. 1949.
39. 23 Jan. 1926; 20 Sept. 1931.
40. Neatby, 404-6 (based on examination of King's correspondence with Julia).
41. Pencil memo of sitting, Diary, 16 Nov. 1935.
42. Neatby, 408-10.
43. 14-17 July 1939.
44. 11 July 1950.
45. *Globe and Mail* (Toronto), 8 Oct. 1975.
46. 29 March-1 April 1923; 31 March-9 April 1928; May 1937.
47. *Citizen* (Ottawa), 11 Aug. 1950.
48. 17 July 1939.
49. Joan Patteson to Violet Markham, 28 July 1950, Markham Carruthers Papers, Public Archives of Canada, M.G. 32, F. 6.
50. 8 May 1928; 22 Aug. 1928.
51. 27, 28, 30, and 31 Aug., 1, 11, and 20-22 Sept., 1 and 3 Oct.,1928. *New York Times*, 21 Apr. 1957.
52. 25 June 1950.

*Little Angel Dogs*

1. 9 and 10 Aug. 1924.
2. 16 June 1931.
3. 16 Dec. 1934.
4. 3 Sept. 1939; 8 Oct. 1939. See Norah M. Holland, "The Little Dog-Angel", in *Spun-Yarn and Spindrift* (London and Toronto, 1918), 7.

5. 12 July 1941.
6. 14 July, 14 and 15 July, 1941.
7. 14 July 1941.
8. 14 and 15 July, 1941 (written on 16th).
9. Minutes of 97th meeting of Cabinet War Committee, 15 July 1941 (P.A.C.).
10. *Journal* (Ottawa), 18 July 1941; Diary 19 July 1941.
11. 11 Oct. 1941; 17 Dec. 1949.
12. Pickersgill and Forster, *Mackenzie King Record*, Vol. 4, 91. 17 Dec. 1949.
13. 11, 12, and 14 Aug., 1947.
14. 18 and 19 July, 7 Aug., 6 Sept., 1948; 17 Dec. 1949.

## PART III: THINGS IN HEAVEN AND EARTH

*Six Candles on the Cake*

1. 9 April, 17 July 1917. Mary W. Tileston, *Daily Strength for Daily Needs* (29th ed., London, 1924).
2. King family tombstone, Mount Pleasant Cemetery, Toronto.
3. 25 Nov. 1916.
4. Dawson, 253. 25 Sept. 1917; January 1917, *passim.*
5. 6 and 10 Feb., 1917.
6. 18 March, 4 April, 1917.
7. 19, 21, and 27, 1917.
8. 29 and 30 Nov. 1917; 2 Dec. 1917.
9. E.g., 9 Dec. 1944.
10. 19 Oct. 1929.
11. 15 Feb. 1918.
12. 25 Dec. 1930.
13. 5, 7, and 8 Jan., 1922.
14. Max King tombstone, Mount Pleasant Cemetery, Toronto. Dawson, 381-3. On Pasteur design, 10 and 11 March, 20 April, 1929.

15. Max King tombstone.
16. 5-9 Aug. 1919. Dawson, 309-10.
17. 2 and 3 May, 1923; 30 Aug. 1948.

*Moving into Spiritualism*

1. 13 and 14 Nov., 1893.
2. 3 June and 22 July, 1894.
3. 1 June 1934.
4. Dawson, 252-3. Stacey, *Arms, Men and Governments*, 471. 15 May 1944.
5. 28 Jan. 1926; 1 Sept. 1939.
6. 13 July 1941.
7. Diary, 1902 (Microfiche transcript 19).
8. *"Our Life After Death" or The Teaching of The Bible concerning the Unseen-World* (Forty-ninth ed., London, 1900).
9. 2 Sept. 1925.
10. 2 May 1896.
11. 20 Oct. 1925.
12. 30 Oct. 1925. See Neatby, 202-3.
13. "Interview with Sir Oliver Lodge, at Lord Grey's House, November 12, 1926", Diary, 1926, M.G. 26, J 13, Vol. 33.
14. E.g., 10 and 30 May, 1927.
15. 6 Oct. 1927.
16. 22 Aug. 1928.
17. 9, 18, and 25 Dec., 1930.
18. 23 Sept. 1931.
19. 3 Jan., 22 Aug., and 23 Sept., 1931.
20. 22-3 Aug. 1931.
21. Neatby, 406.
22. 21 Feb. 1932. Photographs of Mrs. Wriedt in King Collection, P.A.C. 14 April 1933.
23. 26 Feb. 1932.
24. 26, 27, 28, 29, and 30 June, 1932.
25. 29 and 30 Sept., 1 Oct., 1932.
26. 30 June 1932.

27. 8 and 9 Sept., 1932.
28. 6 and 7 Jan., 14, 15, 16, 17, and 18 Apr., 17 Oct., 13, 14, and 15 Dec., 1933.
29. 20 Aug. 1933.

*The Little Table*

1. 18 Nov. 1933.
2. 27 Nov. 1933.
3. Frederic W. H. Myers, *Human Personality and Its Survival of Bodily Death*, 2 vols. (London, 1903), especially Vol. 2, 92 and 474.
4. Note by King in margin of memorandum of sitting at 202 Elgin Street, 25 Mar. 1934.
5. See, e.g., Diary for 17 Dec. 1933.
6. Note of sitting, 202 Elgin Street, 27 Dec. 1936.
7. Sittings of 1 Feb. 1934 (re name Grange) and 25 Mar. 1934 (re name Myers).
8. 13 and 15 April, 1934.
9. 31 Dec. 1933.
10. 27 Jan. 1934.
11. 30 June 1934 (Vol. 2).
12. *Ibid.*
13. 15 April 1934 (Vol. 2).
14. 1 June 1934 (Vol. 2).
15. Stacey, *The Arts of War and Peace*, 196-9.
16. 1 Jan. 1934.
17. Retrospective comment by King, 3 June 1934 (Vol. 2). Notes of sitting, 13 May 1934.
18. *Ibid.*, also Vol. 1.
19. 3 and 4 June, 1934 (Vol. 2).
20. Notes of sittings, Kingsmere, 24 June and 1 July, 1934 (Vol. 2).
21. 2, 4, and 5 July, 1934.

22. 5 and 6 July, 1934.
23. 25-28 Aug. 1934.
24. 12, 14, 23, and 24 Oct., 1934.
25. 29 Oct. 1934.
26. 25 and 27 Nov., 1934.
27. Notes of sittings, 2 and 9 Dec., 1934, King Papers, M.G. 26, J 13, Vol. 120. Cf. 19 Nov. 1934.
28. Neatby, 383-4.
29. King Papers, M.G. 26, J 1, Vol. 43, page 37405. I owe this reference to the kindness of Ramsay Cook.
30. Notes of sitting, Laurier House, 13 Oct. 1935, original Diary, Vol. 122.
31. Diary, Vol. 78, "Loose Items", 4 Dec. 1935.
32. Notes on sitting, Moorside, 17 July 1936.
33. Notes on sitting, Moorside, 26 July 1936.
34. Notes on (second) sitting, Kingsmere, 22 Aug. 1936.
35. Notes on sitting, 22 Aug. 1936.
36. Diary, Vol. 125, memo re meeting with Duchess of Hamilton, Geneva, 3 Oct. 1936; 23, 24, and 27 Oct., 1936.
37. Notes of sitting, 202 Elgin Street, 29 Nov. 1936.
38. 15 and 16 May, 12 June, 1937.
39. 26 Dec. 1936.
40. 25 Dec. 1937.
41. Joachim C. Fest, *Hitler*, trans. Richard and Clara Winston (New York, 1973), 9.
42. E.g., 9 Jan., 24 Feb., 1 May, 1938.
43. 15 Jan., 8 Feb. 1938.
44. *Ibid.*
45. Notes of sitting, 202 Elgin Street, 13 Nov. 1938 (original Diary, 1938, Vol. 131). The portion of these notes relating to Borden is accurately transcribed in a Canadian Press story in the *Globe and Mail* (Toronto), 3 Jan. 1975.
46. See McGregor, *Fall & Rise of Mackenzie King*, 314-15 (Diary, 18 Sept. 1918). Cf. Diary, 17 Dec. 1918 and 7 Aug. 1917.

*War: The Prime Minister Swears Off*

1. Notes of sitting, Kingsmere, 2 Sept. 1939 (original Diary, 1939, Vol. 133).
2. 2 Sept. 1939.
3. August-September 1941. April-May 1944. See especially 5 and 6 Sept., 1941, and 17 May 1944.
4. 17 Oct. 1945.
5. 18 Sept. 1939.
6. Memo (original Diary, Vol. 145, p. 719). Tea-leaves, e.g., 2 July 1943.
7. Notes of sittings, Kingsmere, The Farm, Wednesday, 16 July 1941; Moorside, 3 Aug. 1941; and (no place), 11 Aug. 1941 (original Diary, Vol. 139). Pickersgill and Forster, *Mackenzie King Record*, Vol. 1, 235.
8. 5 Aug. 1942.
9. 2 Feb. 1941. For more probable case, see Diary, 11 Oct. 1942 (transcribed from "Book F").
10. Article by Fred Archer in *Psychic News* (London), reprinted in *Evening Citizen*, Ottawa, 11 Oct. 1950.
11. 17 Dec. 1950 (Markham Carruthers Papers, M.G. 32, F. 6, P.A.C.).
12. "The Secret Life of Mackenzie King, Spiritualist", *Maclean's*, 15 Dec. 1951.
13. Neatby, 407-8.
14. Notes of sittings, 202 Elgin Street, 6 Jan. 1934 [1935], and 13 Jan. 1935 (Diary, 1935).
15. 8 Dec. 1944.
16. Stacey, *Arms, Men and Governments*, 441-59.
17. 30 Oct. 1944.
18. 31 Oct. 1944.
19. *Arms, Men and Governments*, 456-9.
20. *Ibid.*, 466.
21. *Ibid.*, 459-60.

PART IV: THE FINAL YEARS

*The Mediums of England*

1. For the public aspects of these visits, see Pickersgill and Forster, *The Mackenzie King Record*, Vols. 3 and 4.
2. 12 June 1937; 10 Dec. 1944.
3. 15 and 16 Sept., 1942. *New York Times*, 16 Sept. 1942.
4. 7 Oct.–3 Nov. 1945 (especially 17, 25, and 27 Oct.); 19 May–30 May 1946 (especially 23, 28, 29, and 30 May).
5. 22 Nov. 1947. Automatic-writing script, "Saturday afternoon, November 22nd 1947", Cummins Papers, Cork Archives, courtesy of Professor Graeme Patterson.
6. On King and retirement, *Mackenzie King Record*, Vol. 4, 57-60. Geraldine Cummins, *Mind in Life and Death* (London, 1956), 109. Miss Cummins, under pressure from King's Liberal friends, had given a much more guarded version of these events in *Unseen Adventures* (London, 1951), in which she did not identify King and Roosevelt by name. See Fraser, "The Secret Life of Mackenzie King, Spiritualist".
7. Denis Stairs, *The Diplomacy of Constraint: Canada, the Korean War, and the United States* (Toronto and Buffalo, 1974), 10. Cf. William Kilbourn, "The 1950s", in J. M. S. Careless and R. Craig Brown, *The Canadians, 1867-1967* (Toronto, 1967), 328.
8. Automatic-writing script, "Oct 23, 1948. Dorchester Hotel", Cummins Papers, above, note 5. "(Returned by Mr. Mackenzie King's Exors to Miss Gibbes)".
9. Cummins, *Mind in Life and Death*, 112.
10. 25 Nov. 1947.
11. Much detail, *Mackenzie King Record*, Vol. 4, 402-24. 8 and 26 Oct., 1948.
12. 8, 22, 26, and 23 Oct., 1948.
13. Automatic-writing script, note 8 above.
14. 14 Mar. 1949. *Mackenzie King Record*, Vol. 4, 427.

15. 27 Feb., 7 April, 1949.

*The Last Summer*

1. Original of King's will and codicil, Probate No. 27038, Carleton County Court House, Ottawa. 13 May and 11 Dec., 1944.
2. 18 July 1950.
3. 17 and 8 April, 1950.
4. 29 and 11 March, 1950. Cf. *Mackenzie King Record*, Vol. 4, 398-9. King Papers, M.G. 26, J. 4, Vol. 228.
5. *Citizen* (Ottawa), 10 June 1950. Diary, 21 and 30 May, 1 June, 1950.
6. 30 June 1950.
7. 25 Nov. 1934.
8. 7 and 4 July, 1950.
9. 25 June 1950.
10. 6 July 1950.
11. King to Violet Markham, 1 July 1950, Markham Carruthers Papers. Diary, 7 July 1950.
12. Joan Patteson to Violet Markham, 28 July 1950, Markham Carruthers Papers.

APPENDIX: MACKENZIE KING'S PERSONAL FORTUNE AND HIS WILL

1. *Journal* (Ottawa), 8 Aug. 1950.
2. Probate number 27038.
3. *Canada Year Book, 1948*, 87.
4. McGregor, *The Fall & Rise of Mackenzie King*, 271.
5. 22 Jan. 1928.
6. 23 Dec. 1944.
7. 1 Oct. 1944.
8. *Citizen* (Ottawa), 11 Aug. 1950. Probate number 27038, records of Surrogate Court, Carleton County Court House, Ottawa.

# INDEX